Praying Curses

Praying Curses

The Therapeutic and Preaching Value of the Imprecatory Psalms

Daniel Michael Nehrbass

◆PICKWICK *Publications* • Eugene, Oregon

PRAYING CURSES
The Therapeutic and Preaching Value of the Imprecatory Psalms

Copyright © 2013 Daniel Michael Nehrbass. All rights reserved. Except for brief quotations in critical publications or reviews, no part of this book may be reproduced in any manner without prior written permission from the publisher. Write: Permissions, Wipf and Stock Publishers, 199 W. 8th Ave., Suite 3, Eugene, OR 97401.

Pickwick Publications
An Imprint of Wipf and Stock Publishers
199 W. 8th Ave., Suite 3
Eugene, OR 97401

www.wipfandstock.com

ISBN 13: 978-1-62032-749-4

Cataloguing-in-Publication data:

Nehrbass, Daniel Michael.

    Praying curses : the therapeutic and preaching value of the imprecatory psalms / Daniel Michael Nehrbass, with a foreword by David Augsburger.

    xiv + 214 pp. ; 23 cm. Includes bibliographical references.

    ISBN 13: 978-1-62032-749-4

    1. Imprecatory psalms. 2. Bible. Psalms—Criticism, interpretations, etc. 3. Bible. Psalms—Theology. 4. Pastoral theology. I. Augsburger, David W. II. Title.

BS1445.I46 N237 2013

Manufactured in the U.S.A.

Dedicated to my mother and father,
who taught me to love learning and writing

Contents

List of Figures | ix
Foreword by David Augsburger | xi
Acknowledgments | xiii

1 Introduction: The Therapeutic and Preaching Value of the Imprecatory Psalms | 1

Part I: Interpretation

2 History of Interpretation of the Imprecatory Psalms | 13
3 Interpretation of the Imprecatory Psalms through the Eyes of Victims | 53

Part II: Theology

4 Tension in the Canon | 77
5 A Theology of God in the Imprecatory Psalms | 88
6 Human Nature in the Imprecatory Psalms | 101
7 A Practical Theology of the Imprecatory Psalms | 120

Part III: Application

8 The Therapeutic Value of the Imprecatory Psalms | 147
9 Preaching the Imprecatory Psalms | 174
10 Conclusion | 201

Appendix | 207
Bibliography | 211

Figures

1. Figure 2.1 New Testament citations of Psalms by Jesus | 40
2. Figure 2.2 New Testament citations of Psalms in reference to Jesus | 41
3. Figure 2.3 Summary of Interpretations | 49–50
4. Figure 7.1 Imprecatory Psalms in the United Methodist Hymnal | 122
5. Figure 7.2 Imprecatory Psalms in the Revised Common Lectionary | 122
6. Figure 7.3 Episcopal Sunday Lectionary | 122
7. Figure 7.4 Imprecation in the New Testament | 138–39

Foreword

THE *CHRISTIAN CENTURY* REPORTED, May 2012, that Texas District Court Judge Martin Hoffman ruled that praying for God to hurt someone is not illegal.

The case before him was a lawsuit brought against U.S. Navy chaplain, Gordon Klingenschmitt, a Full Gospel minister, who used imprecatory Psalm 109 to curse Mikey Weinstein, a Jewish agnostic and the founder of the Military Religious Freedom Foundation. Klingenschmitt, for good measure, called down God's wrath on Weinstein's family as well. (Psalm 109 calls for the death of an opponent and provides further curses upon the widow and children among other things.) As a result of the imprecatory prayers being posted on the Reverend Klingenschmitt's website, Weinstein has received numerous death threats, had swastikas painted on his house, had his windows shot out and animal carcasses left on his doorstep. If God does not answer, friends of God will.

Weinstein is not the only recent object of imprecatory praying—a number of religious conservatives have invoked Psalm 109 against President Obama. In fact, Mike O'Neal, speaker of the House of Representatives in Kansas, sent a few verses from Psalm 109 to Republican colleagues announcing, "At last—I can honestly voice a biblical prayer for our president."

Anyone who experiences an inability to smile while reading the news notes cited above, may suffer from a critical irony deficiency. In the name of Jesus, forbidden fire is being called down from Heaven. (Luke 9:54). One can only wish that this book by Daniel Nehrbass were available to all of the above. Indeed, virtually all of us share a great deal in common with our imprecatory friends—a need for wise guidance, not just in the practice of prayer, but in managing the vengeful anger that goes with us when we rise to go about relating, serving, counseling, preaching.

Whatever we do in ministry, we do in the light of the Psalter. We counsel, comfort, confront, consciously or unconsciously, from the wisdom of the Psalms. We can hardly worship in any other language than that strongly

Foreword

influenced by the Psalter. We learn to quote it as a child, "The Lord is my Shepherd," we turn to it as we die, "Yea, though I walk through the valley of the shadow of death, I will fear no evil, for Thou . . ."

The Psalter teaches us to pray, comforts us in sorrow, gives language to our gratitude and praise, legitimates our deep feelings of abandonment, betrayal, loneliness, fear, anger, victimization. And the Psalter gives voice to revenge, to the deep desire that justice be seen to be done, and lacking that, for vindication, for retribution, indeed for exorbitant retaliation—not just an eye for an eye, but every enemy eye closed. Praying the Psalms leads us not just into familiar territory of the soul's spiritual homeland, it leads us into "the killing fields" even to the wastelands of genocide. So what do we do with these bloody texts? Bloody prayers? Bloody cries? ("Bloody" in literal sense, not the British contraction of "by-our-Lady").

Praying the Psalms is an audacious act of trust. Not just in the positive bonding Psalms the express love for the Lord and delight in community, but also for the severing Psalms that cut off the violent, the scornful, the slanderous in full recognition of encounter with evil. (It is also a treacherous razor edge to walk when pointing to the malevolence of the foe; in our accusations we accuse ourselves, in our condemnation we condemn ourselves). Some Psalms get sucked into the endless spiral of revenge. The supplicant so rarely can differentiate between seeking retributive justice and praying for parity in justice, for mutuality and transformative justice. One party's justice feels to the other party very much like revenge; "just repayment" leads to a cry for "just counter-repayment" and go on and on. Caught in the spiral of vengeance both parties may seek to triangle God into the dance. It is a rare prayer that humbly surrenders the justice controversy to a higher court. It is not our injured demands for redress that bring a halt to the spiral of vengeance, but forgiveness, When prayers of prosecution turn to prayers of lament, the sufferer ceases giving directions to the Divine and gives up god-like pretentions to administering the universe rightly.

"Repeating the Psalms of lament is a bold act of faith on two accounts," Walter Brueggemann argues. "First, the Psalms insist that we must look at the world and our lives the way they really are, no pretense, no denial. And second, they insist that all such experiences of disorder and dismay are a proper subject of discourse with God." The reality of the world, the truth about ourselves can be brought forward in prayer.[1]

Repeating the Psalms of condemnation is a risky act of requital. The prayer of measure for measure goes from the longing for safety from those who wish or plan your downfall to a plea for reprisal, retribution or revenge

---

1. Brueggemann, *Message of the Psalms*, 52.

Foreword

from a coopted Almighty hand. It presumes the knowledge of what justice entails and does not hesitate to make demands for its delivery. The impulse to make quits fires the passions either of personal quest or in public request for satisfaction of one's most primary needs, "an eye, a tooth, a hand, a child, a life." What shall we do with these concrete thoughts, these regressive drives, these toddler tantrums in ourselves? What shall we do with the tidal waves of desired revenge in our society? What shall we say when such issues issue from our souls even in the hour of *Lectio Divina* or in the liturgical readings of worship? And what do we say under our breath *in extremis?*

What use dare we make of the imprecatory Psalms and scathing, even genocidal readings from the prophets in our spiritual exercises, in our counseling, our teaching or from the pulpit? There they stand stark and unavoidable among our most exemplary and necessary texts. We cannot worship well without recourse to the Psalter nor express our deeper feelings without quoting the Psalms. The fact is we turn to them first and last in our times of sorrow—a believer's funeral is not a Christian funeral without Psalm 23. And Jesus suffering would make little sense, to the Gospel writers or to us, without the interpretive words of the Psalms. We do well to remember that both Mark and Matthew record only one word from the cross, the lament from Psalm 22, "My God, My God, Why hast thou forsaken me?" They take pains to trace nine parallels between Jesus' death and the Psalm. And none of the Gospel writers quote an imprecatory word. Jesus turned to Psalm 22, not Psalm 109. (He is the one who reversed the Law of Lamech—seventy-seven blows returned for every one received—to bring an end to all mathematics of retaliation—forgive seventy-seven times.)

Praying the Psalter might lead one to the greatest reversal of all—the prayer prayed repeatedly, after each hammer blow, jolt of cross erected, each jeer, each wild mob cheer, "Father, forgive them" reverses "Father obliterate them."

In the moment of pain wracked execution, a shriek, a scream came from the cross, as reported by Matthew, (27:50) . It was a wordless cry, according to Mark, (15:37) that followed the lament of Psalm 22. Luke's reports the final cry was "Father into thy hands" (quoting another non-imprecatory lament, Psalm 31:5) but John contradicts him by telling us that Jesus gave up his spirit with a bowed head.

Jürgen Moltmann concludes that the lament from 22 and the wordless cry indicate that Jesus died in despair, not devotion to his cause; and his cry asserted God's absence, not faith in God's presence. So Moltmann concludes that he knew humanity's deepest and darkest desperation and despondency

Foreword

because he was totally abandoned, in fact, absolutely cut off from God; Jesus' death, was more horrendous than any death we might imagine.[2]

Psalm 22 is a cry for help, and in the Psalm, it is answered, it speaks in total certitude of God's presence, compassion, and willingness to rescue the sufferer, so she lays it out before the Highest Judge, so he entrusts his cause to God. In praying this psalm, Jesus joins the great company of those who suffered unjustly, the vast company of the afflicted and identifies with them in their suffering. Jesus died as one of us, as one for us, as one with us so his death is for the evil we suffer as well as for the evil we do, for all sinned against as well as all who sin against. In our blundering and failure, we know what to do with our sins—own, face, forsake, turn. But what do we do with the massive feelings of "sinned against"?

There are questions we cannot avoid without doing violence to our souls.

What do we do with outrage? Where do we put our cumulative disgust? How can we cope with our hate? When do we give up resentments? The Psalms have mechanisms to offer, but do they fit our lives, our relationships, our faith?

If and when we face horror, brutality, inhumane, even bestial behavior, can we bring it up in our prayers? If and when we deal with cries, complaints, contempt at noxious behavior, must we split it off from our better selves, our best intentions? Do we hide it from the face that we put forward when we talk to God?

Daniel Nehrbass is a practical theologian, a truly pastoral theologian, and as you read his work, you will not find answers to these dilemmas, you will find that they are not answerable, but there are clear ways to break new trails through the impenetrable, new openings in the impasses. And they come from these troubling but necessary, these avoided but inescapable texts.

David Augsburger

Notes:

Brueggemann, Walter. *The Message of the Psalms*. Minneapolis: Fortress, 2002.
Miller, Patrick, and Sally Brown. *Lament: Reclaiming Practices in Pulpit, Pew and Public Square*. Louisville: Westminster /John Knox, 2005.
Moltmann, Jürgen *The Gospel of Liberation*. Waco, TX: Word, 1973.

2. Moltmann, *Gospel of Liberation*.

Acknowledgments

MANY THANKS TO DR. David Augsburger for help in every step of this process and thoughtful reflection throughout. I have enjoyed our conversations and your challenges. You approach education with genuine mutuality, expecting to learn as much as you teach. Dr. Leslie Allen was a vital sounding-board and valuable reader as well. Thanks for being so accessible and for spending so much time with this work. I am deeply indebted to Chuck Schussman for helping me think through these issues and present them in an organized manner that is biblically faithful. I am grateful to Dr. Richard and Marilynn Nehrbass and Dr. Kenneth Nehrbass for their reading and constructive comments. Thanks to my wife Kristina Nehrbass and my family for tolerating and supporting me during the length of this project. Thanks to Kathleen McFarland, who by her daily devotion in the Psalms convinced me that this project was worthwhile and possible.

1

Introduction

The Therapeutic and Preaching Value of the Imprecatory Psalms

EACH WEEK I SELECT a Psalm to be read aloud as we start our worship service. I quickly learned that this is not an easy task. If I did not preview them and expected simply to open the Bible and read a psalm, we could be in for an awkward moment. In fact, after exhausting a few of the psalms with which many of us are familiar, I thought: *Why is it so hard to pick one I can read aloud from start to finish without editing out at least a few verses? Someone should come out with an edited book of Psalms that you can use in the worship service, with just the good parts, so you can open up to any part of it and read.* The difficult parts to which I am referring are often called the "imprecatory psalms;" those psalms that articulate anger or cursing, and invoke evil, violence, or hatred toward an enemy. A number of psalms contain this element of calling for the downfall of one's foes; specifically Psalms 7, 35, 58, 59, 69, 83, 109, 137, and 139.

Few books in the last century have focused solely on the imprecatory psalms. Commentaries treat them in passing as one part of the whole psalter. Many offer a hermeneutic and exegetical study of the imprecatory psalms, but lack application for modern prayer or preaching. Books about prayer sometimes contain a section dealing with them as well, but often lack a hermeneutic or historical study. Erich Zenger's *A God of Vengeance* (1996) is probably the most notable book on the subject within the last hundred years. While short, it provides what most commentaries on the subject lack: a section on practical consequences. James Adams' *War Psalms of the Prince of Peace* (1991) is solely dedicated to this topic, but is limited to one nuanced interpretation. In the literature of the imprecatory psalms, three important subjects are still

Introduction

lacking. One missing aspect is a detailed historical study that examines the array of interpretations. Johannes Vos's (1942) article "The Problems of the Imprecatory Psalms" is a good start, but it is not comprehensive and is clearly outdated. A second void is a practical theological method. But perhaps the largest omission is the application of these psalms: how to preach them and how to pray them. This book will offer an updated and comprehensive history of interpretation of the imprecatory psalms, a practical theology, and an extensive application for preaching and for anger therapy.

Though a variety of historical interpretations of the imprecatory psalms have been put forth, there are still not sufficient answers for how these psalms can be applied or practiced in contemporary life. The field offers little help to the preacher who desires to go beyond explaining the cultural setting of these psalms, and provide his or her congregation with a relevant and biblically sound application. Furthermore, the Christian who reads through the psalter on a regular basis as an act of worship and as a means of developing his or her prayer life is left with a serious question: "How am I to pray these prayers?"

Erich Zenger summarizes the problem of the imprecatory prayers in the form of a recurring question: "Do you really think that as Christians (the question is never *as Jews* or *as human beings*, and certainly not *as victims of rape*) we can pray this way?"[1] Preachers are at a loss for how to give these prayers a modern application. Despite C. I. Scofield's high view of Scripture, he said that the imprecatory psalms are a "cry unsuited to the church."[2] If a fundamentalist cannot find practical application for how to pray these psalms, surely we have a problem that requires further research. C. S. Lewis provides a shocking admission of the trouble he faced in finding value within the imprecatory psalms. He writes, "At the outset I felt sure, and I feel sure still, that we must not either try to explain them away or to yield for one moment to the idea that, because it comes in the Bible, all this vindictive hatred must somehow be good and pious. We must face both facts squarely. The hatred is there—festering, gloating, undisguised—and also we should be wicked if we in any way condoned or approved it, or (worse still) used it to justify similar passions in ourselves."[3] Johannes Vos frames the problem in this way: "How can it be right to wish or pray for the destruction or doom of others as is done in the Imprecatory Psalms? Is it right for a Christian to

---

1. Zenger, *A God of Vengeance?* 2.
2. *Scofield Reference Bible*, 599.
3. Lewis, *Reflections on the Psalms*, 22.

Introduction

use the Imprecatory Psalms in the worship of God, and if so, in what sense can he make the language of these Psalms his own?"[4]

The purpose of this study is to build upon the ample exegetical work within the imprecatory psalms and apply this research to the field of practical theology. Specifically, I hope to make a contribution to the area of preaching and pastoral counseling. There are few published sermons which address the imprecatory psalms. And there are also few published resources suggesting modern application of these ancient psalms. In other words, I seek to answer "How can these outpourings of hatred, which go beyond lament to bloodthirstiness, be models for or the medium of our prayers?"[5] Zenger is convinced that there is an answer to this question. He writes, "In order to comprehend this capacity of the biblical psalms of enmity, we must rediscover lament in our liturgical prayer culture."[6] Zenger believes that the preacher and the congregation are capable, and indeed obligated, to find value within the imprecatory psalms. He argues, "*Not a single psalm* may be or need be excluded from the church's official Liturgy of the Hours."[7]

In addition to a better interpretation of the imprecatory psalms, this book offers ways of dealing with anger, hatred, and the desire for vengeance. Brueggemann writes, "The real theological problem, I submit, is not that vengeance is there in the Psalms, but that it is here in our midst. And that it is there and here only reflects how attuned the Psalter is to what is going on among us."[8]

The practical application of the imprecatory psalms leaves us with a few options. Either:

a. God is displeased with these prayers, so we should not pray them;

b. God (Christ) is the only one allowed to pray these prayers;

c. God taught us to pray these prayers, and gave them as an exemplary model for us; or,

d. God neither condones nor commends this type of prayer. Instead, God merely tolerates this type of prayer.

I contend that these psalms are inspired by God and have a legitimate place in the canon. The imprecatory psalms have relevant contemporary value for preaching and practical life. That value is best expressed in an

4. Vos "Ethical Problems of the Imprecatory Psalms," 124.
5. Augsburger, *Hate-Work*, 208.
6. Zenger, *A God of Vengeance?* 88.
7. Ibid., 91.
8. Brueggemann, *Praying the Psalms*, 65.

interpretation of these psalms which assumes the worshiper is voicing his dependence upon God, rather than taking matters into his own hands. This interpretation also assumes that the worshiper is adopting for herself the heart of God, grieving over the things that grieve God, and celebrating the things that God celebrates. The genius of the psalter in addressing heinous evil is that it admonishes believers to defer to the authority and agency of God: to delegate the enemy, the injury, and the injustice to the highest of all courts. We are told in Scripture three times "Vengeance is mine, I will repay."[9] I share Erich Zenger's thesis that "the psalms of enmity are a way of robbing the aggressive images of the enemies of their destructiveness, and transforming them into constructive forces."[10] That thesis, however, is past-focused and provides an exegetical understanding of the psalms, but still does not offer the preacher or the worshiper practical answers for how to preach or pray these psalms. I contend that the modern Christian can still "rob the aggressive images of the enemy and transform them into constructive forces" in the form of imprecatory prayers. I also contend that the modern preacher can do more than explain the *Sitz im Leben* of these psalms, but can offer practical application to the congregation.

A church member heard that I was writing a book on the imprecatory psalms and she asked me, "How many of those psalms end with praise?" I realized that nearly all of them begin and end with praise, and the imprecations themselves affirm praise of God. As Brueggemann points out, all the psalms are about God (not about the enemy). They are *all* songs of worship. He writes, "Even when the disorientation is caused by an enemy, the appeal is still to Yahweh. The appeal is not to the enemy that the enemy should desist, for that is a hopeless plea. The appeal is that Yahweh should intervene to right the situation and to punish the destabilizer. Sometimes Yahweh is blamed, and sometimes not. But when Yahweh is not blamed, he is nonetheless regarded as the only one who can intervene in a decisive and helpful way."[11] God is always the subject of the Psalms, and God is always the object of worship in the Psalms.

Brueggemann conceptualizes the psalms in three categories: psalms of orientation, psalms of disorientation, and psalms of reorientation. He places the imprecatory psalms among those of disorientation. Typically in form criticism these psalms are labeled "lament," and many of these laments contain curses. This book, therefore, assumes that the term "imprecatory

---

9. Deut 32:35; Rom 12:19; Heb 10:30. Unless otherwise noted, all Scripture quotations are from the New International Version [NIV].

10. Zenger, *A God of Vengeance?* vii.

11. Brueggemann, *Message of the Psalms*, 88.

psalm" is somewhat of a misnomer. There are technically no imprecatory psalms; there are only praise psalms. Some of these praise psalms approach God with laments and imprecation.

This study is limited by my choice not to make it exegetical. In addition to the abundant commentaries on the Psalms which have sufficient exegetical work, some studies treat the imprecatory psalms exegetically. This book belongs to the field of practical theology rather than Old Testament studies. Due to the constraints of space, it was also impossible to examine each of the several imprecatory psalms in detail with regard to their preaching and therapeutic value. In the first two sections (theology and interpretation), I take a broad and deep approach to the imprecatory psalms and find consistent themes throughout. But given that there are scores of imprecatory psalms, it would be overwhelming to try to "preach the psalms" in a few sermons. Instead, I limit each sermon to one psalm, and provide five sermons.

The primary sources for this study are specific to each of the three sections: interpretation, theology, and application. With regard to interpretation, Johannes Vos' article "The Problem of the Imprecatory Psalms" is a vital starting point. In this seminal article Vos outlines five historical traditions of interpretation. Other historical sources in this study include Charles Spurgeon's *Treasury of David*, which promotes the prophetic interpretation. This view is also promoted by John Calvin in his *Commentary on the Book of Psalms*. Harold Osgood's article "Dashing the Little Ones against the Rock" argues for an allegorical interpretation. James Sire advocates the "cathartic" view in *Learning to Pray through the Psalms*. C. S. Lewis promotes the "New Testament dispensational view" in his *Reflections on the Psalms*. James Adams argues for a messianic view in *War Psalms of the Prince of Peace*, which was also the view promoted by Dietrich Bonhoeffer in *Psalms: Prayer Book of the Bible*. Though limited to only one psalm, John Chrysostom advocates the "quotation hypothesis" in his commentary on the Psalms. Sigmund Mowinckel argues for the "curse" view in *The Psalms in Israel's Worship*.

A pivotal contemporary source that deals with interpretation is Zephania Kameeta's *Why O Lord, Psalms and Sermons from Namibia*. This is the only book to my knowledge that offers its own "real life" imprecatory prayers. Kameeta models and prays several prayers of imprecation, illustrating that the practice of this type of prayer is not obsolete.

With regard to practical theology, I depend greatly upon Thomas Groome's *Sharing Faith: The Way of Shared Praxis*. Though Groome does not deal with the psalms, he offers a theological method of interpretation and application which will provide the basis for my practical theology. Groome proposes a five movement strategy for working within a community which allows for incorporation of traditional texts. Reinhold

Introduction

Niebuhr's *Nature and Destiny of Man* is the backbone of my theological anthropology within the psalter.

Sources for application of the imprecatory psalms include David Augsburger's *Hate Work*. Augsburger makes the case that there are several types of hate, some more mature than others. He argues, therefore, that not all hatred must be dismissed or eradicated. Donald Shriver's *Ethic for Enemies* and Lytta Baset's *Holy Anger* provide excellent material for developing a therapeutic use of anger, which is clearly fundamental for anyone who wants to incorporate the imprecatory psalms into modern life.

One assumption of this study is that "All Scripture is God-breathed and is useful for teaching, rebuking, correcting and training in righteousness."[12] The psalter, therefore, as a part of Scripture is also inspired. That is not to say that God approves of every action in the Bible. Clearly, the Bible tells us of many things that people did which disappoint God. Nor is every statement in the Bible from the voice of God. We see in the book of Ecclesiastes, for example, two traditions: the worldview "under the sun" and the worldview "under heaven." We are not to take the statements "under the sun" as propositions from the voice of God. In that sense, the Bible can be true in all it teaches, but the Bible does not necessarily teach all that it says. The Bible also faithfully records lies that people have spoken. For example, the Amalakite in 2 Samuel 1:10 says that he killed Saul. But evidently he lied, because we read in 1 Samuel 31:4 that he refused to do the deed. So there are statements made by humans, reported by Scripture that are not true. Yet Scripture is true in that it accurately reports what these people said. When it comes to the imprecatory psalms, therefore, we must remember that these are the prayers of people, but God has seen fit to fix them within his inspired word. If Scripture is true in what it teaches, then our task is to determine what the imprecatory psalms teach. It would be insufficient to say that this portion of Scripture does not belong to the canon, since there are abundant examples of imprecation throughout both the Old and the New Testament, including the words of Jesus (as discussed later).

To say that "all Scripture is inspired by God" does not mean that all Scriptures demand the same rules of interpretation, nor that all Scriptures are equally normative or prescriptive. It is my assumption that sermons are the most prescriptive sections of Scripture, and that the psalms are much less so. Furthermore, the doctrine of inspiration is compatible with some notion of progressive revelation. To some extent, all Christians take for granted progressive revelation: God revealed himself in history, and that revelation expanded in size, clarity, necessity, and sufficiency over time.

12. 1 Tim 3:16

Introduction

But the concept of progressive revelation cannot be used to completely "undo" previous revelation. It is my assumption here that progressive revelation cannot suffice as an answer to the problem of the imprecatory prayers if the solution is phrased as something like: "In former days God allowed people to curse their enemies, but when Christ came he revealed a new way." By attributing this assertion to progressive revelation, one attempts to uphold the doctrine of inspiration, but at the same time undermines the continuity of God's thinking.

Finally, it is my assumption that Christ's teachings and the events of his life interpret all other parts of Scripture. Jesus quotes the imprecatory psalms, but in doing so he also interprets them. There is ample precedent for this methodology in the New Testament. The Gospel writers provide for us a Christocentric interpretation of Old Testament prophecies and psalms—that is, they see Christ as the center of the Bible, including the prophecies and psalms. The author of Hebrews provides for us an interpretation of the Law and the priesthood, and also sees Christ as the primary subject.

Because the imprecatory psalms are a part of Scripture, and because all Scripture is inspired, it is my assumption that these psalms belong in the canon. We cannot simply dismiss them. I assume that the canon is "closed," and that it forever includes these psalms as part of the inspired word of God. Spurgeon admits that while it may be difficult to accept, we must deal with the fact that these psalms belong in Scripture. He writes, "Truly this is one of the hard places of Scripture . . . yet as it is a psalm unto God, given by inspiration, it is not ours to sit in judgment upon it, but to bow our ear to what God the Lord would speak to us therein."[13]

Because the imprecatory psalms belong to Scripture, I assume that we cannot render them irrelevant as an historical phenomenon. The value of these psalms must be greater than the academic curiosity of a cultural practice long ago. James Sire shares this assumption. He writes, "We can trust the psalmist not to mislead us into a prayer that in the final analysis would be incorrect to pray."[14] Not all Christian scholars, admittedly, feel compelled to find value in these psalms. C. S. Lewis writes, "One way of dealing with these terrible or (dare we say?) contemptible Psalms is simply to leave them alone."[15] My assumption, however, is that these psalms of cursing have value. That is my impetus for this study. My faith convinces me that the value must be there; my academic curiosity drives me to find out what it is.

---

13. Spurgeon, *Treasury of David*, Volume 5, 157.
14. Sire, *Learning to Pray Through the Psalms*, 164.
15. Lewis, *Reflections on the Psalms*, 22.

Introduction

It is my assumption that it would be inadequate to determine that the New Testament teaches a different and better way than the Old Testament. If the psalms are not a form of teaching, but merely reporting what men said, then perhaps this division would be arguable (yet still would raise issues of prejudice). But if the psalms teach something valuable (as is my assumption), then I would expect continuity between what God taught both before Christ and after Christ.

Some contemporary scholars find it easy to dismiss the imprecatory psalms because they assert that we are living in a cultural context that is far removed from that of ancient Israel. They assume that all modern readers react to the psalms of anger with repulsion. They reason that in our modern world we have reached consensus that language about hatred and enemies is obsolete. This strikes me as naïve and myopic. People in many developed countries within the last fifty years may have had the privilege of living lives of relative safety. For them, talk of enemies may seem foreign and repulsive. It makes sense that they would find the imprecatory psalms an enigma. But it is my assumption that in much of the developing world where the people have endured centuries of warfare Christians will also find these psalms continue to be relevant. They can readily identify the enemy. In their case, the enemy is not an intangible idea, but a real human being with a weapon pointed in their direction. Christians in war-torn countries can identify with the hatred. Again, not an abstract concept divorced from reality, but as hatred accompanied with genuine personal suffering from the result of another person's actions. Since their life-setting is closer to that of the psalmist's, it is my assumption that we ought to let modern victims of violence teach us of the enduring relevance and interpretation of these psalms.

I follow Thomas Groome's method in *Sharing Fatih* which he calls "shared praxis." This methodology is discussed in detail in chapter seven. As stated in the previous section, I have the assumption that Scripture contains information from God which needed to be revealed and which can be understood. The process of understanding it, however, has always been rooted in a relationship between the individual, the illumination of the Holy Spirit, and one's connection to the community of faith. Many commentators have addressed the psalms with historical criticism, form criticism, text criticism, tradition criticism, etc. The contribution here is to make the leap from exegesis to praxis. This study is practical, and aims at understanding the therapeutic and preaching value of the imprecatory psalms. Borrowing from Groome's language, the methodology here begins with "naming the present action." Within current Christian praxis, there is an apparent contradiction between the imprecations in the psalter and our common understanding of

Introduction

Jesus' ethic in the Sermon on the Mount. Many have chosen to deal with this contradiction by "explaining away" the imprecations. In each chapter I offer a critical reflection on the ways in which the imprecatory psalms have been understood, preached, and practiced. I then explore ways to make this part of the biblical narrative accessible, and how to appropriate the fullness of the Psalter into Christian worship and life.

Part One

Interpretation

2

History of Interpretation of the Imprecatory Psalms

WHEN READING THE IMPRECATORY psalms the reader is faced with an immediate challenge regarding how to interpret these prayers. Is it allowable to pray against one's enemies, given Jesus' teaching on the Sermon on the Mount? Are the enemies spiritual or human? Are these the words of an inspired author, or evidence of a cultural phenomenon? Interpreters have addressed these questions and arrived at a number of systems for interpreting imprecatory psalms. This chapter will examine thirteen typical hermeneutical keys to the psalms of cursing. Each has wide support, often spanning the centuries and the globe. Not all of the following interpretive models are mutually exclusive. It is possible, for instance, to hold both the cathartic and the dependence theory. I divide these theories into the following categories not because they are exclusive, but because each theory below highlights something distinct from the others. The allegorical-historical view is very similar to the socio-historical view, and they are by no means mutually exclusive. But not all socio-historical interpreters see allegory in the psalms, nor do all interpreters who see the psalms as allegorical base this interpretation on historical research. Similarly, the "curses" theory is thoroughly socio-historical, but not all socio-historical interpreters see the psalms as curses. Many scholars who hold the prophetic theory also argue for the covenant theory. But not all interpreters who see the psalms as prophetic use covenant language. For this reason, there is some overlap among the theories, not only in concept, but also among proponents. It should not be assumed, therefore, that the scholars cited below for evidence embrace one and only one theory. Instead, authors are quoted below to help explain the interpretive model, rather than to categorize the authors themselves.

Part One: Interpretation

A. Spiritual/Allegorical Interpretation

Some interpreters have assumed that since these psalms are in Scripture, and it is not possible that God could condone one human being expressing such hatred toward another human being, then the imprecations must be allegorical. The enemy must be abstract, such as evil in general. Or the enemy is only spiritual: the devil or demons. This was the view of Augustine. He interpreted the phrase, "crush the teeth in their mouth" in Psalm 56 to be allegorical of Jesus crushing his enemies by giving superior answers to his opponents who tried to entrap him.[1] Others have read Psalm 137, which speaks of dashing little ones against the stones, to mean that unbelievers (children of evil) will be dashed against (judged by) the rock of Christ. This was Osgood's view:

> Does any intelligent reader interpret literally these sayings by the Savior and of the Savior? Is he to take men and dash them in pieces with a rod of iron and find delight in that work? Are not his words expressive of the terrible results of humanity's own sin, precisely as Jeremiah's breaking the earthen jar before men was a visible type of the ruin sin would bring? If no intelligent reader interprets literally the words quoted by the Savior, why should these same words be interpreted literally in the passages of the Old Testament from which they are quoted?[2]

In other words, the imprecations of the psalms are not literal wishes for physical violence, but hyperbolic expressions of anger. Osgood writes, "To dash down by the cliff is a metaphor that has not imagination but a terrible fact for its basis. But that it is used metaphorically by the author of our psalm, long resident by Babylon's myriad willow-bordered canals, is proved by the fact that Babylon is a perfectly flat alluvial country where no hill, nor stone, nor rock, nor cliff is to be found."[3] According to Osgood, neither the ancient author, nor Jesus, nor the modern interpreter should employ the imprecatory psalms in a strictly literal manner.

Spurgeon shared this allegorical preference. Also writing of Psalm 137 he comments, "Happy is the man who shall help in the overthrow of the spiritual Babylon, which, despite its riches and power, is 'to be destroyed.'"[4] Rather than make an overt defense for the psalm or his hermeneutic, Spurgeon implicitly argues for an allegorical interpretation.

1. Zenger, *A God of Vengeance?* 36.
2. Osgood, "Dashing the Little Ones against the Rock," 34.
3. Ibid., 35.
4. Spurgeon, *Treasury of David*, 188.

History of Interpretation of the Imprecatory Psalms

Mowinckel also prefers an allegorical or spiritual interpretation of these psalms. Birkland observes, "Mowinckel maintained that their subject was a person suffering from sickness. Since the enemies had caused the suffering they must have been sorcerers."[5]

This allegorical interpretation has some advantages. One is that there may be some allegorical references in the Psalms. But even if this is the case, it is certainly not true of all enemies in the Psalter. Another advantage is that it solves the "imprecatory problem" by making these psalms "nicer." As long as either the enemy or the imprecations are figurative, the psalms are vindicated of the so-called "sin of hatred" (presumably it would be a sin to hate a person, but not to hate the devil). In addition, this view is in harmony with the doctrine of inspiration. If the psalms are not directed at human enemies, then they are not necessarily in conflict with the Sermon on the Mount.

One problem with this interpretation is that the text seems quite clear in naming historical human enemies, rather than spiritual ones. The enemies of King David,[6] for instance, are named: Cush the Benjamite,[7] Saul,[8] Edom and the Ishmaelites, Moab and the Hagarites, Gebal, Ammon, Amalek, Philistia, Tyre, Assyria,[9] etc. Another problem with the allegorical interpretation is that it contradicts our own human experience. We have all had our own share of human enemies, so it is not difficult to relate to the psalmist, who names his own human enemies. Perhaps if we had no idea what the writer meant when he spoke of his enemies we would prefer the allegorical interpretation, but our own experience resonates well enough with the author's. Are we to imagine these authors did not have any real human enemies? This interpretation of the psalms might have us think so, but that is unrealistic. Or are we to imagine that they did not hope for the death of their enemies? Why shouldn't they have? This is also unrealistic. Given that the authors undoubtedly had human enemies, like we all do, it is more likely that these would be the enemies addressed in the psalms.

---

5. Birkland, *The Evildoers in the Book of Psalms*, 11.

6. I recognize that many of the psalms were not written by David, and that the *ldwd* prescript does not necessarily mean "written by David." Nevertheless, these psalms clearly have in mind real nations and kings who fight against the Israelites. The debate about the Davidic authorship of the Psalms is beyond the scope of this study. The use of "David" should be seen in respect to the setting within the Psalms, not necessarily with respect to the setting of the composition of the Psalms.

7. Ps 7:1

8. Ps 59:1

9. Ps 83:6–8

Part One: Interpretation

Historical Interpretations

Another interpretation of these imprecatory psalms is that they are merely products of an historical context. They are not necessarily meant to teach anything, or at least need not be a model for prayer today. They simply report what the psalmist prayed about their enemies. On this view, the imprecatory psalms do not represent the thoughts of God on the matter. David, for instance, was a king surrounded by enemies with whom he was at war. This is what David prayed, and perhaps David was wrong to pray in this manner. There are four nuanced versions of historical models.

B. Allegorical-historical

The previous methodology assumes an allegorical enemy or hyperbolic curse with the intent of preserving the harmony of all Scripture (including the Sermon on the Mount, which presumably prohibits hatred), and ameliorating the concerns of divine inspiration (for the Psalms are also inspired). Other authors have similarly argued for an allegorical interpretation, yet their methodology is distinct from more traditional Christian approaches because they do not share the same presupposition of divine inspiration. In this sense the interpretation, while allegorical, is explained in phenomenological terms, rather than theological terms. In other words, there is no effort to explain why God would allow these verses to appear in the Bible; instead there is an attempt to explain how these imprecations emerged from a social group. The socio-historical interpretation deserves (and receives) its own heading below, but I address the issue here because this particular explanation of enemies is distinctly allegorical.

Several authors have outlined the similarities between the imprecatory psalms and ancient Near Eastern (ANE) literature. This argument is presented in Ballard's monograph entitled *The Divine Warrior Motif*, Patrick Miller's *The Divine Warrior in Early Israel*, John Day's *God's Conflict with the Dragon and the Sea*, and Carol Kloos' *YHWH's Combat with the Sea*. Each of these sources attempts to demonstrate a correlation between the imprecatory psalms and the divine warrior motif present in other ANE literature. This hermeneutical method, though ultimately arriving at an allegorical interpretation, takes an historical-critical approach (reflective of the *sitz im leben* of the biblical authors and their neighbors).

Ballard's detailed study includes comparisons to Baal, El, and Resheph, in Ugarit literature, Erra, Inanna, and Ishtar in Akkadian Scriptures, Marduk in Babylon, Assur in Assyria, as well as Seth and Amun-Re in Egypt.

Ballard's thesis is that the divine warrior motifs in all ancient Near Eastern literature shares common characteristics with each other. He observes that the divine warrior is nearly always associated with storms, limited to mythological and military engagements, associated with assorted weaponry, and related to fertility. In addition, the literature containing this motif often illustrates the rise of power of the divine warrior through battle, his/her settlement of jural issues, and his/her association with acts of creation.

A strength of this interpretation is that it is cognizant of the historical context. There are similarities between biblical curses and the allegorical writings of Israel's ancient neighbors. But that this literature is similar does not mean that it is identical, or that it should be interpreted with the same set of assumptions or rules.

One criticism of the allegorical-historical interpretation is that it assumes the psalms arose out of a borrowed worldview, rather than maintaining that the psalms offer a worldview that is divinely revealed. If we maintain a high view of Scripture, we cannot dismiss the worldview of the psalmists on the grounds that it is foreign, outdated, etc. That's because the worldview of the psalmist arises from propositions revealed by God.

A traditional understanding of the inspiration of Scripture assumes an overall propositional quality of the Bible: Its statements must either be accepted or denied. Such a propositional understanding would mean that the worldview of the imprecatory psalmist is now offered to the modern reader for his acceptance or rejection. If we take the propositions of Scripture to be inspired, then we also mean that their origin is divine and therefore not the result of the human author's conditioning.

Strictly speaking, the imprecations of the psalter are not propositions. As such, they do not in themselves offer statements which readers must accept or deny as true. But the imprecations arise out of the psalmist's worldview, which is based on the propositions revealed to Moses and other prophets in the Law. The psalmists knew the difference between right and wrong, good and bad, evildoers and the righteous, from what they read in the Scriptures. They also knew from the Scriptures how God deals with the wicked and metes out judgment. From the propositions of Scripture they were able to utter their imprecations. There is in the psalter, therefore, an implicit revealed worldview.

If we take the propositions of Scripture to be inspired, then we also mean that their origin is divine and therefore not the result of the human author's conditioning. Since this is the case, it is insufficient simply to draw connections between the biblical worldview and that of the author's neighbors. The doctrine of revelation implies that no matter how many similarities to contemporary literature; there is a biblical worldview that is revealed by God to the author. In this sense, that biblical worldview is distinct, even if it bears resemblance to the worldviews of neighboring nations. It is distinct because being divinely revealed, it transcends a social-evolutionary explanation. For this reason, the allegorical-historical model is insufficient for interpreters who accept the doctrine of inspiration. In addition, this allegorical model shares the same disadvantages with the above view: it forgets that Israel had real neighbors who acted as enemies, and gave the nation cause for hatred (whether just or unjust). Why should we see allegorical enemies in the Psalms, when Israel clearly had plenty physical ones as well? Finally, this view does not offer much in the way of modern application or practice.

C. Historical-inspired

Surprisingly, it is possible to hold the view that the psalmists were wrong in what they prayed, and yet the Bible is still inspired by God. The *Halley's Bible Handbook*, for instance, says the imprecatory psalms are the words of man: "They are not God's pronouncements of His wrath on the wicked; but are the prayers of a man for vengeance on his enemies, just the opposite of Jesus' teaching that we should love our enemies."[10] In other words, the Bible is inspired, but the words of the psalmist were not necessarily inspired by God. To speak of the Bible's inspiration in this instance means that the Bible accurately records the words of the psalmist, without endorsing these prayers. The Bible, for instance, records the words that Goliath spoke against David. It even contains a false promise. Goliath threatens: "Come here and I'll give your flesh to the birds and the wild animals."[11] The doctrine of inspiration does not require that Goliath's words were inspired by God, but that the book of Samuel accurately tells us what Goliath said and that God had a divine reason for placing the material in the book. Similarly, some argue, the Psalms do not say anything contrary to fact, because they accurately portray the author's sentiment, though that sentiment is not endorsed by God.[12]

A strength of this view is that it is undoubtedly true that some speakers in the Bible have less authority than others. It also preserves the integrity of the canon. In addition, it is mindful of Jesus' teachings about enemy-love. But this view offers little in the way of application for modern preaching or practice. We are still left wondering, "Why did God place this material in the canon?"

---

10. Adams, *War Psalms of the Prince of Peace*, 9.
11. 1 Sam 17.44
12. A more detailed discussion of this concept is on page 78.

History of Interpretation of the Imprecatory Psalms

D. Historical Non-inspired

It is clear that preserving a strong view of inspiration while also dismissing the imprecatory psalms is a difficult task. Those without a high view of the inspiration of Scripture have an easier task. Obviously, if these psalms are not inspired by God, then one might conclude they "do great damage and represent unbridled hatred and thirst for revenge."[13] C. S. Lewis articulates an historical non-inspired interpretation in *Reflections on the Psalms*. Lewis writes concerning the imprecatory corpus, "the pettiness and vulgarity of it, especially in such surroundings, are hard to endure."[14] Lewis suggests that, "One way of dealing with these terrible or (dare we say?) contemptible Psalms is simply to leave them alone."[15] He admits that he and surely others have reservations about dismissing them, because of their reverence for Scripture. Lewis comments on his initial desire to harmonize these imprecations with the fact that they are included in the Bible. He writes, "At the outset I felt sure, and I feel sure still, that we must not either try to explain them away or to yield for one moment to the idea that, because it comes in the Bible, all this vindictive hatred must somehow be good and pious. We must face both facts squarely. The hatred is there—festering, gloating, undisguised—and also we should be wicked if we in any way condoned or approved it, or (worse still) used it to justify similar passions in ourselves."[16]

Lewis warns, however, that just because these sentiments are in Scripture, they are not commendable or allowable. This vehement tone, he fears, "encourages a man to think that his own worst passions are holy."[17] Lewis is confident in calling the psalmist's vitriol sin. He writes, "The Jews sinned in this matter worse than the Pagans not because they were further from God but because they were nearer to him."[18] The specific sin at issue, for Lewis, is pride. He says, "It leads straight to 'Pharisaism' in the sense which Our Lord's own teaching has given to that word. This I assume from the outset, and I think that even in the psalms this evil is already at work."[19]

Having dismissed the notion that these psalms are God-inspired allows the interpreter to take an historical-critical approach while at the same time having no obligation to defend the thoughts in the Psalms. Cross writes,

13. Zenger, *A God of Vengeance?* 22.
14. Lewis, *Reflections on the Psalms*, 21.
15. Ibid., 22.
16. Ibid., 22.
17. Ibid., 31.
18. Ibid., 31.
19. Ibid., 66–67.

"There is a considerable list of Psalms which the Christian Church would do well to preserve only in the ancient record as evidence of the pit from whence we have been dug."[20] Similarly, Farndale comments, "All this, set against the Imprecatory Psalms, pulls us up and makes us realize acutely how far the ethical ideal and standard has been raised for humanity by Jesus."[21]

For some interpreters, the apparent evolution of ethics from the imprecatory psalms to the New Testament is justified by progressive revelation. This concept will be examined later. But for other interpreters, the so-called "ethical improvement" is the result of social evolution. Craigie writes, "These psalms are not the oracles of God; they are Israel's response to God's revelation emerging from the painful realities of human life, and thus they open a window into the soul of the psalmist."[22] Craigie explains how one can call the Psalms inspired, yet dismiss their message. He argues that the Psalter, like all Scripture, is "literature which purports to be primarily a human creation." Craigie continues, "The book of Psalms is thus recognized as 'revelation,' or inspired, by virtue of its inclusion in the canon of Holy Scripture, rather than by any internal characteristics specifying God's direct self-revelation *in* word."[23]

A strength of this view is that it is realistic about human nature: it assumes the Israelites had real enemies, and that they desired to see them avenged. This view arises from a plain reading of the text. But it has the obvious disadvantage that it is inconsistent with the doctrine of inspiration, and offers no contemporary application.

E. Sociological-historical

The previous interpretive model overtly states that the imprecatory portions of Scripture are not inspired. Other authors simply do not address the topic of inspiration. Instead, some interpreters take a sociological-historical approach. Birkland's thesis is that the Psalms evolved out of a social context where cursing enemies was not only socially acceptable, but became formulaic and banal. His approach does not engage with issues of revelation and inspiration, but interprets the psalms solely from a socio-historical perspective. Central to Birkland's explanation is the observation that, "the enemies of the individual were in principle identical with those of the nation."[24] This

---

20. Quoted by Cheong in *Biblical Basis of the Imprecatory Psalms*, 86.
21. Ibid., 109.
22. Ibid., 128.
23. Quoted by Cheong in ibid., 129.
24. Birkland, *The Evildoers in the Book of Psalms*, 9.

observation is vital for several other theories of interpretation, so it is not unique to the historical perspective. In contrast to the allegorical-historical situation described above, however, "the sufferings in the psalms are real sufferings caused by historical events, not cultic sufferings."[25]

Birkland sees in the imprecatory psalms a pattern of cursing, directed at the wicked (*rᵉšāʾîm*). He explains,

> The existence of a *Hebrew* pattern of *rᵉšāʾîm* as pointed out, cannot be doubted. The stereotyped monotony of their description in the psalms is sufficient evidence. It is absolutely obvious that the psalmists are operating with a socially recognized ideology concerning the qualities of evildoers. They know what to say about evildoers whoever they are, and they say it.[26]

Birkland's approach renders as ridiculous most of the ethical questions associated with the imprecatory psalms. These questions include: "Should cursing continue? Has God changed his mind about cursing? Is there a New versus Old Testament dispensation for cursing? Was cursing enemies a sin at the time?" The reason these questions are deemed ridiculous is that the interpreter assumes the curses were socially required, and therefore raised no ethical problems for the original audience. Furthermore, it is not that God has changed over time, but that cultures have changed. So following Birlkand's model it goes without saying that this formula of cursing is not required or appropriate for all cultures. He explains, "The author is bound by social patterns whenever he is *expressing* (form!) an *idea* (ideological pattern)."[27]

Birkland does not simply ignore the question of inspiration or revelation. He sees the development of these psalms as products of culture, rather than decidedly teaching religious propositions. He writes,

> Their literary value is indeed mostly greater than that of their religious content, which keeps to the nationalistic core of extreme exclusivity revealing itself especially clearly in the patternized descriptions of national enemies. But it must be kept in mind that this pattern has been created by society, not by outstanding spiritual leaders.[28]

These historical approaches have some common weaknesses. At best, they lack engagement with the issues of revelation and inspiration and render these psalms irrelevant to Christian practice and preaching. At worst,

25. Ibid., 16.
26. Ibid., 24.
27. Ibid., 28.
28. Ibid., 46.

they deny these doctrines. McKenzie notes, "It has been suggested that the imprecatory psalms be explained according to the poetically exaggerated mode of composition found in many of the ancient literary remains of the Babylonians."[29] But, he points out, "This explanation does not touch the heart of the question, which is not the formulae employed, but the hatred which these formulae express."[30] Taken alone, therefore, the historical approach is difficult to harmonize with the desire equate the imprecatory psalms with God's word. These historical interpretations leave us asking, "Why God would allow these portions of non-inspired material to remain in the canon. What are we to do with such a large portion of the canon that has no relevance to modern life?"

But that does not mean the whole approach must be abandoned. Birkland contends, "Sociological viewpoints are needed to understand this ideology. The notion of social patterns is required to clarify the problem of the psalms as literary units."[31] His point is well-taken, but may not be the exclusive key to understanding these psalms.

Some point out that the psalmist had a worldview colored by his ANE environment. His treatment of enemies was typical of other ancient Near Eastern writers. While this is of course true, we must remember that the psalmist not only had an ancient Near Eastern worldview, he also had a biblical worldview. This was a worldview that he did inherit from his environment, but one specially revealed by God to him. To relegate these psalms merely to their historical setting would be a failure to preach "the whole counsel of God."[32]

Another problem with the historical models, is that if we say the psalms are typical of the world in which the psalmist lived, what type of world do we live in now? In our world violence is endemic to society. In the last 100 years there has never been a time of peace. Ours is a world where—despite the existence of superpower nations—relatively insignificant dictators have been able to perpetuate atrocities while the rest of the world watched in apathy, ignorance, or fear. With regard to the presence of violent and unjust enemies, our world is not substantially different than that of the psalmist. Since this is the case, there is no reason to argue that the psalms that arose out of our similar predicament are now somehow irrelevant. This interpretive method is probably too charitable to modern readers, and assumes that we find the imprecatory psalms more reprehensible than we actually do.

29. McKenzie, "The Imprecations of the Psalter," 83.
30. Ibid., 85.
31. Birkland, *The Evildoers in the Book of Psalms*, 93.
32. Acts 20:27

These historical interpretations, therefore, do not offer a contemporary application for preaching or prayer. They fail to answer the basic questions: "So what? What shall we do?"

F. Catharsis/Poetic Form

Another approach to these imprecations is to see them as cathartic[33] or poetic in form. In other words, they express an honest human sentiment of anger, and the cathartic method legitimates the expressing of that anger without legitimating the actual imprecations. In this sense, the imprecations are not propositional: They do not offer a truth that must either be accepted or denied. Nor are they moral in the sense of providing a model for how we ought to pray. But instead, they are tolerable. They are acceptable to God, but not as sweet aromas rising to heaven. God, as a wise and tolerant parent, can put up with his children's complaints. Explaining this approach to the psalms, Vos wrote that some see the curses as "outbursts of the moral feeling of humanity called forth by unusually brutal or inhuman crimes."[34]

The ability to see the psalms as inspired, while seeing the imprecations therein as deeply human is rooted in assumptions about the function of the psalms within theology. Some see the psalms as examples of allowable expressions from people to God, but not as propositions from God to people. Gunn explains, "The caution has often been given by many writers on the Psalms both in Britain and in Germany that we should not allow ourselves to speak of their theology but only of their piety."[35] The function of the psalms is poetic, therefore, and not didactic.

Even if we acknowledge that the imprecatory psalms are a cathartic form endorsed by God, it is vital to remember that they belong to the genre of poetry, and not moral prescriptions. Martin points out that thirteen of the eighteen imprecatory psalms have the ascription "of David." David is clearly associated with cursing his enemies, of which he had many. Yet David repeatedly spared the lives of his enemies: Absalom, Saul (twice), Abner, Gilboa, and Ishbosheth.[36] Though David prayed prayers against his enemies, he did not always act upon this desire for revenge. Clearly, then, the psalms served a cathartic purpose which curtailed the need for personal vengeance.

---

33. A detailed discussion of the therapeutic limits of catharsis (verses ventilation) is found in chapter 8, section E.

34. Vos, "Ethical Problems of the Imprecatory Psalms," 129.

35. Gunn, *God in the Psalms*, 3.

36. Martin, "Imprecations in the Psalms," 542.

Part One: Interpretation

One value of this hermeneutic is that it does not necessarily exclude a high view of divine inspiration. Taking the view that all the psalms are God's word, Davison writes, "We cannot listen to the psalmist praying as we listen to the prophet preaching; the prophet is the spokesman of God, and the psalmist is at best only the representative of humanity, speaking for them to God."[37]

James Sire is adamant that all Scripture is God's word, yet he sees in the psalms a thoroughly human sentiment, as well as human function, perhaps best described as a catharsis. He writes, "The curses that proceed from the mouth of the psalmist are painfully true to human nature. Even when we are horrified by the expressions we read, we know that, faced with the same situation we could say the same thing, even in our guarded moments, and have probably done so. It is this utter realism about human nature that is, I think, the key to how we are to pray these psalms."[38]

Considering the thorough human composition of the psalms could lead to an ambiguous moral lesson. Martin, for example, concludes that these imprecations are sinful, but that does not mean they do not belong in the Bible. That should not be a shocking oxymoron, for

> Not everything is commendable which the Bible records; no more, it is suggested, is all the religious experience that finds expression in the psalms necessarily endorsed as pleasing in God's sight and meant for the imitation of those who read. However manifestly some of them may embody the thoughts and feelings begotten by such cruel experiences as David's outlaw life or his flight from Absalom, it is plain that they must have been composed at leisure; and while we may make excuse for harsh words uttered in the heat of anger, we cannot excuse the embodiment of the same words in permanent literary form. Imprecations on one's enemies should be repented of, not written down for others to read.[39]

Admittedly, there are many events recorded in the Bible which seem reprehensible, and yet the Bible remains the inspired Word of God. Sire disagrees that this means the imprecations in the Psalter must be easily excluded morally. He writes, "We can trust the psalmist not to mislead us into a prayer that in the final analysis would be incorrect to pray."[40] That assurance is surely the heart of the issue. Are the psalms as value-neutral as the historical

---

37. Gunn, *God in the Psalms*, 4.
38. Sire, *Learning to Pray through the Psalms*, 164.
39. Martin, "Imprecations in the Psalms," 540.
40. Sire, *Learning to Pray through the Psalms*, 164.

narrative in Judges? The author of Judges does not make it a point to say that each evil action was wrong. That it was wrong for Judah to rape Tamar is self-evident, and the narrative needs no moral commentary or Greek chorus to hurl moral vindictive. But in the Psalms we are not certain whether we are reading a value-neutral imprecation, or a style endorsed implicitly by God.

Sire is less concerned whether that imprecatory style is *endorsed*, however, and more willing to say that it is *tolerable*. He writes, "True spirituality is true to our broken nature. It derives not from perfect prayer but from honest prayer."[41] In this sense, the presence of imprecations in the Psalter is an accommodation by God for our benefit. They do not represent the mind of God, but they concede to the mind of man, and accommodate our need for catharsis. Sire explains, "If we are honest with ourselves, we can say anything to God. He can take it. We can call on him to do whatever violent or mischievous thing we can imagine. Why? Because we can trust him not to do what is wrong, even if we ask it in all sincerity."[42]

Another advantage of this hermeneutic is that it adequately deals with the tension in Scripture between enemy-love and enemy-hate. The notion that these psalms are cathartic does not "explain away" the hate, but gives this voice its due attention in Scripture. This school of thought also has the advantage that it is compatible with other views (such as the covenant theory and the dependence theory). It is not exclusive, but can augment other theories regarding the nature and interpretation of the imprecatory psalms. Furthermore, the catharsis theory allows for present-day application (it argues that one can still pray these psalms).

But a weakness is that it contains an ambiguous moral lesson, and therefore it has diminished relevance. Using the same hermeneutic of catharsis, one concludes that we ought not curse, and another concludes that we may curse. Of these two, it seems that the doctrine of inspiration lends itself more to the conclusion that the psalms not only allow, but in some way model imprecation. Martin explains that an implicit endorsement is inherent to the poetic form. He writes that poetry, "Is in its very nature an expression of the poet's personal feeling, and involves an implicit claim that this feeling is in some sense true and right such as others should sympathize with and, it may be, adopt as their own."[43]

---

41. Ibid., 165.
42. Ibid., 167.
43. Martin, "Imprecations in the Psalms," 540.

Part One: Interpretation

G. Pre-New Testament Dispensation

The New Testament dispensational approach to these psalms relies heavily on the idea that God reveals himself progressively over time. On this view, the psalms were revealed relatively early, and while true for their original audience, are no longer useful to us in light of the fuller, New Testament revelation. Some say that the New Testament teaching (specifically the Sermon on the Mount) has replaced the Old Testament teaching. They point out that Jesus said, "You have heard that it was said, 'Love your neighbor and hate your enemy.' But I tell you: Love your enemies and pray for those who persecute you."[44] We notice, however, that nowhere in the Old Testament does it teach "love your neighbor and hate your enemy." Those in Jesus' audience must have "heard it said" from somewhere other than the Bible. Admittedly the New Testament does give a fuller perspective, and God has progressively revealed himself, which is equivalent to admitting that God didn't regressively reveal himself, nor did he reveal himself all at once.

To say that this view is dispensational does not mean that it subscribes to all the tenets of Scofield's dispensationalism (though Scofield did hold to this interpretation of the imprecatory psalms). Any substantial division between theology at one time and theology at another, recognizes distinctions between dispensations. At minimum, therefore, this theory states that there was an Old Testament way of dealing with enemies that was God-inspired, but that epoch has passed and we now have a new calling in the New Testament. Kidner summarizes the view in this way, "Our response should be to recognize that our calling, *since* the cross, is to pray down conciliation, not judgment."[45] We read,

> It is not open to us simply to occupy the ground on which [the psalmists] stood. Between our day and theirs, our calling and theirs, stands the cross. We are ministers of reconciliation, and this is a day of good tidings. To the question, Can a Christian use these cries for vengeance as his own? The short answer must surely be No.[46]

The New Testament Dispensational view is probably the longest standing and widest held interpretation of the imprecatory psalms. Spurgeon interprets the curses with a sharp division between the Old and New covenant. He writes, "The desire for righteous retribution is rather the spirit of the law than of the gospel; and yet in moments of righteous wrath the old fire will

---

44. Matt 5:43–44
45. Kidner, *Psalms 73–50*, 461.
46. Kidner, *Psalms 1–72*, 31–32.

burn; and while justice survives in the human breast it will not lack for fuel among the various tyrannies which still survive."[47]

Of Psalm 141:10, Spurgeon wrote,

> It may not be a Christian prayer, but it is a very just one, and it takes a great deal of grace to refrain from crying Amen to it; in fact, grace does not work towards making us wish otherwise concerning the enemies of holy men. Do we not all wish the innocent to be delivered, and the guilty to repent as a result of their own malice? Of course we do, if we are just men. There can be no wrong in desiring that to happen in our own case which we wish for all good men. Yet there is a more excellent way.[48]

That excellent way is presumably always to pray for the blessing of one's enemies, rather than their destruction. Bruce Waltke agrees that the imprecations may have been allowable at one point in redemptive history, but there is a more excellent way for Christians. He writes,

> Though theologically sound . . . these petitions for retribution are inappropriate for the church because, among other reasons, judgment will occur in the eschaton . . . sin and sinner are now more distinctly differentiated, allowing the saint both to hate sin and to love sinner . . . and the saint's struggle is against spiritual power of darkness, where he conquers by turning the other cheek and by praying for the forgiveness of enemies.[49]

Laney also claims that the dispensation for cursing has passed. He says,

> In the light of the fact that the Abrahamic covenant reflects God's promise to Abraham and his descendants, it would be inappropriate for a church-age believer to call down God's judgment on the wicked. One can appreciate the Old Testament setting of the imprecatory psalms and teach and preach from them. However, like the ceremonial dietary laws of the Old Testament, the imprecations in the Psalms should not be applied to church-age saints.[50]

Mays expresses the dispensational view when he writes, "Jesus and Paul instruct Christians to love, bless and pray for their enemies. That instruction forbids prayer against our human enemies. The use of the imprecations

---

47. Spurgeon, *Treasury of David*, 188.
48. Ibid., 279.
49. Waltke, "Theology of the *Psalms*," 1106.
50. Laney, "A Fresh Look at the Imprecatory Psalms," 44.

Part One: Interpretation

in liturgy in any plain or literal sense is rejected."[51] Similarly, Anderson says, "Admittedly, the laments of the Psalter are raised from the depths of human anxiety, from which the emotions of bitterness and hatred often well up. The Psalter, like the Old Testament as a whole, is very earthly—all the moods and passions of human life find expression here."[52] If it is earthly, then presumably it is more primitive and somehow less divine (or less inspired).

Driver also argues for the passing of the Old Testament dispensation. Commenting on Psalm 109 he writes, "The spirit of the older dispensation is not the spirit of Christ."[53] It is clear that he regards not only the end of one era and the coming of another, but he places the New Testament ethic in a superior position. He writes,

> The passages must be regarded as passages in which the voice of God is not heard with the clearness and directness which is usual in Scripture. The psalmists do largely express their own personal experiences and feelings; and their feelings and thoughts possess unquestionably, as a rule, the highest spirituality; but there are instances in which the case is different; and in these we are obliged to suppose that they have not been completely subordinate to the spirit of God, and that the voice of human passion is heard in them in a manner which is intelligible, perhaps even justifiable, in the age in which the authors wrote, but which is not in harmony with the higher moral level on which Christ has placed us.[54]

Finally, Delitzsch writes, "It is zeal for God that puts such harsh words into the poet's mouth; but they do not suit the mouth of the New Testament Church."[55]

The rationale for why the Bible sanctions two opposing views of cursing is thought to be explained by New Testament Dispensational hermeneutic. The imprecations make sense within their place of progressive revelation because of the presumed undeveloped theology of the psalmist. However, some interpreters in this school may go too far. For example, Gunn writes, that it is important to remember, "That the men who wrote these psalms were probably deficient in any sure conviction of a future life, and a final judgment, and so they desire and expected to see a present, visible destruction of the wicked."[56] Gunn's comments are difficult to harmonize with a ro-

---

51. Mays, *The Lord Reigns*, 38.
52. Anderson, *Out of the Depths*, 71.
53. Driver, *Studies in the Psalms*, 213.
54. Ibid., 225.
55. Cheong, *Biblical Basis of the Imprecatory Psalms*, 55.
56. Gunn, *God in the Psalms*, 104.

bust view of the inspiration of Scripture. He not only says that the psalmists were more primitive in their theology (which must be admitted), but that they believed and wrote theology that was contrary to fact. Their writings were based upon faulty presuppositions (no afterlife, etc.), so there was a faulty conclusion (imprecations). This raises problems for those who see continuity in the theology of the Bible, since it is inspired by a coherent God who does not change.

One of the problems with this dispensational view is that it denies the reality of our own experience. This dispensational view would have us believe that somehow human nature has changed to a degree that what ancient people thought was normal, modern people think is reprehensible. But is that really the state of modern reality? Do we really think these psalms are as reprehensible as the dispensationalist authors contend? Or do we think we are supposed to find them reprehensible, but still privately cherish the practice of imprecating enemies? I argue that human nature has not substantially changed. The ancients were probably not as hate-filled as this dispensational view assumes, nor are we as charitable as the view pretends. I do not think that three thousand years is enough time for us to evolve away from something as basic as hate for enemies.

Furthermore, an alarming characteristic of the dispensational view is its anti-Jewish bias. It seems implied that the Jews evolved to a lesser state of maturity than Christians. Heinrich Junker reflects this sentiment: "mature worshipers will be able to read the psalms realizing that these are ancient thoughts, but they do not do this pridefully, they realize they are on the same plane and liable to succumb to the same temptation to utter vengeful prayers."[57] It is impossible to have a dispensational interpretation without implying the inferiority of one system to another. That hierarchy ends up characterizing Jewish thought as more primitive, and Christian thought as more advanced. Zenger summarizes the idea: "The only advantage [Christians] have is they have been shown a higher ideal and more sublime commandment."[58] Zenger contends that this dichotomy reveals Christian prejudice. He speaks of the, "Vapid cliché of violence/God of violence = Old Testament, Judaism; non-violence/God of non-violence = New Testament, Christianity."[59] The dispensational view does not help eradicate this vapid cliché.

Another problem with this school of thought is that it ignores imprecation in the New Testament. For instance, the book of Acts quotes

---

57. Zenger, *A God of Vengeance?* 17.
58. Ibid., 17.
59. Ibid., 80.

imprecatory Psalms 69 and 109 approvingly with respect to Judas.[60] The usage of the imprecatory psalms in the New Testament indicates that the dispensation has not passed. Christian authors still saw fit to incorporate them into their theology and even Christology. What's more, the abundance of fresh imprecations (not taken from the Psalms) in the New Testament illustrates that the dispensation of cursing had not really passed. The distinction required by the New Testament dispensational model looks quite arbitrary, in light of the long list of New Testament curses.

In Galatians 5:12, for instance, the Judaizers were demanding circumcision of the Gentiles. Paul saw these false teachers as enemies, and said that he wished they would emasculate themselves. In Mark 11:13–14 we read that Jesus cursed a fig tree, which subsequently withered (to the disciples' surprise). Some may think it a stretch to apply this action as an ethic that Christians are meant to employ on their enemies, except that Jesus goes on to say that his disciples should have faith that God will answer any prayer they ask, apparently including destruction (v. 24). It is in this context of acceptable prayer before God that Jesus utters his well-known words about commanding a mountain to be hurled into the sea and destroyed (v. 23). In 1 Corinthians 16:22 Paul invokes a curse on anyone who does not love the Lord Jesus Christ. In Galatians 1:8–9 Paul says twice that anyone who preaches a gospel other than the one he preached should be condemned or accursed. And there are others in the New Testament. Allen lists: Acts 23:1–6, 1 Timothy 1:19–20, 2 Timothy 4:4, James 5:1–6, Revelation 6:9–10, and Matthew 23:32–35.[61] If there were such a strong distinction between the Old and New dispensation, as is necessary for the New Testament Dispensation hermeneutic to remain viable, no curses should exist in the New Testament. The presence of the imprecations in the New Testament, however, exposes the contrived nature of the distinction—a distinction motivated not by good exegesis, but an unsound theological presupposition that imprecations must be wrong for the modern believer. Since imprecations are part of the New Testament, we would be misguided to argue that we can simply abandon the imprecatory psalms in favor of the teachings in the Sermon on the Mount. Nor would we be advised to dismiss Jesus' teachings on mercy

---

60. Acts 1:20. It must be admitted here that while Luke references the psalms in relation to Judas, the context and tone is different. The Psalms in mind are clearly imprecatory. Acts, on the other hand, is more of an historical commentary about who Judas was. As historical narrative, Luke is not cursing Judas here. Jesus, however, did say of Judas "But woe to that man who betrays the Son of Man! It would be better for him if he had not been born" (Mark 14:21).

61. Allen, *Psalms 101–150*, 74. A detailed table of New Testament Imprecation is on page 137, guideline 7.

History of Interpretation of the Imprecatory Psalms

and forgiveness found in the Sermon on the Mount. Instead, I suggest that we must reconcile these two as complementary and inspired Scriptures. We may strive to preserve the theology and the passion of these psalms, while also loving our enemy and praying for him.

An additional disadvantage with this interpretive model is the problem it raises for the doctrine of inspiration. The notion of progressive revelation is not enough to explain the imprecatory problem. Progress in thought is one thing, but a complete reversal in morality is another. To see in the Sermon on the Mount a moral teaching that is antithetical to moral teaching given in the Psalms would mean that God is confused or capricious, or that one of these sections was not inspired by God. McKenzie explains,

> It has been said that the imprecatory psalms must be understood in the light of the imperfect morality of the Old Testament. It is often, though carelessly, said that these things were lawful in the Old Testament which are not lawful in the New. So it is proposed that the imprecations of the psalms proceed from the less enlightened conscience of the writer. This explanation seems not merely inadequate, but positively dangerous to the doctrine of inspiration.[62]

The New Testament Dispensational model poses serious problems for the integrity of God's thinking. Because of this, the model raises problems for the doctrine of inspiration.

A further criticism of this dispensational view is that it denies that the Old Testament promotes the love of one's enemy. In the Law we discover that this concept is not as new as the proponents of this dispensational view contend. We read, "You shall not hate your brother in your heart. You shall surely rebuke your neighbor, and not bear sin because of him. You shall not take vengeance, nor bear any grudge against the children of your people, but you shall love your neighbor as yourself. I am the Lord." (Lev 19:17–18). The Wisdom literature also promotes love of enemy. We read, "Do not rejoice when your enemy falls, and do not let your heart be glad when he stumbles; Lest the Lord see it and it displease him, and he turn away his wrath from him" (Prov 24:17–18). Similarly, "If your enemy is hungry, give him bread to eat; and if he is thirsty, give him water to drink; for so you will heap coals of fire on his head, and the Lord will reward you" (Prov 25:21–22).

Denying the presence of this teaching in the Old Testament has the effect of perpetuating the notion above that Christians have dug themselves out of a pit of old Jewish teaching. The simplistic division between two dispensations, one hateful and the other loving, also provides an overly simplistic

---

62. McKenzie, "The Imprecations of the Psalter," 82–83.

hermeneutic when reading either testament. This is a narrow interpretive lens through which to understand the world of biblical literature. Furthermore, we want to be trained in the "whole counsel of God," but the dispensational view keeps us ignorant of a certain aspect of Old Testament teaching.

Finally, a persistent problem with dispensationalism of any kind is the question of relevance. Generally the proponents of dispensational views have a high regard for Scripture, otherwise they would have dismissed the "problem of the imprecatory psalms" as an historical phenomenon. But because they have a high view of Scripture, they seek to reconcile the imprecatory psalms with their view of God. This high view of Scripture generally compels people to find the relevance and application of Scripture in modern life. And this is one of the peculiar self-defeating problems with any dispensational view. Dispensationalists arrive at their conclusions in part because they believe Scripture, but their conclusion leaves almost no room for modern day application. This is clearly seen in dispensational eschatology, for instance. The passages about the end times refer to the end times, so there is no application for life today. Those passages were written for someone else. This seems like a bizarre destination for people to arrive at because they take Scripture seriously. The same problem applies to a dispensational view of the imprecatory psalms. If the imprecations in the Psalter reflect a bygone era, and the cross has changed everything, then what are we to do with them? It seems that the only thing to do with them is appreciate "the pit from which we have been dug." By this logic, we can marvel at these psalms, but we cannot apply anything to our lives from them.

H. Quotation Hypothesis

In this section, we examine the quotation hypothesis in regard to the imprecatory psalms. It turns out that maybe the psalmists were not saying all those imprecations in the first place. The justification for the Quotation Hypothesis is grounded in the fact that the oldest copies of the Hebrew OT lack any punctuation—including quotation marks. This lack of punctuation has required modern translators to make the decision when quotation marks are necessary. Often the clues are obvious, but in some cases the placement of quotation marks is an interpretive decision, based on context or theological assumptions. Some interpreters, therefore, have argued that we should place quotation marks around the imprecatory statements, thereby making these the statements of the adversary, and not the psalmist.[63] By taking this

63. Vos and Laney each state that the quotation hypothesis is a historic method for dealing with the imprecatory Psalms, but they do not cite sources. McKenzie attributes this view to Boylon, but gives no citation.

History of Interpretation of the Imprecatory Psalms

approach, the apparent moral problem of God's people cursing their enemies is solved, though the textual basis for doing so can be dubious.

At times, the quotation hypothesis may be justified. The New Revised Standard Version of the Bible (NRSV), for instance, places Psalm 109:6–19 in the voice of the accuser.[64] The interpretation of these curses as from the mouth of the enemy, however, is not motivated by a theological commitment that imprecations are sinful. The text seems to warrant the use of quotations *in this instance*. This must be the case whenever we make an interpretive decision of this kind. Allen writes of the rationale for placing quotation marks in Psalm 109, "it is to be hoped that the aim of all serious scholars, whichever view they hold, is that theology should grow out of exegesis and not vice versa."[65] Zenger says of this psalm in particular, "For exegetical, not apologetic reasons, I myself consider the so-called quotation hypothesis the most adequate explanation of the series of curses in verse 6–19."[66] But the NRSV does not supply the quotations each time imprecations appear in other psalms. There is not a systematic attempt to explain away curses, but an isolated attempt to grasp the best reading of Psalm 109. So in this case, the quotations do not solve the "problem" of imprecations, since the remainder of the Psalter supplies plenty other curses. Furthermore, Allen points out that even if we see verses 6–20 as the words of the accuser, in verse 20 the psalmist still asks God to do what has previously been wished for by his enemies.[67]

Chrysostom had a modified view of the quotation hypothesis. Rather than seeing the imprecations as the utterance of the adversary, he sees the psalmist as representing the view of his people (though the psalmist may not necessarily agree). Chrysostom writes of Psalm 137, "When he tells of the sufferings of others, he depicts their anger, their pain, which is what he did in this case, bringing to the fore the desire of the Jews, who let their rage extend even to such a young age."[68] In other words, the psalmist is not quoting the enemy, but the sentiment of others in his nation. Chrysostom's assumption presumably is that it would be wrong for the psalmist to imprecate, but not for him to report what his countrymen are saying. McKenzie argues that Herkenne also proposed a modified view of the quotation hypothesis: "Herkenne's proposal that Ps. 108:6–19 is spoken as the words of God Himself is merely

---

64. This is a departure from the reading of the RSV text, which has no quotation marks.
65. Allen, *Psalms 101–150*, 73.
66. Zenger, *A God of Vengeance?* 59.
67. Allen, *Psalms 101–150*, 73.
68. Chrysostom, *Commentary on the Psalms*, 233.

Part One: Interpretation

a modification of the same view and is no more acceptable."[69] The alleged speakers in the quotation hypothesis range from the ungodly adversary, to the community, to God. But in each case the imprecatory problem is "solved" because the curses are not spoken by godly people, but by God himself, who presumably has the right to judge in this way.

An obvious problem with the quotation hypothesis is that even if it could be employed legitimately (based on textual evidence in a few instances), nearly a third of the psalms have an imprecatory element. There is no textual basis for attributing the imprecation to the enemy in each of these curses. Therefore, if one were to do so in these cases their action would be based on a prior theological assumption that it is morally wrong for men of God to pray for the downfall of their enemies. It would be erroneous to begin with such an assumption, since the Old Testament prohibits revenge (Lev 19:18), but does not actually prohibit imprecation. Furthermore, the use of imprecatory language extends into the New Testament through the lips of Jesus and other writers. There is not sufficient theological evidence to say that imprecation is wrong, and to justify placing these words in the mouth of adversaries. So the quotation hypothesis fails on the grounds that there is not enough exegetical and theological evidence.

I. Spells

Some scholars insist that the best interpretation of these imprecations is to see them as magical spells. Other scholars are less adamant, but say that the curses at least have the remnant of spells, or that they were modeled after magical practices. In either case, this is a more nuanced form of the sociological-historical interpretation.

To see the curses in the psalms as prayers to God against an adversary implies that there is in fact an adversary. This more literal interpretation of the curses places them in an historical context with real enemies and battles. But those who see the psalms as spells arrive at this conclusion because they have removed the psalms from real historical events. Such authors see the psalms as a later liturgical, ritualized development. They contend that the genre of imprecatory speech follows a ritualized pattern: "When you are afflicted, say these words." The practice of repeating such a ritualized curse, Mowinckel argued, is rooted in magic. Since neighboring nations employed magical spells which invoked the language of mythical battles, proponents of this view state that these "curse formulas" in

---

69. McKenzie, "The Imprecations of the Psalter," 86. Referring to Herkenne in *Das Buch Der Psalmen*.

History of Interpretation of the Imprecatory Psalms

the psalms also address mythical, rather than historical battles. Birkland writes, "Mowinckel interprets the sayings of the psalms in question [of an annual enthronement of Yahweh] as founded on a mythical battle, so that e.g., the investigation of the walls and towers of Zion in 48.13f would have no real, historic basis."[70] In other words, Brichto summarizes Hempel's and Mowinckel's view that, "beneath the Old Testament conceptions of curse and blessing there can be discovered—despite all the sublimation—their origin in magical practices."[71] The psalmist may have had an enemy in mind, but the Psalm itself does not tell us who the present enemy was (perhaps the enemy in mind was a demon, a disease, disaster, or neighboring nation). The stated enemies in the Psalms, instead, are believed to be mythical, since presumably the Jews borrowed this practice from other nations invoked mythical battles in their magical curse formulas.

As evidence for this position, Hempel offers the following examples of magical practices in the Old Testament: "Joshua's stretching out of the javelin (Joshua 8.18), the pointing of the finger (Isaiah 58.9), spitting (Deuteronomy 25.9)."[72] Brichto explains that according to proponents of this view, "All these are devices to effect a kind of contract between subject and object, i.e., the imprecator and his victim. Also rooted in magic is the use of the right hand in blessing (Genesis 48.13)."[73]

The key concept that would make a curse a spell, rather than simply a prayer, is whether the spoken word is self-causal. Do the words effect change in themselves, or must God approve the prayer? Mowinckel thinks some of the curses in the Old Testament are effectual. Speaking of Deuteronomy 30, he writes, "We find a formula which still brings out the earlier conception about the self-acting power of the 'water of curse.'"[74] And regarding the Psalms, Mowinckel says, "A prayer like the one in 83.10ff with its elaborate description of the disaster imprecated on the enemies of the people is evidently connected with the ancient cursing formulas, such as seers and other 'divine men' and possessors of the effectual word would use against the enemy before the battle; with such words Balak expected Balaam to slay the Israelites for him."[75]

Gunkel's conclusion is somewhat modified from Mowinckel's. He sees the remnant of magic, if not the blatant use of it. Gunkel writes, "In the

---

70. Birkland, *The Evildoers in the Book of Psalms*, 77.
71. Brichto, *The Problem of Curse in the Hebrew Bible*, 4.
72. Ibid., 5.
73. Ibid., 5.
74. Mowinckel, *The Psalms in Israel's Worship*, Volume 2, 29.
75. Ibid., 51.

extant biblical songs magic is completely lacking or, at least, has receded far into the background."[76] Mowinckel and Hempel are confident to equate the curses with spells, but Brichto offers a qualified position. In a detailed Hebrew word study, Brichto examines the synonyms for curse and oath, and concludes that at least one Hebrew word is similar to the concept of a spell. He explains, "The stem 'rr in both its verbal and nominal occurrences has the force of 'curse' only in the operative sense of the word. As such, its basic sense is best rendered by 'spell.' Spell is imagined as something like a magic circle, which bars that which is within from that which is without."[77]

But Brichto qualifies his position that the curses are magical in a strict sense. He writes, "Oaths are contingent or conditional curses."[78] In this sense, curses may be magical, but the effect of the curse is not guaranteed, nor is the person praying the agent of affliction. Instead, the prayer is offered to God as the sovereign agent of affliction or blessing. Nevertheless, according to Brichto, the prayers are irrevocable, formulaic, and even transferable.

So if the worshiper was not consciously aware that he was offering a magical spell, Brichto still thinks the formula for the prayer derived from such practices. He writes, "Now it is true that atavistic superstitions die hard, but the rites accompanying them do not necessarily involve a consciousness of magical potency."[79]

One problem with this interpretation is the level to which magic, sorcery, and the consulting of mediums is forbidden in the Old Testament. The Bible proclaims a curse on those who engage in such practices: "A man or woman who is a medium or spiritist among you must be put to death" (Lev 20:27). So if one takes the position that the Bible presents a unified theology (because it is inspired by a coherent God), it is impossible to reconcile the "spell theory" with the biblical stance concerning magic. Even putting the inspiration of Scripture aside, and approaching this issue from an historical-critical angle, it is difficult to see how the ancient readers would have tolerated such an inconsistency. Given the deeply fundamental taboo of magic in Jewish thought, they would have eradicated the remnant of it in their Scriptures. Furthermore, it seems that the proponents of this theory have confused symbolic acts (blessing with the right hand) with magic. These two concepts are not necessarily related, and certainly not synonymous. In addition, this theory has the same weakness of the historical theories: it does not offer a present day application. We are still left with the question, "what should we do?"

---

76. Gunkel. *The Psalms*, 21–22.
77. Brichto, *The Problem of Curse in the Hebrew Bible*, 114.
78. Ibid., 40.
79. Ibid., 207.

History of Interpretation of the Imprecatory Psalms

J. Prophetic

A traditional way of accepting the inspiration of the imprecatory psalms while excusing, justifying, or dismissing the tone of the curses, is to see them as prophetic. The theory admirably starts with the assumption that the Bible presents a unified, inspired theology. But there is an assumption that one should always and only pray favorably for his enemies. This would ostensibly be the theology of the New Testament. This is reminiscent of the NT Dispensation view which postulates a contradiction between the Old and New Testaments in regard to cursing. To preserve the integrity of the inspired word, one must see the curses as something other than prayers against the enemy. So according to the prophetic view, the imprecatory psalms are not prayers but rather are prophecies of what will inevitably happen to the unrighteous. This psalms can be interpreted within a prophetic-proverbial structure, or a prophetic-eschatological framework. Prophetic-proverbial means that the curses prophesy what inevitably befalls a person in his own lifetime. Like the tone of the proverbs, there is a "what goes around, comes around" sentiment in the imprecatory prayers. On the other hand, prophetic-eschatological means that the psalms decry what will befall the wicked on the final Day of Judgment.

Calvin was a strong proponent of the prophetic theory.[80] Regarding Psalm 129:5 he writes, "Whether we take this as a prayer or a promise, the prophet has a respect to the time to come. Since all the verbs are in the future tense, it is certainly a very appropriate interpretation to understand him as deriving from times past instruction as to what is to be hoped for in future, even to the end."[81]

Similarly, Calvin says of Psalm 137, "This is not the language of imprecation, but of prophecy, and predicts the horrors which would accompany the taking and sacking of the city of Babylon; and amongst these atrocious the cruelty of 'dashing the children against the stones.'"[82] Matthew Henry also took the prophetic approach. He wrote of Psalm 137, "The Lord will not forsake his church in her low estate. He will execute *predicted* vengeance on all her persecutors, and if professors join such in their prosperity, they will be joined with them in the day of wrath."[83]

---

80. Calvin was also an adamant covenantal theologian. These views are not mutually exclusive, and he should be seen as a proponent of both views. These views are separated in this discussion because not all advocates of the prophetic theory use covenantal language.

81. Calvin, *Commentary on the Book of Psalms*, Vol. 5, 125.

82. Ibid., 194–95.

83. Henry, *Matthew Henry Commentary*, Vol. 2, 319.

Part One: Interpretation

Spurgeon also seems to prefer the prophetic theory. Also speaking of Psalm 137, he cites William Wilson, "We are not to regard the imprecations of this psalm in any other light than as prophetical."[84] Spurgeon further cites Adam Clarke regarding the same psalm, "These prophetic declarations contain no excitement to any person or persons to commit acts of cruelty and barbarity; but are simply declarative of what would take place in the order of the retributive providence and justice of God, and the general opinion that should in consequence be expressed on the subject; therefore praying for the destruction of our enemies is totally out of the question."[85]

The prophetic theory clearly has strong support throughout history, with adherents such as Calvin, Spurgeon, and Clarke. It was even endorsed by John Chrysostom, who wrote of Psalm 109, "[This] inspired composition is composed in the form of a curse, announcing and foretelling the fate of Judas, and then dealing with another topic after him, even reaching on some people who rebelled against the priesthood."[86]

A strength of the prophetic theory is that the rest of Scripture confirms the eschatological hope that God will make all things right, and that he will establish justice. Regardless of whether the best interpretation of the Psalms is prophetic, the general concept behind this theory is true. The question, however, is not whether God will avenge his enemies, but whether that is the best reading of the Psalms.

One problem with this theory is that it is meant to soften what otherwise sounds like a vehement attitude. The prophetic theory tries to "solve" the imprecatory problem by alleging that the authors did not wish any ill-will; they merely predicted it. But McKenzie agrees that the prophetic interpretation does not solve the imprecatory problem. In response to Augustine's prophetic treatment of Psalm 109, he writes,

> This explanation is simply not valid for the greater part of the imprecatory passages; and the more common opinion of modern exegetes does not accept it even in Pss. 68 and 108,[87] where the Fathers introduce it. And even if it could be demonstrated for some passages, we should still face the question of the joy which the Psalmist feels and expresses at the evils which are to

---

84. Spurgeon, *Treasury of David*, 199.

85. Ibid., 200. It should be noted that Adam Clarke's conclusion is a non sequitur: given that Scripture contains prophecies of future revenge, it does not necessarily follow that praying for this destruction is out of the question.

86. Chrysostom, *Commentary on the Psalms*, 5.

87. McKenzie is using the Psalm numbering from the Vulgate, which would correspond to Psalms 69 and 109.

befall his enemies—a sentiment of hatred which also is prohibited by the law of charity.[88]

As McKenzie points out, in order for the prophetic theory to solve the imprecatory problem, we must imagine that the psalmist harbored no ill feelings toward his neighbor, and was filled with no hatred. But this is clearly not the case. The psalms are either a cesspool or treasure trove (depending on how you look at it) of emotional language. No other place in Scripture, or even ancient literature, comes close to expressing the depth of emotion. It seems unrealistic to read the psalms and imagine that the authors were emotionally detached from their so-called prophesies.

Like the historical models, this interpretive method does not offer much in the way of contemporary application: it does not help us pray the psalms except as prophecies. In addition, like the allegorical models, this school of thought does not correspond to our experience. If we have wished the downfall of our enemies, why should not the psalmist have had this same wish?

Another problem with the theory, at least the prophetic-proverbial model, is that it does not always turn out to be true. Quite often enemies do not fall into their own nets. Many enemies live to old age and always have the upper hand. So these curses could not be prophetic in the immediate sense; they could only be proverbial at best. The only way to preserve them as prophetic without the obvious observation that the prophecy did not come true, is to see them as eschatological.

This, however, is unnecessary, because the Bible does not need such a forced interpretation in order to allow for the presence of these imprecations. It is difficult to conclude that the unified biblical theology is exclusively to pray "nicely" for enemies. True, Jesus did teach on the Sermon on the Mount that we ought to pray for our enemies. But (as stated in section four) imprecations are found throughout the Old and New Testament.

---

88. McKenzie, "The Imprecations of the Psalter," 86.

Part One: Interpretation

K. Messianic

Similar to the prophetic theory, there is an interpretation of the imprecatory psalms that might be called "messianic." This theory sees EACH of the psalms as prayers of Christ. In this sense they are prophetic, because they are the prayers that will be prayed by Christ at some point. There is some rationale for this theory, in that Christ did pray the psalms on several occasions. Furthermore, many of the psalms have blatant messianic prophecies in them. Other psalms are nevertheless cited by New Testament authors as being messianic prophecies. Below is a table of instances where Jesus directly cites the Psalms.

Figure 2.1: New Testament citations of Psalms by Jesus

Psalm	New Testament Citation by Jesus	Text of Psalm in NIV
8:2	Matt 21:16	Through the praise of children and infants you have established a stronghold against your enemies, to silence the foe and the avenger.
22:1	Matt 27:46 Mark 15:34	My God, my God, why have you forsaken me? Why are you so far from saving me, so far from my cries of anguish?
31:5	Luke 23:46	Into your hands I commit my spirit; deliver me, LORD, my faithful God
41:9	Matt 21:16 John 13:18	Even my close friend, someone I trusted, one who shared my bread, has turned against me.
82:6	John 10:34	I said, "You are 'Gods'; you are all sons of the Most High."
91:11–12	Matt 4:6 Luke 4:10–11	For he will command his angels concerning you to guard you in all your ways; they will lift you up in their hands, so that you will not strike your foot against a stone.
110:1	Matt 22:44 Mark 12:36 Luke 20:42–43	The LORD says to my lord: "Sit at my right hand until I make your enemies a footstool for your feet."
118:26	Matt 21:9 Luke 13:35; 19:38 John 12:13	Blessed is he who comes in the name of the LORD. From the house of the LORD we bless you.

History of Interpretation of the Imprecatory Psalms

In addition, there are psalms which are interpreted by New Testament authors to have been messianic.

Figure 2.2: New Testament citations of Psalms in reference to Jesus

Psalm	New Testament use in reference to Jesus	Text of Psalm in NIV
22:18	Matt 27:35 John 19:24	They divide my clothes among them and cast lots for my garment.
34:20	John 19:36	he protects all his bones, not one of them will be broken.
69:4–9	John 2:17 John 12:25	for zeal for your house consumes me, and the insults of those who insult you fall on me.
78:2	Matt 13:35	I will open my mouth with a parable; I will utter hidden things, things from of old—
118:22–23	Matt 21:42 Mark 12:10 Luke 20:17	The stone the builders rejected has become the cornerstone; the LORD has done this, and it is marvelous in our eyes

Clearly the Jesus himself and the New Testament authors viewed some of the psalms as either explicitly messianic, containing messianic elements, or containing messianic typology. But the fact that Christ prayed the psalms, and that the New Testament authors consider the psalms messianic is not the only consideration for the messianic model for interpreting the imprecatory psalms. There is a further moral issue in play. If one starts with the assumption that imprecations are sinful, there must be an account for how they ended up in the Bible. James Adams concluded that we are not afforded the permission to pray these curses, though God is allowed to pray them, since God is more just and holy than we. In other words, the imprecations are not our prayers. Adams claims that his view was also that of Webster, Luther, and Calvin.[89]

As proof Adams offers Psalm 22, and observes that David did not experience many of the things listed in the psalm, but Christ in fact did. He reasons, therefore, that the prayer is more suited for Christ than for David, and must therefore be a prophetic embodiment of a messianic prayer.

Mays also subscribes to this view. He points out that the writers of the New Testament saw predictions of the Messiah in the psalms. Mays also looks to Psalm 2 and asserts that it contains both a messianic and imprecatory element.[90] He writes that the psalm predicts, "The entire life of Jesus,

---

89. Adams, *War Psalms of the Prince of Peace*, 20, 32.
90. Mays, *The Lord Reigns*, 51, 89.

Part One: Interpretation

from baptism to crucifixion, his accession, his public presentation to the nation as their ruler, as the Messiah. This means that the psalm has a new setting in the Gospel. It is here now, not in a palace in the midst of royal ritual, but in a ritual of repentance-baptism."[91] Mays summarizes the messianic position, "It is also generally agreed that by the time the Psalter was being completed, the psalms dealing with the kingship of the Lord were understood as eschatological. They no longer refer only to what was enacted in cult, but refer as well to what was promised in prophecy."[92]

Luther's interpretation of the imprecatory psalms was thoroughly messianic. His interpretation is uniquely nuanced, and follows a strict pattern. In each imprecation, Jesus is the speaker; the victim. The Jews are the perpetrators, for they are the ones who called for his crucifixion. And the punishment invoked in the Psalms is the Jews exclusion from salvation. Luther places Psalm 68 entirely in the context of the future, illustrated by the title of his sermon on that Psalm: "About Easter, Ascension, and Pentecost." The Psalm begins "May God arise, may his enemies be scattered; may his foes flee before him." Commenting on this Scripture, Luther writes, "When Christ died, God feigned sleep and pretended that He did not see the raging Jews. He permitted them to rally and gather strength, whereas the poor disciples fled and scattered. And now, when the Jews assumed that they had carried the day and that Christ had been laid low, God woke up again and raised Christ from the dead."[93] Similarly, in Psalm 109:9 we read "let his children be fatherless and his wife a widow." Luther writes, "(that is, his[94] good works without Christ to acknowledge them), and his wife a widow, that is, may the soul remain without Christ, the husband."[95] Of Psalm 2, Luther says, "Behold now the catalog of the dreadful punishments that are prepared for the crucifiers of Christ."[96]

Bonhoeffer also interpreted the psalms as wholly messianic, albeit in a different manner than Luther. Whereas Luther sees the wrath of God poured out on the Jews, Bonhoeffer sees God's wrath satisfied in Jesus. He writes, "The prayers of David were prayed also by Christ. Or better, Christ himself prayed them through his forerunner David."[97] Bonhoeffer's interpretation is that the retribution asked for in the imprecatory psalms was fulfilled on the cross. He says, "I pray the imprecatory psalms in the certainty of their

91. Ibid., 115.
92. Ibid., 133.
93. Luther, *Luther's Works*, Vol. 13, 3.
94. Referring to the enemy of the author of Psalm 109.
95. Luther, *Luther's Works*, Vol. 11, 356.
96. Ibid., Vol. 14, 323.
97. Bonhoeffer, *Psalms*, 19.

marvelous fulfillment. I leave the vengeance to God and ask him to execute his righteousness to all his enemies, knowing that God has remained true to himself and has himself secured justice in his wrathful judgment on the cross, and that this wrath has become grace and joy for us."[98] He references Galatians 1:8, 1 Corinthians 16:22, Revelation 18:19 and 20:11 as examples of God pouring his wrath upon Christ, rather than upon humans. So when Bonhoeffer prays the imprecatory prayers, he is mindful that Christ bore the punishment that each of us is due. He says, "In this way the crucified Jesus teaches us to pray the imprecatory psalms correctly."[99]

A strength of this view is that undoubtedly some of the psalms are messianic. As seen in the above chart, the New Testament employs this interpretive model for many of the imprecatory psalms. But it would be a stretch to say that every psalm is messianic. In addition, this theory poses no problems for the doctrine of inspiration, and seems to "solve" the imprecatory problem.

One of the weaknesses of the prophetic theory above is that it manipulates the grammar of specific passages in order to achieve moral vindication for the Psalms. The messianic theory is even more contrived. It seems that the theory is not based on good exegesis, but on a moral assumption. If one assumes that fallible human beings have no moral justification for praying a curse on their enemies, then work must be done to reconcile the fact that godly, inspired authors of the Bible did in fact pray those prayers. The messianic theory sufficiently solves that moral dilemma. But the whole theory rests on the assumption that only God has the right to imprecate, and godly people do not have the right to pray curses. But how can we justify such an assumption? We could only arrive at such a moral conclusion by looking to Scripture. But when we look to Scripture, we see godly people praying curses.

Similar to the prophetic theory, the messianic theory also lacks contemporary application and is inconsistent with human nature. If the psalms were the prayers of Christ, then they are not our prayers. There is not much for us to "do" with them. And as the prayers of Christ, we are to imagine that these psalms were not the prayers of the victim. But why should the victim not have prayed against his enemies?

L. Covenantal Theory

Commenting on Psalm 143:12, Calvin writes, "Whatever severity may appear on the part of God when he destroys the wicked, David affirms that the

---

98. Ibid., 59.
99. Ibid., 60.

Part One: Interpretation

vengeance taken upon them would be a proof of fatherly mercy to him."[100] Calvin's interpretation of this imprecatory psalm may be called the "covenantal theory." This theory reads the imprecations as appeals for God to make good on his promises. The promises include the prosperity of a chosen people, judgment of the wicked, blessing of the righteous, and that God would be slow to anger, and abounding in love. When the psalmist prays, he is calling out to God to be faithful to his character.

Jungho Kim summarizes the view in this way; "A covenantal perspective brings the theology of imprecations . . . into proper view. The psalmist utters covenantal curses against his enemies according to Yahweh's covenantal character. Covenant curses are the psalmist's spiritual weapon."[101]

An important aspect of the covenantal interpretation is that we recognize the psalmist was not praying according to his own will, nor against his personal enemies. Instead, "The enemies turn out to be the foes of Yahweh's covenant." For instance, "The covenant breakers in Psalm 35 are identical to the covenant foes. The covenant breakers are those who violate Yahweh's moral law."[102] If this is true, then the prayers are words of agreement with what we already know about God. Seen in this light, it is hard to see how a moral dilemma would arise about whether it is permissible to pray these prayers. That is, it cannot be wrong to pray that God will be faithful to his character.

Kim explains the function of imprecatory prayers within the covenantal context. He says, "The poet's imprecations are a covenant appeal to Yahweh for justice to fulfill His promise."[103] This theory shares a similar basis to the prophetic theory. Both are premised on a belief of what God will surely do to the wicked. In the prophetic view the psalmist can prophesy the destruction of the wicked because he knows the character of God. Similarly, in the covenant view, the psalmist can pray for God to be faithful to his character. Kim explains, "In return for his covenant faithfulness to Yahweh, he asks Yahweh to demonstrate his faithfulness by executing His covenant curses against the psalmist's oppressors."[104]

A key difference between the prophetic and covenantal view, however, is the level of emotion that we see in the psalms. The prophetic view seems to expect us to believe that the psalmist did not desire or enjoy the downfall of his enemy. But the covenantal view allows for the presence of

---

100. Calvin, *Commentary on the Book of Psalms*, 258.

101. Kim, *A Literary and Theological Study of Imprecatory Psalms 35 and 137 as a Defense for their Integrity*, 65

102. Ibid., 81–82.

103. Ibid., 203.

104. Ibid., 204.

anger and hatred. Kim writes, "Imprecations are a covenant appeal to the God of justice to implement His promise; imprecations express concern for the reputation and sovereignty of God and the salvation of his people; and, imprecations are a reflection of hatred of sin."[105]

An advantage of the covenantal theory is that it recognizes the presence of imprecations throughout Scripture. Any good theory of the imprecatory psalms must do this. But the covenantal theory goes further than identifying other imprecations; it demonstrates that cursing is fundamental to the concept of covenant. Cheong writes,

> The Abrahamic Covenant lays a foundation for a curse on national enemies who would annoy Israel's descendants. The Mosaic Covenant binds every person to God and neighbors, vertically and horizontally, so that people who violate the Mosaic Covenant by doing considerable harm to neighbors are to be cursed according to God's law. The Davidic Covenant deals with both the national enemy and the personal enemy because David was a representative of God's Kingdom. The biblical ground on which one may justify the imprecations is the covenantal basis for curses on enemies.[106]

In other words, not only is there evidence of imprecations throughout the Bible, these curses are inherently necessary to the concept of covenant. The modern reader may ask why the curses are inherent to the concept of covenant, and many may wish to separate the two. But upon studying the curses of Deuteronomy 27–28, for example, we see that the purpose of the curses upon the wicked was to establish an "in-group" and an "out-group." This line of demarcation is clearly inherent to the concept of covenant, for it declares who will be the recipient of God's promises, and who will be left out.

As a sociological explanation, the covenantal theory seems sufficient. Any ancient historian, regardless of theology, would agree the psalmists had an underlying assumption of covenant, and that these curses established the in-group. The covenantal theory also fits well within a dispensational framework,[107] with the assumption that the imprecations were appropriate as long as they appealed to the particular covenantal promise of the day. Laney explains how the covenantal view fits within a dispensational hermeneutic, while also harmonizing with the modern aversion to curses: "In light of the fact that the Abrahamic covenant reflects God's promise to Abraham

---

105. Ibid., 215.

106. Cheong, *Biblical Basis of the Imprecatory Psalms*, 29–30.

107. That is, any interpretation that divides history into at least two epochs, and assigns different ethics or theological programs to these time periods.

and his descendants, it would be inappropriate for a church-age believers to call down God's judgment on the wicked."[108]

The covenant theory, therefore, preserves the doctrine of inspiration. It allows for contemporary application, in that God's covenant people are still permitted to ask God to make good on his promises. And it is consistent with human experience: it assumes that we have enemies, and that we wish to see them avenged.

M. Dependence Theory

The final view presented in this study I term "Dependence theory." This notion affirms that the psalms were written by inspired, mature people who suffered at the hands of hard-hearted enemies. The psalmists knew that God was grieved by the plight of the helpless, and he was more capable of exacting justified vengeance than they. So they transferred their own schemes of vengeance to a sovereign God who, though just, defends the innocent. In short, the imprecations are prayers of dependence upon God. This theory is similar to covenantal theory; so similar, in fact, that it may seem difficult to distinguish the two. They are placed in distinct categories here simply because some authors who subscribe to the dependence theory do not use covenantal language.

Though Erich Zenger does not use the term "dependence theory" (he does not give his interpretation any title), he clearly advocates it. Zenger wrote, "When those who pray call to their God as a righteous judge they avert vengeance from themselves. They appeal to a God who, as a God of justice, considers, decides, and punishes, this last not out of a pleasure in punishment but in order to restore and defend the damaged order of law."[109] Perhaps another suitable name for this interpretation would be "transference theory." Writing about Psalm 137, for instance, Zenger says it is, "an attempt, in the face of the most profound humiliation and helplessness, to suppress the primitive human lust for violence in one's own heart, by surrendering *everything* to God."[110] Through imprecation, the psalmist transfers the need to take action and the desire for vengeance from himself to God. I prefer the term dependence, however, because the work is not done once the desire for vengeance is transferred. The psalmist must continue to depend upon God to act.

Several recent authors read the imprecatory psalms as prayers of dependence. Laney, for instance, writes, "David had a perfect right as the

---

108. Laney, "A Fresh Look at the Imprecatory Psalms," 44.

109. Zenger, *A God of Vengeance?* 71.

110. Ibid., 48.

representative of the nation to pray that God would effect what he had promised, cursing on those who cursed or attacked Israel."[111] In other words, David had the opportunity to take matters in his own hands, but he depended upon God (usually) to live up to God's character and promises. John Day also sees in the imprecations a prayer for God to fulfill his promises. He writes,

> Although Christians must continually seek reconciliation and practice longsuffering, forgiveness, and kindness, times come when justice must be enacted—whether from God directly or through his representatives.... Since God has promised to take revenge and repay those who hate him, it is not wrong for believers to petition him to fulfill these promises.[112]

The key concept to this theory is the observation that those who prayed for justice did not take matters into their own hands. They depended upon God to act. Kelly writes, "Prayers for vengeance were never accompanied by acts of violence against one's enemies. On the contrary such prayers were a renunciation of the principle of retaliation and a recognition that the authority to avenge wrongs rested only with God."[113] Shepherd also advocates an interpretation of dependence upon God. He writes,

> The covenantal basis of Psalm 109 is very clear, as is David's appeal to God to accomplish the judgment for which he calls. This is a very important point, not simply demonstrating the faith of the psalmist in God's power to save, but showing his desire to put his troubles and, more particularly, the fate of his enemies in the hands of God. David himself is not planning revenge; that's why he prays to God.[114]

Lind argues that the concept of dependence extends well beyond the Psalms, but pervades the whole Old Testament: "Yahweh, Israel's only war hero, became Yahweh, Israel's only king. Thus the principle of reliance upon Yahweh alone for military succor became imbedded in Israel's political structure."[115]

Vos explains that the moral permissibility of these imprecations requires the person praying to transfer his personal desires of revenge into the hands of God. This utter dependence upon the character of God is what makes the prayers "allowable." Vos writes,

---

111. Laney, "A Fresh Look at the Imprecatory Psalms," 42.
112. Day, "The Imprecatory Psalms and Christian Ethics," 169.
113. Kelly, "Prayers of Troubled Saints," 380.
114. Shepherd, "The Place of the Imprecatory Psalms in the Canon of Scripture," 42.
115. Lind, *Yahweh is a Warrior*, 32.

Part One: Interpretation

> The destruction of the wicked which is prayed for in the Imprecatory Psalms, then, is not murder but execution. These Psalms do not seek the unjust destruction of the life of man; on the contrary they are in essence an appeal to the justice of God and a prayer for that justice to execute sentence upon the wicked. The whole question of the morality of such prayers hinges upon the question of the compatibility of the thing prayed for with the nature of God.[116]

An advantage of the dependence theory is that it preserves the modern relevance of these prayers better than any other (with the exception of the covenant theory). The other theories examined in this study imply that the purpose that these psalms served has now passed. If they arose out of a particular historical situation, that era has faded. If they were "placed" in a particular dispensation, we now live in a new one. If they are solely messianic, then we leave them to be prayed by the Messiah. Other interpretations of the psalms attempt to make an excuse for the presence of imprecations in the inspired canon, or to render them obsolete. But the dependence theory gives the curses a rightful place not only within the canon, but also within worship. Few authors have had either the desire or the courage to give believers the green light to pray these prayers of imprecation. Vos does exactly that. He writes,

> Ultimately, then, it was right for the psalmists to pray for the destruction of the wicked because they were praying for God to do something which it was in harmony with God's nature for him to do, because the act of God which was prayed for conflicted with no actual rights of men, and because the prayers themselves were uttered by the inspiration of the Holy Spirit and therefore must have been right prayers and could not have been immoral.[117]

John Day also argues for continued usage of imprecation. He says, "The imprecatory psalms are at times appropriate on the lips of New Testament believers. Cursing and calling for divine vengeance and their extreme ethic may be voiced in extreme circumstances against hardened, deceitful, violent, immoral, and unjust sinners."[118]

Another advantage of the dependence theory is that it corresponds to the reality that many people actually do have human enemies. It also does not attempt to sweep away the fact that hatred is seen in the psalms. In this sense, it is faithful to the plainest reading of the psalms. The theory allows the psalms to have continued relevance for modern readers.

---

116. Vos, "Ethical Problems of the Imprecatory Psalms," 136.
117. Ibid., 134.
118. Day, "The Imprecatory Psalms and Christian Ethics," 168.

One disadvantage of the "dependence" theory is that it assumes, for instance, that after King David prayed against his enemies, he subsequently lost the urge personally to fight his enemies. Having transferred the responsibility of the problem to God, we are to imagine that David then intended not to take matters into his own hands. Although there are instances where David did refrain from taking matters into his own hands (as examined in section three), clearly these were the exception and not the rule. Most often, it appears that David prayed, and then he fought. He was a man of war. So much so, this prevented him from having the blessing of building the temple. This criticism, at least in regard to David, depends upon the Davidic authorship of at least some of the imprecatory psalms.

If one argues for later authorship of these psalms, then the dependence theory is immune to this criticism. That is, if one assumes the imprecatory psalms were written by people powerless to fight their enemies, and they had no other recourse but to call out to the Lord, then they are more likely to be expressions of dependence. In this case, however, a new question emerges, namely, "how serious is dependence when it is the only option?" Dependence is more authentic when it is the willful choice over independence, rather than the only available option. Nevertheless, God expects his people to be dependent upon him in all circumstances: good or bad, either when we are powerful or powerless.

N. Conclusion

I have discussed thirteen hermeneutical approaches toward the imprecatory psalms. Some of these approaches have been argued since the early church fathers; others are more recent theories. Figure 2.3 summarizes these models.

Figure 2.3: Summary of Interpretations[119]

1. Interpretive Model	Proponents
2. Spiritual-allegorical	Harold Osgood Charles Spurgeon Augustine

---

119. Note that these theories are not always explicitly named by the author, nor do all authors subscribe to these theories alone. I have tried to express the general thrust of their arguments, allowing that sometimes these authors advocate a combination of more than one interpretive model.

Part One: Interpretation

3.	Allegorical-historical	Patrick Miller Harold Ballard Carol Kloos
4.	Historical-inspired	*Halley's Bible Handbook* J. L. McKenzie
5.	Historical non-inspired	C. S. Lewis W. E. Farndale Peter Craigie
6.	Sociological-historical	Harris Birkland Millard Lind
7.	Cathartic	James Sire Chalmers Martin
8.	Pre New Testament (dispensational)	Bruce Waltke Derek Kidner Carl Laney James Mays Samuel Driver Bernhard Anderson Franz Delitzch
9.	Quotation	Heinrich Herkenne John Chrysostom
10.	Spells	Sigmund Mowinckel H. C. Brichto Herman Gunkel
11.	Prophetic	John Calvin Matthew Henry Charles Spurgeon Adam Clarke
12.	Messianic	James Adams James Mays Dietrich Bonhoeffer
13.	Covenant	Jungho Kim Eun Chae Cheong John Calvin
14.	Dependence	Erich Zenger Johannes G. Vos John Shepherd Leslie Allen Walter Brueggemann

In conclusion, it appears that many of the theories outlined in this study have the purpose of defending the psalms from the charge of advocating hatred, which is presumably a sin. This purpose seems misguided.

History of Interpretation of the Imprecatory Psalms

Most scholars of the psalms refer to them as horrific or at least distasteful. However, that sentiment seems to reflect a narrow worldview. It lacks global experience and is not empathetic to "the other half of the world" where many people live in daily terror of human enemies. As Allen contends, "Perhaps the citizen of a European country who has experienced its invasion and destruction would be the best exegete of such a psalm."[120] Many who have softened the tone of the imprecatory psalms have probably lacked such an experience. But this insulation from attack does not speak for the rest of the world, so interpreters would be wise not to assume that all readers find the imprecations in the Psalter repulsive.

The spiritual/allegorical interpretation is faulty because it ignores or denies the simple fact that we all have real human enemies. With so many actual enemies, why assume the psalmists were referring to spiritual ones? There is something unrealistic about the allegorical reading. As Brueggemann states, "Let us begin with two acts of realism. First, the yearning for vengeance is there in the Psalms. . . . And the counterpart, a second act of realism, is that the yearning for vengeance is here, among us and within us and with power."[121]

The historical-critical theory (taken alone) lacks engagement with a sense of divine revelation, so it renders this portion of Scripture irrelevant. The imprecatory psalms are an interesting phenomenon, but not a gift of revelation from God. The cathartic theory is a good model for understanding the psalms, and is compatible with other theories, so it need not stand alone. The dispensational model has several downfalls: it is prejudicial, renders prior dispensations irrelevant (such as the period from which we get the psalms), and makes false assumption about the New Testament (that it prohibits imprecations). There is almost no exegetical basis for the quotation hypothesis, so it must be rejected except where the text clearly justifies the placement of the imprecations in the mouth of the enemy. The theory that the imprecatory psalms are spells is incompatible with a doctrine of holistic revealed theology. It asks us to allow for the presence of magic in one biblical book, while we have the prohibition of magic in another, yet the whole Scripture is inspired by the same God. The prophetic view also lacks exegetical basis. It denies the obvious observation that the psalmists were enraged with their enemies. The messianic theory seems contrived and forced in some cases, though it is clearly applicable in others. It cannot, however, serve as a systematic theory of the imprecatory psalms. The covenantal theory is faithful to the plain reading of the text, allowing for

---

120. Allen, *Psalms 101–150*, 242.
121. Brueggemann, *Praying the Psalms*, 64.

hatred and the desire for violence. Depending on how one understands the concept of covenant, however, it could include a misleading endorsement of different dispensations with different covenants. Like the covenant theory, the dependence theory also captures the plain reading of the text. It allows for anger, hatred, and the desire for violence. It allows for the presence of real enemies. In addition, it is compatible with the doctrine of revelation.

Finally, many of the theories examined in this chapter seem contrived: they attempt to force a simple solution upon a complex problem. The dispensational, prophetic, allegorical, messianic, and quotation theories are intolerant of any tension in Scripture. It seems that these interpreters need Scripture to produce a monolithic message. This may not be necessary, even with a high view of Scripture and canon. The dependence, covenant, and catharsis theories allow one to maintain a high view of the Bible, while also recognizing that Scripture presents a more complex view of how to deal with enemies.

3

Interpretation of the Imprecatory Psalms through the Eyes of Victims

To this point, we have evaluated thirteen hermeneutical approaches to the Psalms. We have essentially asked, Is imprecation godly? Does it belong in the Christian life today? Perhaps one place to go in answering this question is among contemporary victims of violence. That is because the imprecatory psalms are written from the perspective of the victim. Most often, this victim of violence asserts his innocence, while crying out to God for revenge and justice. The victim appeal's to God because he lacks the power to deliver himself and judge the oppressor on his own. The perspective of the victim is a unique feature of the Bible, according to Culbertson. She writes, "Both Hebrew and Christian Scripture are unique in the world for their attention to the innocent victim. This privileging of the victim grounds both Judaism and Christianity in an ethic of compassion that has had profound consequences in the history of culture and civilizations. In the Psalms . . . we see the world through the eyes of the victim."[1] One reason this observation is important is that even if the Psalms are filled with rage and hatred, they cannot be a realistic call to arms. The victim is in no position to fight back, even if he wants to. Yet not every innocent victim in the Bible entertains this desire to fight back. Culbertson writes, "Jesus' death on the cross is properly interpreted as an end to all sacrifice."[2] Her comments are not directed at imprecations, but at the practice of sacrifice. Yet her interpretation of Christ's death is pertinent to the psalms. Her general question is "What does violence in the Bible teach us?" And her answer, with the paramount example of Christ's death, is that we "see violence from the perspective of the victim,

1. Culbertson, "Preaching the Word in a Culture of Violence," 61.
2. Ibid., 61.

especially this victim, whose forgiveness transformed human violence into love."³

The therapeutic and theological value of the imprecatory psalms, therefore, is that we identify with the oppressed and the victims of violence. In this identification, we never see retaliation carried out. Instead, we see the plans for retaliation transferred to God, who will supervene over the situation, even as he does over all history.

A. Hope for the Hopeless

Not surprisingly, Gustavo Gutierrez, the Peruvian regarded as the "father of Liberation theology," sees in the imprecatory psalms an assurance of future liberation. This is an eschatological hope, where God will make all things right. In Psalm 137:4 the psalmist asks, "How can we sing the songs of the LORD while in a foreign land?" Gutierrez comments, "It was a painful question for the psalmist; it is painful for the Latin American people as well. How can we sing to God from this strange world of the poor? Without songs—without thanksgiving for God's love—we have no Christian life. But how can we thank God for the gift of life in the reality of early and unjust death?"⁴ Gutierrez sees an eschatological hope of resurrection as the vital message for victims of oppression. He states, "According to Deuteronomy 30:15 we need to choose between death and life. Spiritualty—that is, a way to be Christian disciples—means to choose life. And to choose life in Latin America is to announce resurrection from the context of solidarity with the poor. When we talk about liberation, we talk about life."⁵ For Gutierrez, the imprecatory psalms impart hope for the hopeless.

Alvaro Salomon is a liberation scholar and pastor in Montevideo, Uruguay. In his, "Pastoral Reflections on the Psalms" he reveals his eschatological interpretation of the psalms. Specifically, in Psalm 37 he sees our hope realized in the *eschaton*. Salomon writes,

> El cristianismo prolonga esta esperanza en la proyección de la eternidad. Las Bienaventuranzas que Jesús pronunció y que el cristianismo primitivo tomó como fundamento de ética y seguimiento, comienzan a ser válidas en nuestra vida pero tendrán su cumplimiento final cuando el Reino de Dios se instale plenamente.⁶ [Christianity prolongs this hope in the projection

3. Ibid., 61.
4. Gutierrez, "A Spirituality of Liberation," 42
5. Ibid., 43.
6. Salomon, "Reflexiones Pastorales Sobre algunos Salmos," 265.

of eternity. The Beatitudes that Jesus pronounced and that early Christianity took as fundamental ethics, and following become validated in our life, must have their final completion when the Reign of God is fully installed.]

Salomon sees an ethic of justice in the Psalms that is typified by Christ. Jesus became the example of suffering when he refused to retaliate. But the story did not end there. Jesus was victorious over death and promises to create a just world in the future at his Second Coming. Salomon writes about the example of Christ's ethic in his reflection on Psalm 37,

> Sea ahora, o sea en la eternidad, el modelo de vida en justicia, en humildad y en verdad que viene del judaismo y que Jesús encarnó como nadie, sigue siendo válido para todos nosotros. La auténtica vida (y la que nos predispone a participar de un estado espiritual más cerca de Cristo) es la que nos señala el mensaje bíblico.[7] [Whether now, or whether in eternity, the model of life in justice, in humility, and in truth that comes from Judaism and that Jesus incarnated like no one else, seems valid for all of us. The authentic life (and that which disposes us to participate in the spiritual state closer to Christ) is that which the biblical message signals to us.]

Much has been written about the Psalms as a prophetic vision. This was perhaps the dominant reading of the imprecatory psalms throughout the Reformation and Enlightenment. But the eschatological hope expressed by these liberation scholars is distinct in a few ways. First, the traditional scholars who see the imprecations as prophetic make apologies for the unacceptable tone of the psalms. They find the curses unworthy of Godly desires, and insist that the imprecations are statements of fact (not wish). But the liberation theologians do not apologize for the harsh tone, nor do they pretend that retribution is not one of their desires. A second difference is that the prophetic interpretation does not necessarily see the retribution of sin in the *eschaton*. Those who hold that the curses are prophesies allow for the fulfillment of these prophesies even within the immediate generation. Not all liberation theologians insist that the "righting of wrongs" will occur at the End of the Age, but that is what Gutierrez and Salomon envision. This fulfillment in the *eschaton* is distinct from the prophetic interpretation. Brueggemann explains the relationship between hope and imprecation:

> But even the venom is left in God's hands. Perhaps there is a division of labor here to be celebrated: Israel hopes; Yahweh

---

7. Ibid., 265.

Part One: Interpretation

avenges as he chooses. The capacity to leave vengeance to God may free Israel for its primary vocation, which is the tenacious hope that prevents sell-out. Indeed, one may speculate that if Israel could not boldly leave vengeance to God and had worried about vengeance on its own, Israel might have had no energy or freedom to hope. Perhaps it is precisely this capacity to turn that over to God which leaves Israel free to hope for the New Jerusalem.[8]

Contemporary liberation authors share the same eschatological hope with the ancient authors of the imprecatory psalms.

B. Power for the Powerless

The skeptic may wonder whether it is legitimate to see in these war-filled psalms a call for peace. Is this not a supreme example of modern, bourgeois, "re-imagining" of the text? Can we really see peace in psalms that call for violence? To begin answering that question, we can ask whether the ancient psalmist had any realistic expectation of taking up arms himself to win the battles which he envisions. Many of the imprecatory psalms were composed during the Babylonian exile. The victims who endured the Babylonian exile had no realistic opportunity to take matters into their own hands. They were powerless to execute the judgment that they desired. Clearly, their prayers were of complete dependence upon divine intervention. Lind sees this relationship between powerlessness and pacifism throughout the Old Testament. He writes, "The pacifist nature of the patriarchal narratives may have been conditioned by the political weakness of the clans."[9] Themes of pacifism, however, did not cease once Israel became powerful. Even in times of military strength, there is a persistent theology that upholds a form of pacifism, because the nation was wholly dependent upon a powerful God: "Divine help made it unnecessary for the warriors to fight."[10]

In this sense, their prayers were not a call to arms, but a cry to God. The dependence upon God (and the worshiper's feeling of complete powerlessness) had the effect of a peaceful resolution. The worshiper says, "I cannot fight this battle. I depend upon God." According to Brueggemann, "It is important to recognize that these verbal assaults of imagination and hyperbole are verbal. They speak wishes and prayers. But the speaker does

---

8. Brueggemann, *Message of the Psalms*, 77.
9. Lind, *Yahweh is a Warrior*, 36.
10. Ibid., 24.

Interpretation of the Imprecatory Psalms through the Eyes of Victims

not do anything beyond speak. So far as we know, even in the most violent cries for vengeance, no action is taken."[11]

Though God is asked to fight, the worshiper is now at peace. This same scenario unfolds in the modern world among the powerless who invoke battle imagery in their prayers. They have no realistic opportunity to take up arms, yet they ask God to fight. Is such a prayer a call for peace, or war? While the imagery may be war-like, one of the final effects is that the worshiper is at peace. God may still establish justice and defeat the enemy. But the Christian does not assume he will be the party through whom this justice comes.

We see evidence for this in the writings of Zephania Kameeta, who calls upon God to fight for a people who have no ability to fight on their own. Out of this powerlessness, the people become dependent upon God. Kameeta, is the author of, *Why O Lord, Songs and Psalms from Namibia*. He was Vice President of the Evangelical Lutheran Church in Namibia. He participated in his nation's struggle for independence, and against apartheid. One might expect modern interpreters living in peaceful, prosperous nations to insist on a pacifist reading of the imprecatory psalms. Those of us living in relative luxury and quiet can allegorize or spiritualize the imprecations in the psalms. But when reading the international conversation about imprecatory language, one might expect the opposite interpretation among the oppressed. If anyone has reason to see in these psalms a call to arms, it is the victims of violence. It is striking, therefore, that the corpus of literature from the perspective of victims is unequivocally peace-making. The urgency of a peaceful resolution is heightened among the writers closest to oppressive regimes and institutions. In *Songs from Namibia*, Kameeta quotes a resolution from his denomination's conference, "Christians are peacemakers. They are not cowardly pacifists, but they are pacifists who are sent out into the storm in order to change, in a non-violent struggle, oppressive structures and conditions."[12]

Kameeta's prayers are thoroughly peace-making. In his section on Psalm 115, he writes, "To you alone, O Lord our Liberator, to you alone and not to us—whom you use as your instruments of peace—must glory be given, because of your constant love and faithfulness, because you oppose all powers of oppression."[13] The Namibian Pastor believes that the way God intends to fight oppression is with love. Kameeta's prayers are that love will be victorious. He clearly has no intention of fighting the aggressors with aggression. One might assert that he is in no position to call for aggression.

---

11. Brueggemann, *Praying the Psalms*, 67.
12. Kameeta, *Why O Lord?* 14. From FELKSA conference, Feb 11–13, 1975
13. Ibid., 42.

Part One: Interpretation

He sides with the weak, so a call to arms would be futile or suicidal. But Kameeta's aversion to violence is not simply motivated by self-preservation. He does not love peace merely because he has no other choice (since he is in no position to fight). His love of peace is rooted in his theology: the character of God, the image of God in all people, and the example of Christ who did not retaliate. God himself will establish justice in the future, but Jesus gave us the example for how we ought to act in the present.

Enzo Cortese, a liberation scholar in Italy, sees a call for peace in the imprecatory Psalms. In his article, "Psalm 37, An interpretation in dialogue with the Third World," he writes,

> Tales promesas, lejos de dar occasion a una espera pasiva, no eximen al justo de la oblgacion de llevar a cabo una lucha contra la injusticia. Pero una lucha sin violencia, que cuente ante todo con la ayuda que Dios ha prometido.[14] [Such promises, far from giving occasion for a passive hope, do not exempt the just from the obligation of bringing to an end the struggle against injustice. But a struggle without violence, that demonstrates in everything the help that God has promised].[15]

Martin Luther King was deeply convinced that non-violence was the greatest weapon. His reflection on imprecation was deeply experiential (as a black man) and academic (as a Ph.D. in Theology from Union theological Seminary). Regarding non-violence, King often remarked, "Jesus gave us the message. Gandhi gave us the method." King wrote about non-violence as an offensive position:

> Communism will never be defeated by the use of atomic bombs or nuclear weapons. These are the days when Christians must evince wise restraint and calm reasonableness. We must not engage in a negative anti-communism but rather in a positive thrust for democracy, realizing that our greatest defense against communism is to take offensive action in behalf of justice and righteousness.[16]

Like Kameeta, King did not resort to non-violence merely because there was no other realistic option. His commitment to non-violence was inherently theological. He wrote, "The nonviolent approach does something to the hearts and souls of those committed to it. It gives them new self-respect. It calls up resources of strength and courage that they did not know they

---

14. Cortese, "Salmo 37: Una Interpretacion en Dialogo con el Tercer Mundo," 39.
15. My translation.
16. King, *Strength to Love*, 105.

Interpretation of the Imprecatory Psalms through the Eyes of Victims

had. Finally, it so stirs the conscience of the opponent that reconciliation becomes a reality."[17] These examples of Christians who struggled against injustice illustrate that imprecatory prayer can have a non-violent effect for the worshiper. That is because the prayers ask God to do something humans cannot. We do not assume, however, that God is limited in the same way. So the cry to God is not one of resignation, but of dependence.

C. Validation for the Invalidated

Alvaro Salomon sees the psalms as providing a form of therapy. The cries to God about injustice give a voice to the worshiper. Writing about Psalm 31:22, Salomon states, "'Porque has visto mi aflicción, has conocido las angustias de mi alma.' El orante siente que Dios lo escuchó. La experiencia de sentirse escuchado es fundamental para una terapia mental y spiritual."[18] ["'Because you have seen my affliction, you have known the anxieties of my soul.' The prayer senses that God has heard him. The experience of feeling heard is fundamental for a mental and spiritual therapy."][19] Some may see this interpretation as cathartic: a cleansing of something impure or a release of pressure. But the concept is instead one of solidarity and validation. The psalmist has a sense of healing (therapy) because he knows that God stands with him in his suffering. God hears his call, and he knows that he is not alone.

D. Victory for the Vanquished

Similar to the prophetic interpretation of the imprecatory Psalms, Zephania Kameeta prays his own imprecations with assurance of a just outcome. Many of his prayers are phrased in such a way that they are not begging or asking for deliverance, but certain of it. Writing in the spirit of Psalm 4 he says, "History is in your hands, O Lord, and it will condemn and punish what they say and do; their own plots will cause their ruin."[20] And he charges, "Remember that the Lord will stop all this. For we are not calling unto him only with words, but also with our tears and blood, yes with our lives . . . be our guard in this time of trouble."[21] It is debatable whether this is an imprecation or a prophecy, yet we have the same debate within the Psalter as well.

---

17. Ibid., 151.
18. Salomon, "Reflexiones Pastorales Sobre algunos Salmos," 264.
19. My translation.
20. Kameeta, *Why, O Lord?* 26.
21. Ibid., 35.

Part One: Interpretation

We can question Kameeta's motive or rationale for articulating these prayers in the form of a prophecy, rather than as explicit curses. Perhaps he is too kind-hearted. Is it cowardice? Or do imprecations strike him as unchristian? We cannot know with certainty the true motive behind his decision to write in this way. But we do know that one reason for framing the imprecations as prophecies is that by doing so we move from focus on what we want and begin to focus on who God is. Perhaps Kameeta is able to pray in this prophetic spirit because he is confident that it will come to pass. He writes inspirited by Psalm 5, "He will scatter all the enemies of justice and peace; in sudden confusion they will be driven away."[22] And similarly in his section on Psalm 27, "When their 'security forces' attack me, they stumble and fall."[23] Regardless of whether we think Kameeta is too charitable or too timid, he is right about God. God will not tolerate oppression forever. God did hate apartheid. And all "security forces" will fall in God's presence. So Kameeta successfully changes the focus from our condition and desires toward God's character and promises.

Most likely, however, Kameeta's motive for praying these imprecations as promises rather than as curses is that he genuinely believes in love as a powerful force of change. Inspired by Zechariah 1, he writes, "Together with him we will break the chains of slavery and break down the walls of separation. In the footsteps of the prophets and martyrs we will confront, with the confession of God's love, the powers of hatred and destruction in this world."[24]

In this sense, Kameeta makes a wise bet. He seems to put no stock in what he could ask God to do. Instead, he places complete confidence in God remaining faithful to his own character. What the sufferer wants is irrelevant. Who God is, however, is truly pertinent. So Kameeta writes in the spirit of Psalm 54, "God is our helper; the Lord is our defender; he will destroy their evil plans because of his faithfulness."[25] And he says with confidence, "I know that I will live to see in this present life the Lord's victory over the enemies of the oppressed people in Southern Africa."[26]

Alvaro Salomon also sees in the imprecations a prophetic promise. Writing about the psalms of lament and anguish, he summarizes, "Para los cristianos, la persona de Jesús es la garantía de que el futuro nuestro y del

---

22. Ibid., 27.
23. Ibid., 30.
24. Ibid., 18.
25. Ibid., 33.
26. Ibid., 31.

Interpretation of the Imprecatory Psalms through the Eyes of Victims

mundo está en manos de Dios."²⁷ ["For Christians, the person of Jesus is the guarantee that our future and the world is in the hands of God."]²⁸

Biblical scholars debate the nature of God presented in the Psalms with respect to God's final victory. Specifically within Psalm 7, there is debate whether God is a cosmic judge or the overseer of a system. J. R. John Samuel Raj addresses this question. In that article, he resolves the debate by positing a paradoxical conclusion. He writes, "It is possible to recognize in Psalm 7 the fusion of, and not the conflict between ideas. The legal language with its emphasis on judgment, and the automatic action-result on orderliness complement each other. . . . His legal verdict is aimed at the restoration of order, which ensures deliverance (salvation) of the innocent."²⁹ Raj demonstrates that God's future victory is promised in the imprecatory psalms, and this victory is a result of God's faithfulness to his own character.

Cheryl Gilkes sees in the imprecatory psalms an assurance of future victory. Gilkes is a black woman, and professor of sociology at Colby College. Her exposition on Psalm 68 is profound and thorough. Psalm 68 contains the phrase "a father to the fatherless." In black folksong and folklore, the phrase was amended to say "a father to the fatherless, and a mother to the motherless." Gilkes asserts that the addition to this text has been popularly canonized. She has a detailed theory for how and why this came about, but in short she believes that historically blacks have not lacked a father—although the slave owners did a sufficient job playing the role of "father" to them. What they lacked was a mother, that is, someone to nurture and look out for them. Gilkes says the adaptation of this psalm remedied that problem. Long before Gustavo Gutierrez began writing, black slaves in America developed their own liberation theology. She writes, "What has been done in the past, using Psalm 68 as only one example, represents a strategy of the cultural production of hope in oppressive and depressing circumstances."³⁰ Historically, when blacks have read Psalm 68, they have seen themselves in the psalm. This is for a variety of reasons. There is the obvious identification with the oppressed, and the more subtle identification with the "fatherless" (and the "motherless"). But there is also the reference in the Psalm to two African countries: Egypt and Ethiopia. Gilkes explains, "The Afrocentric folktext, as a theological interpretation of spiritual and social experience does what liberation theology is supposed to do. Welch describes liberation

---

27 Salomon, "Reflexiones Pastorales Sobre algunos Salmos ," 261.

28. My translation.

29. Raj, "Cosmic Judge or Overseer of the World-Order? The Role of Yahweh as Portrayed in Psalm 7," 8.

30. Gilkes, "Mother to the Motherless, Father to the Fatherless," 78.

Part One: Interpretation

theology as the 'preservation of dangerous memory . . . of resistance and liberation declaring 'the possibility of freedom and justice.'"[31]

Gilkes says that historically scholars have had no idea how to categorize Psalm 68, and are baffled by it, especially since it appears to lack a central theme. But the powerless see that it is about power throughout. She believes that the psalm (and we might say all imprecatory psalms) remains an enigma unless it is seen through the eyes of victims. Reading these psalms through the eyes and experiences of slaves provides us with a key to their interpretation. The psalm served to create hope among the oppressed, and assure the victims of God's ultimate victory.

Martin Luther King spoke of God's future victory with assurance. He wrote, "When slumbering giants of injustice emerge in the earth, we need to know that there is a God of power who can cut them down like grass and leave them withering like the green herb."[32] This statement from King has an imprecatory tone to it: it is threatening and reveals a desire for vengeance. But it is more than a wish; King expresses certainty about what God is able to do, and what God will do. There is more to this imprecation than prophecy, however. It would be a mistake to equate any of the above authors' assurance of God's future victory with the traditional "prophetic interpretation" of the imprecatory psalms. What these authors capture in their vision of the future is not a stoic picture of what God will do. Instead, these modern victims of violence and oppression rely upon God to do what they cannot do. These assurances of future victory are songs of utter dependence.

E. Prayers for the Prayer-less

Kameeta's prayer is not solely prophetic. He does take the opportunity to petition God with what he wants to happen. Pastor Zephania's prayers are a rare find in literature of the imprecatory psalms. He models for us what a prayer of imprecation looks like through the mouth of a modern-day victim. He writes, "Fill our callous, empty hands with your good gifts. Crush the copper gates and shatter the iron locks of Robben Island. Break up the prison camps where our brethren are captive and tortured. Help them, Lord."[33] He not only prays for an end of the problem, but to frustrate the perpetrators. In his reflection on Psalm 55 he writes, "O Lord, confuse the plans of our enemies. You, O Lord, will bring those murders, liars and

---

31. Gilkes, "Mother to the Motherless, Father to the Fatherless," 69.
32. King, *Strength to Love*, 20.
33. Kameeta, *Why, O Lord?* 2–3.

traitors to their shame and defeat."[34] Clearly, Kameeta does not find the imprecatory psalms troubling or irrelevant. He practiced imprecatory prayer, and was not reticent to pray for the plans of the wicked to fail.

Dietrich Bonhoeffer had reason to pray against those who plotted evil. He was jailed and executed in 1945 in Germany for participating in a plot to assassinate Hitler. Bonhoeffer, a Doctor of Theology from the University of Berlin, addresses the imprecatory psalms in several of his works, including: *Life Together, Letters from Prison,* and *Psalms: Prayer Book of the Bible.* Evidently, the imprecatory psalms were more than a scholarly enigma to him. They became a regular part of his prayer life. He writes in *Psalms,*

> The prayer for the vengeance of God is the prayer for the execution of his righteousness in the judgment of sin. This judgment must be made public if God is to stand by his word. It must also be promulgated among those whom it concerns. I myself, with my sin, belong to this judgment. I have no right to want to hinder this judgment. It must be fulfilled for God's sake and it has been fulfilled, certainly, in wonderful ways.[35]

The following quotations from Bonhoeffer do not reveal *what* he thought about the imprecatory prayers, but they do demonstrate that these cursing psalms occupied an important place in his life. In *Letters from Prison,* Bonhoeffer writes, "If you think of me, in the next days and weeks, please do so in this way (Psalm 60:12)."[36] How did Bonhoeffer want his friend to think of him? With this verse in mind: "With God we will gain the victory, and he will trample down our enemies." Similarly, he writes, "Certainly one must try everything, but only to become more certain what God's way is and to be able to pray Psalm 91 with great confidence."[37] The psalm that Bonhoeffer says one must pray with great confidence says in verse 8, "You will only observe with your eyes and see the punishment of the wicked." In addition, he writes, "I cannot now read Psalms 3, 47, 70 and others without hearing them in the [musical] settings by Heinrich Schutz."[38] Later of the same psalm Bonhoeffer says, "I wish I could play the G minor sonata with you and sing some Schutz, and hear you sing Psalms 70 and 47; that was what you did best."[39] Psalm 70, which Bonhoeffer says continues to play through his mind, says the following:

34. Ibid., 34.
35. Bonhoeffer, *Psalms,* 57
36. Bonhoeffer, *Letters and Papers from Prison,* 174.
37. Ibid., 320.
38. Ibid., 40.
39. Ibid., 134.

Part One: Interpretation

> May those who want to take my life
> be put to shame and confusion;
> may all who desire my ruin
> be turned back in disgrace.
> May those who say to me, "Aha! Aha!"
> turn back because of their shame.[40]

Again, these quotations from Bonhoeffer do not explain his interpretation of the imprecatory psalms (I will examine this later), but they do show that the prayers of cursing were dear to him. He found meaning and value in these psalms that nourished him and enabled him to endure prison with a hopeful countenance.

F. The Imprecatory Psalms Model Prayers for Conversion

One of the lingering debates surrounding canonical imprecatory language is whether it is necessary to pray for the conversion of one's enemies. Some theologians insist that prayer for conversion is the only legitimate way to pray for enemies. Others insist that we may pray for the downfall of our enemies, but at the same time must explicitly pray for their conversion as well. Still others say that the prayer for enemies to be converted is always implicit, even if not explicitly stated. They see these desires for conversion of enemies implicitly underlying the imprecatory Psalms, even if explicit evidence is sparse. Still, there are some who think no such desire for enemies to repent or covert is needed or even possible. They see enemies as vessels of wrath, created for destruction (inspired by Romans 9:22).[41]

But how do modern day victims of oppression view this debate? Kameeta is willing to pray explicitly for the conversion of his enemies. Writing on Psalm 68, he says, "Rebuke those nations who supply it [the government] with weapons to kill the people, until they bow down before you and repent."[42]

Alvaro Salomon also shares the position that imprecatory prayers should explicitly name the desire for one's enemies to repent. Quoting Luis Alonso Schökel, he writes,

> A ejemplo de Cristo, el cristiano perseguido, calumniado, injustamente condenado, puede hacer suyo este salmo, aunque pidiendo

---

40. Ps 70:2–3

41. What if God, although willing to demonstrate his wrath and to make his power known, endured with much patience vessels of wrath prepared for destruction? [NAS]

42. Kameeta, *Why, O Lord?* 38.

la conversión más que el castigo de los malvados.[43] [Following the example of Christ, the persecuted Christian, suffering, unjustly condemned, can make this psalm his own, while asking for the conversion more than the punishment of the evil doers.][44]

Martin Luther King also shared the desire for his enemies to convert. On several occasions King prayed for this, stated it prophetically, or expressed it as his earnest desire. King wrote, "Generations will rise and fall; men will continue to worship the God of revenge and bow before the altar of retaliation; but ever and again this noble lesson of Calvary will be a nagging reminder that only goodness can drive out evil and only love can conquer hate."[45] King sincerely desired to forgive his enemies, and asked God and others to do the same. We read, "Millions of Negros have been crucified by conscientious blindness. With Jesus on the cross we must look lovingly at our oppressors and say, 'Father, forgive them; for they know not what they do.'"[46] King quotes Abraham Lincoln as he explains how he intends to deal with his enemies: "Madam, do I not destroy my enemies when I make them my friends?"[47] Though Martin Luther King was not averse to imprecate, these prayers for victory were almost always coupled with a desire for reconciliation. He wrote, "This simply means that there is some good in the worst of us and some evil in the best of us. When we discover this, we are less prone to hate our enemies. We must not seek to defeat or humiliate the enemy but to win his friendship and understanding."[48]

Conversion Versus Attunement of One's Attitude toward the Enemy

There is another way to approach this theme of conversion, which is instead to focus on the attitude of the psalmist. Though biblical evidence for prayers of conversion is scant (but not absent), there is ample evidence that the worshiper prays for a right attitude. This theme is difficult to find at first glance, but that is not because it is cryptic. The difficulty of seeing this theme is that we have little understanding ourselves about the nature, definition, and shape of reconciliation. So to find a reconciling attitude in the psalms,

43. Schökel, 188.
44. My translation.
45. King, *Strength to Love*, 42.
46. Ibid., 46.
47. Ibid., 55.
48. Ibid., 51.

we first have to describe what reconciliation looks like. Then we can find evidence of these categories in the Psalms.

According to Augsburger's *Hate-Work*, reconciliation requires memory. Contrary to the popular adage that "to forgive is to forget," reconciliation experts agree that memory is required for movement toward one another. Elie Wiesel states that memory builds a bridge. It allows us to begin speaking to the other party. It pulls us out of denial, and allows us to become "unstuck." Clearly, the Psalter is filled with memory. Psalm 35:15–16 is a good example: "But when I stumbled, they gathered in glee; assailants gathered against me without my knowledge. They slandered me without ceasing. Like the ungodly they maliciously mocked; they gnashed their teeth at me." Memory is not sufficient for reconciliation, but it is necessary. It is low on the spectrum of "types of hate." Even malicious hatred invokes memory. But memory is a vital element for forgiveness.

Proper attunement of one's attitude toward his enemy also requires empathy. In the *Sunflower*, Milton Konvitz writes a response to Wiesenthal's question about how to respond to the Nazi who begs for forgiveness. Konvitz states that he might have said, "My broken heart pleads with your broken heart."[49] This is not the whole answer that the Nazi is looking for: it does not absolve any guilt. Nor is it a sufficient answer, because it does not seek justice. But the ability to see the human face of the enemy, according to Augsburger, is what divides principled hatred from moral hatred. Empathy is a vital element of reconciliation. I argue earlier,[50] based on the text from Leviticus 19, Proverbs 24, and Proverbs 25, that the Old Testament does acknowledge the human face of the enemy. This background, though not a loud voice in the Psalter, is nevertheless present.

A third necessary element in an attitude of reconciliation is the passionate pursuit of justice. It is the relentless work toward justice that according to Augsburger (*Hate-Work*) separates just hatred from moral hatred, because it metamorphoses hate into seeking all that is good. In the book *Amish Grace*, we consider the responses of victims and observers after a school shooting in Amish country. Jeff Jacoby wrote an op-ed piece that was reprinted regularly in newspapers throughout the nation, and included in the book. Jacoby is largely critical of the Amish response. He thinks the forgiveness offered was premature and insufficient. He says, "How many of us would really want to live in a society in which no one gets angry when children are slaughtered?"[51] Jacoby contends that a passionate pursuit of justice is a necessary attitude

---

49. Wiesenthal, *The Sunflower*, 160.
50. Especially in chapter 2, section D.
51. Kraybill, *Amish Grace*, 129.

toward one's enemy. It is possible to embrace the Amish response, however, without neglecting the pursuit of justice. Undoubtedly, this is one of the strongest themes in the imprecatory psalms. In Psalm 7 the evil doers are put on trial. We read, "Bring to an end the violence of the wicked and make the righteous secure—you, the righteous God who probes minds and hearts."[52] If the pursuit of justice is necessary for attunement of one's attitude toward his enemy, the Psalms greatly exceed this criterion.

Taking personal responsibility for one's own sin is another necessary attitude of reconciliation. I would argue that the Psalter also provides ample explicit evidence of this. Psalm 139, that beautiful song with the peculiar boasting of perfect hatred, includes in verses 23–24, "Search me, O God, and know my heart, try me, and know my anxieties; and see if there is any wicked way in me, and lead me in the way everlasting."[53] Psalm 7:3–4, "If there is iniquity in my hands . . . or if I have plundered my enemy without cause." Psalm 25:18, "look on my affliction and my pain, and forgive all my sins." Psalm 40:12, "My iniquities have overtaken me, so that I am not able to look up." Psalm 51:2, "Blot out my transgressions." Clearly the Psalter offers this facet of attuning one's attitude for reconciliation.

Interestingly, hatred is a necessary facet of a reconciling attitude as well. And here the Psalter has no shortage. In *Helping People Forgive*, Augsburger contends that hatred is necessary for reconciliation because it allows one to differentiate himself from two poles. On the one hand, hatred differentiates us from the "other." But it can also differentiate us from "rage." In *Hate-Work*, Augsburger says "in this sense, just hatred is nearly synonymous with love." That is because just hatred has similar qualities to the love described in 1 Corinthians 13: it is not self-seeking, it always hopes, always endures, is not proud, etc. To refuse to hate means that we remain in denial, and cannot move toward reconciliation. Refusal to hate diminishes one or both of the parties involved. If I refuse to hate it may be that I do not have the self-respect to see that what someone else has done to me is wrong. Or if I refuse to hate it may be that I do not respect the other person enough to see that his actions are worthy of my contemplation and response. In either case, hatred provides the necessary differentiation to respect both parties. I should not need to answer whether this element of a reconciling attitude is found in the Psalms.

Another attitude required for reconciliation is objectivity. In *Hate-Work* Augsburger states that the line between retributive and principled hatred is crossed when we begin to differentiate between actor and action. Retributive

---

52. Ps 7:9

53. This verse is somewhat problematic, in that it may be understood as a psalm of innocence.

Part One: Interpretation

hatred is subjective, but principled hatred it objective. With increased objectivity, we are increasingly able to "hate the sin but love the sinner." Psalm 109 draws some distinction here between the actor and the action. It focuses on specific conduct: "The mouth of the wicked and the mouth of the deceitful have opened against me: they have spoken against me with a lying tongue. They have surrounded me with words of hatred, and fought against me without a cause. In return for my love they are my accusers."[54]

Finally, a necessary element of reconciliation is a communal sense of victim/perpetrator rather than an individual sense. One of the reasons that the imprecatory psalms have posed such an enigma to modern Western authors is that our biblical interpretation is largely individualistic, since our society is largely individualistic. If we are right in seeing individualism in the Psalter, then the hatred of the imprecatory psalms is quite shocking. But if we remember that the psalms were preserved and sung by a community, and the enemies described are also often communities, then it is apparent that the hatred in the Psalter is not merely malicious or retributive. The hatred is thought-out, developed, deeply experienced, and aimed at profound issues. In *Amish Grace*, this communal mindset is credited for why the Amish have been able to offer reconciliation in the midst of tragedy. The authors assert that, "modern people are practically obsessed with their personal desires. In contrast, the core value of Amish culture is community."[55] If we ask ourselves, "Do I feel like forgiving? Do I want to forgive?" the answer will likely be "no" for a long time, and perhaps even forever. But personal feeling and desire is not hermeneutic with which the Amish make decisions. The question instead is, "What shall we do?" Put in this light, individuals are able to do things that they may not desire, because the duty or calling of the community requires them to do so.

Elements Missing from the Psalter

It would be misleading to say that the Psalter offers a comprehensive teaching on reconciliation. Some key elements of reconciliation are missing. That lack is not to say that the ancient Hebrew people were missing the proper attitude: only that some of these elements are not explicit in the Psalter.

---

54. I am not implying that the Psalms always focus on behavior, and not on people. Certainly the Psalms are replete with references to "wicked and deceitful men" among other ad hominem charges. Instead, I am pointing out that the focus on actions is a valuable and redemptive practice.

55. Kraybill, *Amish Grace*, 93. The book cites Kenneth Gergen in *The Saturated Self* for this assertion.

Interpretation of the Imprecatory Psalms through the Eyes of Victims

Perhaps the void is due to the fact that the Psalter has a different purpose. As Walter Brueggemann points out, enemies are never the primary subject of the psalms. Even imprecatory prayers look more like praise songs. That is because enemies in the psalms are merely the background for illustrating the greatness of God. The psalms are really about God; not enemies. If they teach, they teach dependence and praise. They do not teach reconciliation; at least, that is not their intended function.

According to Augsburger (*Hate-Work*), a key element to reconciliation is the ability to transcend "absolute" thinking. He does not offer "relative" thinking in its place, but instead "visional" thinking. This is a key trait found in *just hatred*—however, "visional" thinking is noticeably absent from both *moral hatred* and the Psalter. There does not appear to be a desire of the psalmist to think forward in such a way that includes the enemy.

Another aspect missing in the Psalter is the desire for an apology from the enemy. Furthermore, should an apology be offered, we are not certain what the psalmist would say. Jeffrie Murphy explains that an apology and acceptance are key factors in reconciliation. He argues that the apology can only be accepted if the other party is deserving (i.e., truly repentant), and if the victim can maintain self-respect.[56] I agree that this is an inevitable facet of reconciliation, and it is a theme neglected by the imprecatory psalms. Augsburger states in *Helping People Forgive* that seeking an apology from the other party keeps us (the injured party) from falling into either of two mistakes: Either we tend to appease the other party, or we tend to exonerate. Instead, seeking apology is the more appropriate effort.

Contemporary writers about reconciliation agree that a sense of "togetherness" is required. Zephania Kameeta never forgets that he is working with his enemy, not against him. Martin Luther King wanted to work together with politicians and corporations, not against them. Gandhi felt profoundly that his greatest enemy was himself. These peacemakers have an attitude that seems absent from the Psalter. We do not get the impression that the psalmist "needs" his enemy, or that his world is somehow better with his enemy in it.

G. The Enemy is the System and the Structure

Pastor Zephania Kameeta seems reluctant to name individuals as the enemy in his *Songs from Namibia*. It is doubtful that he does not have any individuals in mind. Perhaps he sees the individual perpetrators as part of a system that continues whether these actors participate or not. In his reflections on

---

56. Murphy, *Forgiveness and Mercy*.

Psalm 4, Kameeta writes, "You hate apartheid. You will destroy it with all its violent manifestations."[57] The theology behind this statement is undeniable. Had he named the specific persons from whom he had seen oppression through apartheid, the certainty of the statement would be lost.

It may be, however, that the naming of individuals is just too barbaric for Kameeta. In his reflection on Psalm 137 he writes, "Happy is the man who pays you back for what you have done to us—who takes your rotten system of apartheid and smashes it against a rock."[58] But it may also be that the desire for physical retribution is truly not what Kameeta has in mind. He believes that ultimately violence will be vanquished by peace. The victory Pastor Zephania envisions is through Christ's example in suffering. He reflects, "Those who are converted are used by God as instruments of liberation—to cast down powers, structures and governments which build these walls between people and people and between people and God, by the word of the cross, the sword of the spirit."[59]

The interpretation of the enemy as an institution has a long-standing and ancient tradition. There is an allegorical nature to this interpretation, and it has been shared by theologians from the apostolic age onward. Paul Kalluvettil, writing in India's *Journal of Dharma*, considers the Warrior God motif in the psalter. In Psalm 24, for instance, he sees the Canaanite pattern of poetry and believes that the battle is cosmogonic, and not physical.[60] He states, "The Christian community is "not battling against people, but against the structures of evil, which lie behind them."[61] Kalluvettil also says about Matthew 10:34, (where Jesus says he has come to bring a sword), "He is not advocating physical violence. Rather his words are to be understood in a metaphorical sense. Thus the language of Jesus' Kingdom refers to ideological or moral aggression."[62] Those who advocate an allegorical interpretation of the enemy, whether as a spiritual enemy or an institutional one, tend to see the battle as figurative as well. As a result, they also see the victory as metaphorical. Kalluvettil writes, "The intervention of Yahweh is for the liberation of the marginalized, oppressed and exploited people. Of course, the God of the Bible does not use physical force or military equipment."[63] Some interpreters see the enemy as spiritual (i.e., the devil) and others believe the

---

57. Kameeta, *Why, O Lord?* 26.
58. Ibid., 48.
59. Ibid., 22.
60. Kalluvettil, "The Warrior God and the Prince of Peace," 298.
61. Ibid., 302.
62. Ibid., 302.
63. Ibid., 298.

enemy is institutional (such as the system of slavery). In either case, these interpretations are allegorical.

Martin Luther King, Jr. also imprecates an institutional enemy in *Strength to Love*. He writes, "In our nation today a mighty struggle is taking place. It is a struggle to conquer the reign of an evil monster called segregation and its inseparable twin called discrimination—a monster that has wandered through this land for well-nigh one hundred years, stripping millions of Negro people of their sense of dignity and robbing them of their birthright of freedom."[64]

Allegorical readings have a profound impact on how we might practice imprecatory prayers. If we believe the enemy is the devil, we will pray for Satan's downfall. If the enemy is the system of slavery, we will pray for an end to that institution. But if the enemy were to be a human being, we would pray for destruction to befall that person.

H. The Psalms Note Personal Responsibility

Though the psalter is replete with cries from worshipers maintaining their innocence, there are a couple occasions where personal sin is acknowledged. Alvaro Salomon notes this in Psalm 40:12. He writes,

> Se mezclan las responsabilidades de otras personas en las aflicciones personales, con las propias responsabilidades (v.12). El salmista sabe que es pecador, y que parte de su preocupación es su propio pecado. Siente culpa por ello pero también angustia por aquellas personas que se burlan y quieren su mal.[65] [The responsibilities of other persons and the personal afflictions are mixed, with his own responsibilities. The psalmist knows that he is a sinner, and that part of his preoccupation is his own sin. He feels fault for this, but also anguish for other persons that taunt him and wish him evil.][66]

Enzo Cortese echoes the call for personal responsibility. In his article on Psalm 37 he writes, "No somos realmente malvados, al menos como participantes en la culpa?"[67] ["Are we not in reality the evil doers? At least, participants in the fault?"][68] In other words, Cortese is mindful that even

---

64. King, *Strength to Love*, 37.
65. Salomon, "Reflexiones Pastorales Sobre algunos Salmos," 266.
66. My translation.
67. Cortese, "Salmo 37: Una Interpretacion en Dialogo con el Tercer Mundo," 39.
68. My translation.

the victim must take some measure of personal responsibility for his own sin before God.

Bonhoeffer also reads in the imprecatory psalms a sense of personal responsibility for his own sin. He writes, "Is this fearful psalm of vengeance to be our prayer? May we pray in this way? Certainly not! We bear much guilt of our own for the action of any enemies who cause us suffering. How then should we, who are guilty ourselves and deserving of God's wrath call down God's vengeance upon our enemies? Will not this vengeance much more strike us? No, we cannot pray this psalm, not because we are too good for it (what a superficial idea, what colossal pride!), but because we are too sinful, too evil for it!"[69] For Bonhoeffer, the imprecatory psalms lead us to humility and repentance, recognizing that we are no better than anyone else.

I. The Psalms are the Prayers of Christ

As the body of Christ, there is an appropriate manner in which we can own these imprecatory psalms. For Bonhoeffer, the imprecatory prayers are not the prayers of an oppressed individual. For an individual to assert his own perfect innocence and then curse someone else would be an act of hubris. These prayers are instead the prayer of a community, but only in so far as that community is an extension of the body of Christ. The church is also imperfect and unable to assert its own innocence. But Since Christ was perfect and he suffered at the hands of oppressors, he was able to pray these psalms. As Christ's body, the church can echo these prayers.

Bonhoeffer writes in *Life Together*, "These prayers are words of Holy Scripture which a believing Christian cannot simply dismiss as outworn and obsolete, as 'early stages of religion.' A psalm that we cannot utter as a prayer, that makes us falter and horrifies us, is a hint to us that here someone else is praying, not we; that the one who is here protesting his innocence, who is invoking God's judgment, who has come to such infinite depths of suffering, is none other than Jesus Christ himself."[70] Bonhoeffer is not saying that these psalms are irrelevant or that they should be dismissed from the canon. Instead, he is arguing that the imprecatory psalms are rightly understood (and practiced) when we see them as Christ's prayers. He continues,

> Can we, then, pray the imprecatory psalms? In so far as we are sinners and express evil thoughts in a prayer of vengeance, we dare not do so. But in so far as Christ is in us, the Christ who

---

69. Bonhoeffer, *Meditating on the Word*.
70. Bonhoeffer, *Life Together*, 45.

took all the vengeance of God upon himself, who met God's vengeance in our stead, who thus—stricken by the wrath of God—and in no other way could forgive his enemies, who himself suffered the wrath that his enemies might go free—we, too, as member of this Jesus Christ, can pray these psalms, through Jesus Christ, from the heart of Jesus Christ.[71]

Bonhoeffer reiterates this Christocentric position in *Psalms: Prayer Book of the Bible*: "God's vengeance did not strike the sinners, but the one sinless man who stood in the sinner's place, namely God's own son. Jesus Christ bore the wrath of God, for the execution of which the psalm prays. He stilled God's wrath toward sin and prayed in the hour of the execution of the divine judgment: 'Father, forgive them, for they do not know what they do.' No other than he, who himself bore the wrath of God, could pray in this way."[72]

This Christocentric reading has several unique features. One must not equate the eschatological or prophetic readings with the Christocentric interpretation. Bonhoeffer, for instance, is not saying that in the psalter Christ was praying for a future vengeance upon his enemies. Instead, Christ becomes the object of this vengeance. He *becomes* the enemy and incurs the wrath of God. He writes, "I pray the imprecatory psalms in the certainty of their marvelous fulfillment. I leave the vengeance to God and ask him to execute his righteousness to all his enemies, knowing that God has remained true to himself and has himself secured justice in his wrathful judgment on the cross, and that this wrath as become grace and joy for us."[73]

We may ask, if these are not our prayers (but instead are the prayers of Christ), what is the relevance of the Psalms? The Christocentric reading accomplishes several objectives. It achieves the goal of making the psalms more tasteful, so that the reader does not need to invoke evil upon others. And by making these prayers the words of Christ, it justifies their inclusion in the canon. But for Bonhoeffer this interpretation also achieved relevance of these prayers in his own life. He explains, "I cannot forgive the enemies of God out of my own resources. Only the crucified Christ can do that, and I through him. Thus the carrying out of vengeance becomes grace for all men in Jesus Christ."[74] Because Christ became the object of God's wrath for all people, we no longer have enemies. And because God forgave all sin through the cross, we are able to forgive all sin as well. Bonhoeffer

---

71. Ibid., 47.
72. Bonhoeffer, *Psalms*, 58.
73. Ibid., 59.
74. Ibid., 59.

summarizes, "In this way the crucified Jesus teaches us to pray the imprecatory psalms correctly."[75]

Admittedly, there is an air of Christian triumphalism in the interpretation that the imprecatory psalms have all along been the prayers of Christ. Proponents of this view try to preserve relevance to all believers by saying that we can all pray these psalms, provided that we do so with Christ in mind. But achieving this relevance for the modern Christian renders the psalms practically irrelevant to the ancient Jew (who not only wrote them, but prayed them and preserved them for thousands of years). It seems that even if Christ is the paramount example of how to deal with enemies, and even if Christ will be the ultimate victor over all enemies, nevertheless, the psalms must have also had immediate value to the ancient Israelite community.

J. Conclusion

Scholarship benefits from reading the imprecatory psalms through the eyes of victims. One notable contribution is the focus upon eschatological hope. The traditional prophetic interpretations do not fully capture the reality that Jesus will make all things right in the final age. Of the various interpretations scholars have presented for the imprecatory psalms, the school of thought consistently promoted through the eyes of victims is the "dependence model." In other words, victims of oppression who read these psalms see them as a cry to God for help. The powerless recognize their inability to respond to their oppressors, so they depend upon God for assistance. Though not a prophecy in the traditional sense, victims find in these psalms assurance that God will cause righteousness to prevail. I say that it is not a "prophecy" because the victims are banking on the character of God. And "not in the traditional sense" because scholars have typically used the interpretive model of prophecy in order to distance the psalmist from any sense of personal hatred. The victims of oppression in this study are unapologetically in touch with their hatred and anger. Through the eyes of modern victims we see that the practice of imprecatory prayer still exists today. To them this is not a barbaric practice, not a pre-Christian one, nor do they make apologies for praying against their enemies. That being said, each of the authors studied in this section make an explicit prayer for the conversion of their enemies. In addition, many of these victims are more ready to indict a "system" rather than individuals. And these authors are also ready to admit their own responsibility and sin.

75. Ibid., 60.

Part Two

Theology

4

Tension in the Canon

THE PRESENCE OF THE imprecatory psalms alongside the rest of sacred Scripture highlights an apparent contradiction within the canon. Jesus teaches in the Sermon on the Mount that we should love our enemies, but the psalms implicitly endorse cursing them. This tension could be the result of a combination of factors.

A. Dispensation

One way that tension in the Bible has been addressed is by recognizing different dispensations. Many interpreters have "solved" the tension caused by the imprecatory psalms by saying that hatred of enemies belongs to one dispensation (the Old Testament) while the love of enemies belongs to another (the New Testament). This theory, and the problems associated with it, was explored in detail in chapter 2. A milder version of the dispensational view is that of progressive revelation. Progressive revelation, however, is not sufficient to "solve" the imprecatory problem. First, the theory of progressive revelation requires us to believe that the people of the Old Testament were fundamentally different than ourselves in relation to their capacity to love enemies. Progressive revelation is sufficient for understanding how we can be saved, since our salvation is rooted in an historical event (and therefore, was progressively revealed). But there is no compelling reason why ethical standards should be progressively revealed—as they are rooted in the character of God, and not in any historical events. Second, to say that the Old Testament teaches hatred of enemies, while the New Testament teaches love of enemies indicates too great a shift in God's thinking to be characterized as "progressive revelation." This would be more than progressive, it would be contradictory. If such a great contradiction actually exists in Scripture, then God has changed his mind. This type of revelation would involve more than disclosing additional information; it would also entail abrogating the previous revelation.[1] I propose, therefore, that neither dispensational distinction nor progressive revelation solve the imprecatory problem. Below are ways of dealing with this tension in Scripture concerning how we should deal with our enemies.

B. Mystery

It is neither necessary, nor possible, nor intellectually responsible to resolve every apparent conflict in the Bible. Deuteronomy reads, "The secret things belong to the LORD our God, but the things revealed belong to us and to our children forever, that we may follow all the words of this law."[2] Tension in the Bible may result from the simple fact that God has not given us all the answers. In this case, resolving the tension would not be possible. Furthermore, it is intellectually irresponsible to try to solve all points of tension in Scripture. To do so would sometimes require simplistic or contrived solutions. Rather than force solutions on the canon, we would do well to remember that "God is in heaven, and you are on earth, so let your words be few."[3]

C. Authority of the Speaker

While we trust that all Scripture is inspired by God, we know that not everything that everyone said in the Bible is true. Saul's armor bearer bragged that he killed Saul (2 Sam 1:10), while the readers know that he is lying, based on the account just a few verses earlier (1 Sam 31:4). In other words, even though Scripture correctly records the words of the armor bearer, what the armor bearer said was not true. So to state that all Scripture is true does not necessarily mean that every statement made by people in the Bible is true (only that the Bible is true in reporting what they said). Even theological statements can be untrue, as in the case of Job's friends. Bildad told Job, "When your children sinned against him, he gave them over to the penalty of their sin."[4] But Job's children did not die as a result of their sin. Bildad's words represent in Scripture a theological statement that is untrue.

---

1. Abrogation is allowable or even foundational to other religious systems, such as Islam, but is foreign to biblical revelation.
2. Deut 29:29
3. Eccl 5:2
4. Job 8:4

Tension in the Canon

The book of Ecclesiastes is a dialogue between two worldviews: life under the sun, and life under heaven. For that reason, half of the book is "bad theology." The reader trusts the Teacher's authority, since he has lived with both philosophies, and concludes that life under heaven is better. Nevertheless, a tension exists in the book as a result of the fact that there are two voices. These two speakers present opposite worldviews. Regarding the Psalms, is it possible that they contain bad theology? As I previously noted, other wisdom books do. But there is significant difference between these wisdom books and the Psalms. Job's friends are clearly the antagonists, and the conflicting voice in Ecclesiastes is clearly refuted. The Psalms, on the other hand, are the voice of the community. There is more unity to the message of the Psalms than in other wisdom literature, in that there is no antagonist. We must be conscious that the Psalms are not the voice of God. On the other hand, Jesus preached the Sermon on the Mount. Jesus is more dependable than Saul's armor bearer or than Bildad. And he is even more authoritative than the voice of the community found in the Psalms. The tension between Jesus' sermon and Israel's cry results from the varying authority of the voice.

Specifically in regard to the imprecatory psalms, McKenzie explains the relationship between the inspiration of Scripture and the nature of authority from the author himself. Lest anyone doubt McKenzie's high view of Scripture, he states,

> Let me make clear at once that no catholic exegete can admit a truly irreducible contradiction between the psalms and the gospels. The dogma of inspiration prohibits the attribution of any kind of error to the inspired writers. Any explanation which is proposed must safeguard this fundamental dogma, and must be judged successful in so far as it does safeguard it. To fail in this respect is to fail in the essential.[5]

Having established his confidence in the inspiration of Scripture, he goes on to write that this does not mean every voice in Scripture should be understood as teaching theology. For example, the role of narrative history is to accurately report what happened, not necessarily to teach morality or theology. McKenzie argues that the Psalms are similar to narrative passages:

> Biblical inspiration is a divine impulse to *write*, not to think or feel. The mental and emotional processes of the author do not take place under the influence of inspiration except in so far as they enter into the actual composition of the book. If the author

---

5. McKenzie, "The Imprecations of the Psalter," 82.

> merely records his past experiences, we cannot affirm that these experiences occurred under divine inspiration; and their record in an inspired book is in itself no assurance that these experiences are free from error or sin. They are to be interpreted according to the same principles by which we interpret any Scripture narrative or an event or of the words of some person other than the author; and the author is not presumed to approve of the words or actions narrated merely because he passes no moral judgment. The content of such narratives is the word of God *ratione consignationis*; the narrative or record is inspired, but not the transactions which are contained therein.[6]

In other words, we can trust that the Psalms accurately reflect what the community believed about their situation, their enemies, and about God. But we may not necessarily make the leap to conclude that the Psalms model "the right way to pray."

D. Difference in Form

An important aspect of the tension in Scripture is the difference in genre or form. Because the Psalms and the Sermon on the Mount belong to different genres, we would expect there to be differences in the way thoughts are expressed, as well as in the guidelines for interpreting these texts. Kidner explains:

> In the Wisdom books the tone of voice and even the speakers have changed. The blunt "Thou shalt" or "shalt not" of the Law, and the urgent "thus saith the Lord" of the prophets, are joined now by the cooler comments of the teacher and the often anguished questions of the learner. Where the bulk of the Old Testament calls us simply to obey and to believe, this part of it [wisdom books] (although wisdom is a thread that runs through every part) summons us to think hard as well as humbly; to keep our eyes open, to use our conscience and our common sense, and not to shrink the most disturbing questions.[7]

Many of the imperative moral statements of the New Testament belong to the genre of epistle, gospel, or sermon. But in the Wisdom literature, imperative statements are rare. When they do occur, they do not have the same *absolute* quality that we would expect in other genres. Kidner explains

---

6. Ibid., 87.
7. Kidner, *The Wisdom of the Proverbs, Job, and Ecclesiastes*, 11.

that Job "accepts the general rule that wickedness will get what it deserves, but not the friend's insistence that there are no exceptions; still less that he himself is reaping what he has sown."[8] In other words, the genre of Wisdom literature tolerates a great deal of tension. Job can at the same time believe in general that the innocent prosper, but also believe that he is innocent, despite the fact that he is not prospering. If Wisdom literature can tolerate this tension, so too can the canon tolerate tension between genres: especially between wisdom literature and sermon.

Kidner observes that Proverbs, Job, and Ecclesiastes essentially promote three apparently contradictory worldviews. He uses the analogy of three houses: arguing that Proverbs speaks of the prosperous house, Job speaks of the stricken house, and Ecclesiastes speaks of the decaying house. Proverbs promises that the righteous will prosper. But Job discovers that this is not always true. And Ecclesiastes says that there is no rhyme or reason to who prospers at all! How can the canon tolerate this tension? Kidner explains:

> It is worth pointing out that this single-minded pursuit of their respective interests is typical of the Old Testament's way of doing things. It tends to give itself wholly to one thing at a time, saying it with maximum force and leaving any resulting imbalance to be corrected in due course by an equally massive counterweight. In this way more justice can be done to a many-sided subject than by steering a middle course between its extremes.[9]

E. Difference in Purpose

The Sermon on the Mount belongs to the genre of sermons, or teaching. It is didactic in nature. In the sermon, Jesus instructs us how to live our lives, and how to deal with others. The imprecatory psalms, on the other hand, belong to the genre of psalms (songs), within the body of wisdom literature. Although the Psalms communicate teaching, they are in the poetic, rather than didactic category of literature. If we see the concept of "command" in both the Sermon on the Mount and the imprecatory psalms, there is indeed a difficult contradiction. But the Psalms do not function as commands. Yet the Old Testament is obviously not void of commands. As a result, some have assumed that there is a contradiction between the commands in the Old Testament and in the New Testament. Yet nowhere in the Old Testament are we commanded to hate our enemies. In chapter 2 it was shown

---

8. Ibid., 79.
9. Ibid., 124.

Part Two: Theology

that the Old Testament commands enemy-love. Wesley summarized: "Then from all this we learn there is no contradiction at all between the law and the gospel. . . . The law, for instance, requires us to love God and our neighbor. It requires us to be meek, humble, and holy."[10]

Throughout Scripture there is a spectrum of purpose from descriptive to prescriptive. Samson killed thirty Philistines in order to pay off a bet, but there is no ethical evaluation of his action. The Bible does not say "that was wrong and selfish" or "you shouldn't pay off your bets that way." Nor does it say "God was pleased" or "the Philistines deserved it." The ethical commentary is lacking because the primary purpose of the narrative is to tell the story—to describe what happened. But when Jesus said, "turn the other cheek" he was not telling a story. The purpose of his sermon was to prescribe what we ought to do. Between these two obvious extremes of description and prescription we have a spectrum of clarity and a wide range of options. Perhaps the middle ground between prescription and description could be called "healthy model." In Acts 2:42, for instance, we read that the early church had "all things in common." This is not a prescription: it does not tell us that true Christians should share all their possessions. But it is insufficient to say this is merely a description about what happened. Luke is excited and impressed about the generosity of the church. He writes about this fact because it is a worthy example and model of what happens when the Gospel is the first priority. Their generosity was more than *interesting*, it was also *good* (but not commanded).

The question arises, then, what is the purpose of the Psalms? Where do the Psalms lie on the continuum between description and prescription? Nearly all scholars agree that the psalms are not prescriptive. It does not follow that because the psalmist cursed his enemy, we are commanded to do the same. But those who have a high view of inspiration hesitate to say that the psalms are merely descriptive. These Psalms are the prayer book and song book of Israel. They are the nation's liturgy. They were read, memorized, and sung regularly and publicly. They do not merely report what happened, but instead they call the people to repeat the words as they draw near to worship God. I propose, therefore, that the psalms are a model of prayer, somewhere between prescription and description. I agree with Sire that, "We can trust the psalmist not to mislead us into a prayer that in the final analysis would be incorrect to pray."[11] In other words, we are at least allowed, but not commanded to pray the way the psalmists do. But "allowed" is somewhere on the spectrum between descriptive and modeled. To say

---

10. Wesley, *The Nature of the Kingdom*, 127–28.
11. Sire, *Learning to Pray through the Psalms*, 164.

that something is a model means more than that it is allowed; it implies that the act is also encouraged. Unarguably, the Israelites were encouraged to sing the psalms. So within the prescription/description spectrum, I would place the psalms in the middle with the purpose of modeling prayer.

This distinction is helpful for understanding the tension between the Sermon on the Mount and the imprecatory psalms. One would certainly expect not only tension but contradiction between prescription and description. Judah raped Tamar, but rape is forbidden. To a lesser extent, one would also expect the middle of the spectrum to also be in tension with what is prescribed. Paul prescribed that Gentiles not be circumcised, lest their faith turn to works and their salvation be in vain. Yet this same Paul circumcised Timothy, so he would not be a stumbling block to Jews. Paul's circumcision of Timothy is not merely described: It is offered as a model for "becoming all things to all people." Yet in no way did Paul command anyone to be circumcised. The tension between Paul's command and his action is partially accounted for by the fact that the literature about Paul has varying purposes.

F. The Bible Offers a Wealth of Options

Another reason for tension within Scripture is that even if every statement of the Bible were prescriptive, it would not necessarily follow that each verse is a prescription for how we should act in every instance. Nor does every verse prescribe the only way ever to act. Paul commands the Corinthians to have nothing to do with a sexually immoral man. He says they should not eat with him, nor fellowship with him. This is a prescriptive statement. But James says, "Speak and act as those who are going to be judged by the law that gives freedom, because judgment without mercy will be shown to anyone who has not been merciful. Mercy triumphs over judgment."[12] This is also a prescriptive statement. We are to act mercifully and also to expel sinners. But how can we do both? Sometimes it is impossible to carry out two commands at the same time, and not all prescriptions are absolute.

Another fitting example of this "dual truth" of Scripture is in Proverbs: "Do not answer a fool according to his folly, or you yourself will be just like him."[13] But immediately afterward, the proverb says, "Answer a fool according to his folly, or he will be wise in his own eyes."[14] Which shall we do? Answer the fool, or not answer him? They are both true, because different situations

---

12. Jas 2:12–13
13. Prov 26:4
14. Prov 26:5

Part Two: Theology

call for different approaches. I would argue that what makes the difference in this case is whether the fool is likely to be receptive to correction.

So it is up to us to use our best judgment. What is the right prescription at this time? Generally the Bible teaches its points forcefully and without qualification. It tells us to be merciful. Elsewhere it tells us not to tolerate sin. Occasionally, it prescribes both mercy and justice in the same breath. Jude says, "Be merciful to those who doubt; save others by snatching them from the fire; to others show mercy, mixed with fear—hating even the clothing stained by corrupted flesh."[15] In other words, show mercy but at the same time be careful every time you do, because mercy can lead to licentiousness (so also know when to stop showing mercy).

Similarly, Jesus told his disciples in Matthew 18 that if their brother sinned against them, they should go privately and show him his fault. But Jesus does not teach that this is the *only* way to deal with a brother who sins. When he was on the cross, he bore his humiliation silently. Both options are available to us: confrontation and silence. God has given us his spirit and our brains in order to help us decide which is the best option.

Regarding the tension between loving enemies and cursing them, even Jesus was capable of both. Jesus called the Pharisees white-washed tombs. Six times in Matthew 23 Jesus said, "Woe to you Pharisees, hypocrites!" He called the Pharisees a "brood of vipers" (Matt 12:34). He cursed Bethsaida and Chorazin for ignoring the signs he performed in their cities (Matt 11:21). He wove a whip and drove out the money changers from the temple courts. But severity was not his only approach to his enemies. When his disciples asked if he wished them to call down fire from heaven to consume Samaria, Jesus rebuked them (Luke 9:54). And of course, "He was oppressed and afflicted, yet he did not open his mouth" (Isa 53:7). All this is to say that Jesus was not monochromatic. The Sermon on the Mount does not offer the *only* way to deal with enemies, not even for Jesus.

One of the reasons the Bible contains apparently conflicting exhortation, is that people who have different problems need to hear different messages. There is a great tension in the Bible about the role of works in salvation. Paul says that "we maintain that a person is justified by faith apart from the works of the law."[16] James says "You see that a person is considered righteous by what they do and not by faith alone."[17] We can ask, what problem was Paul's audience struggling with? Paul's recipients were trying to earn their salvation. This futile quest led to constant fear that they were

15. Jude 22–23
16. Rom 3:28
17. Jas 2:24

Tension in the Canon

not good enough, and fear that they would not be saved. It also apparently led to pride, so that some believed they could boast in their good works. Furthermore, the Gentiles did not receive or keep the Jewish law, so they feared (and the Jews warned) that they would not be saved. In order to humble his audience, and to assure them that they did not need to worry about their salvation, and to assure them that the Gentiles would be included, Paul says that we are saved by faith. James' audience, on the other hand, needed to hear a different message because they were apparently struggling with a different issue. From his epistle it is clear that they wished the needy well, but did nothing to help. They were taking their salvation for granted. They needed a warning, and a motivation to live out the gospel. So James tells them that faith without deeds is dead.[18]

In the same way, perhaps the Bible gives apparently conflicting advice for how to deal with enemies, because different enemies need different responses. Why did Jesus curse the Pharisees? It seems that given their position and knowledge, curses are for the hard of heart; for people who should know better. But when on the cross, Jesus said "Father forgive them, for they do not know what they are doing."[19] In this case, Jesus seems to be thinking about his enemies' ignorance, rather than about hardness of heart. In light of this tension, it is possible to maintain that the love of enemies commanded in the Sermon on the Mount is absolutely true, but that it is not the only truth.

The approach of Desmond Tutu toward his former enemies provides a modern example of what we have been discussing. Throughout the reconciliation process after apartheid, Tutu was committed to peace and forgiveness. He led the Truth and Reconciliation Commission to grant amnesty to offenders in exchange for an admission of guilt. This raised the question, Does love abrogate justice? In other words, people who were worthy of imprisonment and death went unpunished. This seemed to be a breach of justice. Tutu's commitment to this arrangement, however, did not stem from an absolute conviction that this was the only way to deal with enemies. His strategy was pragmatic: he believed it was the best strategy at the time to prevent further bloodshed. He wrote, "It is important to note that the amnesty provision is an ad hoc arrangement meant for this specific purpose. This is not how justice is to be administered in South Africa forever. It is for a limited and definite period and purpose."[20]

---

18. Jas 2:26
19. Luke 23:34
20. Tutu, *No Future without Forgiveness*, 54.

Part Two: Theology

G. The Difference of Context

Another important consideration in dealing with tension in Scripture is the context. Jesus commands his disciples to love his enemies in the Sermon on the Mount. But God commands the nation of Israel at times to go to war. On a simplistic reading it might appear that God is conflicted. However, the commands in the passages are directed to different people in different situations. In the Sermon on the Mount the commands are directed to individuals, in relation to other individuals. On the other hand, the call to war in the Old Testament is directed to kings and prophets, in relation to other nations. The difference in context explains the discrepancy in conduct. Regarding Matthew 5:9 (blessed are the peacemakers), Luther writes,

> There is more needed to begin a war than that you have a good cause. For although we are not forbidden here to carry on a war, as above said, Christ here does not mean to detract anything from the powers that be and their official authority, but is teaching only individual people who wish to lead for themselves a Christian life; yet it is not right that a prince determines to have a war with his neighbor, even though (I say) he has a good cause and his neighbor is in the wrong; but the meaning is: blessed are the peacemakers; so that he who wants to be a Christian and a child of God, not only does not begin war and strife, but helps and advises for peace, whenever he can, although there was reason and cause enough for going to war. It is enough, if one has tried his best for peace and all avails nothing, that one acts on the defensive, to protect land and people.[21]

In other words, Luther understood that there were two messages in Scripture: one a call for peace, and the other a call for war. He did not see the Sermon on the Mount as the only way of dealing with conflict. Nor was it the standard of comparison for other passages. Instead, Luther saw that Jesus' call here is for disciples to be peacemakers inasmuch as they are able. But Jesus was not commanding the government or the nation as a whole that this is the only course of action. Luther continues,

> It is also meant here, if injustice and violence are done to you, that it is not right for you to consult your own foolish head, and begin right away to take vengeance and strike back; but you are to think

---

21. Luther, *Sermon on the Mount*, 72. It should be noted here that Luther made a sharp split between the public and the private Christian, and between the church and the state. He argued for a great deal of dissonance between the way that a Christian relates to individuals and how one could relate as a citizen. I do not endorse this split, nor do I think that it is even possible.

over it and try to bear it and have peace. If that will not answer, and you cannot endure it, you have the law and governmental authority in the land, where you can seek relief in a regular way.[22]

H. Conclusion

We often make misguided attempts to make sense of the canon. Admittedly, there is a discrepancy between Jesus' call to "turn the other cheek" and the way that the psalmists dealt with their enemies. The first step in dealing with such a discrepancy faithfully is to allow it to exist. We should not negate Jesus' sermon by implying that he actually meant something else, nor should we nullify the psalms by implying that they do not actually contain hatred, anger, or a desire for vengeance. Rather than dismiss the contradiction, or radically re-interpret these passages in such a way as to eliminate the discrepancy, we should take into account some of the more complicated issues. These include noting the intended authority of the speaker: To what extent is the passage we are reading *descriptive* or *prescriptive*? We must also note the genre: Are we reading a sermon, letter, prayer, song, command, etc.? We must also ask whether what we are reading is the only way to respond in every situation, or if the passage is offering a way of wisdom in certain situations.

---

22. Ibid., 73.

5

A Theology of God in the Imprecatory Psalms

Consistent with What?

ONE OF THE REASONS we have difficulty understanding inconsistency in Scripture is that we are unclear what the standard of comparison is. In other words, the imprecatory psalms seem obsolete because they appear inconsistent with the Sermon on the Mount. This statement implies that the Sermon on the Mount is the sole or primary standard against which these psalms must be compared. But we could approach this issue with a different question: what are the imprecatory psalms consistent with?

A. The Imprecatory Psalms are Consistent with the Covenant Promises

Several commentators have noted the theme of covenant throughout the imprecatory psalms. This school of interpretation is examined in detail in chapter 2, but we will revisit the concept briefly here. God promised Abraham: "I will make you into a great nation, and I will bless you; I will make your name great, and you will be a blessing. I will bless those who bless you, and whoever curses you I will curse; and all people on earth will be blessed through you."[1] Following this God made a covenant with Moses that those who kept his commands would be blessed, and those who were lawbreakers would be cursed. According to the Bible, God's revelation to Moses was an

---

1. Gen 12:2–3

extension of his earlier revelation to Abraham.² The Psalms are replete with echoes of the covenant.³ When the people of Israel sang the psalms they reminded themselves of the covenants. They affirmed the blessedness of the righteous, and resolved that they would remain righteous in order to remain on God's side. They affirmed their belief that God would be faithful to his promise to protect his people. In other words, the imprecatory prayers were consistent with what God promised to do to his enemies.

B. The Imprecatory Psalms are Consistent with Imprecatory Prophecy

Isaiah wrote, "Ar in Moab is ruined, destroyed in a night! Kir in Moab is ruined, destroyed in a night!"[4] Amos prophesied destruction in Damascus, Gaza, Tyre, Edom, Ammon, Moab (and Judah). The whole content of Obadiah is a prophecy against Edom. Jonah prophesies the immanent destruction of Nineveh. The whole content of Nahum is a prophecy against Nineveh. Zephaniah prophesies against Philistia, Moab, Ammon, Cush, and Assyria. Ezekiel prophesies against Ammon, Moab, Edom, Philistia, Tyre, Sidon, and Egypt. The "imprecatory problem" does not go away if we somehow solve it for the Psalms. We still have the consistent message in the prophets that the enemies of God will be destroyed. This is larger than an ethical problem (whether it is permissible for us to wish, pray for, or declare the destruction of our enemies). The presence of these imprecatory prophecies invokes a doctrine of God that presents tension between God's love and God's severity.

C. The Imprecatory Psalms are Consistent with the Warnings of Scripture

The psalms were sung as an assembly, and as such they have a public function of instruction. Psalm 1 begins, "Blessed is the one who does not walk in step with the wicked." The psalm is a warning. It contains an imprecation: "Not so the wicked! They are like chaff that the wind blows away." Though the psalm is a prayer, and God is undoubtedly listening, the song also teaches as the assembly is listening. In this way, the imprecations are both prayers and a form of catechism. A pervasive tension exists in the Bible with respect to the theme

---

2. See Paul's discussion in Galatians 3

3. See, for example, Pss 25:10, 14; 44:17; 50:5, 16; 55:20; 60:1; 74:20; 78:10, 37; 80:1; 89:3, 28, 34, 39; 103:18; 105:8, 9, 10; 106:45; 111:5, 9; 132:12.

4. Isa 15:1

of warning. John says, "I write these things to you who believe in the name of the son of God so that you may know that you have eternal life."[5] His audience is apparently in need of assurance; perhaps they doubt their salvation. But Hebrews says, "It is impossible for those who have once been enlightened, who have tasted the heavenly gift, who have shared in the Holy Spirit, who have tasted the goodness of the word of God and the powers of the coming age, and have fallen away, to be brought back to repentance."[6] Evidently this audience was in need of warning; perhaps they thought they should sin all the more so that grace would abound! There are two apparently conflicting messages here, but that is the nature of rebuke. Those who have been warned and have heeded the caution are in need of assurance. Those who have, or have ignored the caution are in need of a stern rebuke. When Jesus calls his disciples to love their enemies in the Sermon on the Mount, there is no context of warning. But both testaments are replete with warnings, and some of them quite formalized. We see in the wisdom literature (including the Psalms) the most formalized instances of them.

D. The Imprecatory Psalms are Consistent with New Testament Imprecation

As I stated earlier, even Jesus practiced imprecation at times. In chapter seven there is a lengthy discussion of New Testament imprecation as well.[7] Suffice it to say here that the psalms are not an isolated incidence of imprecation, and the practice is found throughout the Bible.

E. The Imprecatory Psalms are Consistent with a Biblical Doctrine of God.

A fundamental reason that we see tension between the call to love enemies in the Sermon on the Mount and the imprecatory psalms is that we assume love and judgment are incompatible. At stake here is more than an ethic of which to prefer: the Sermon on the Mount or the Psalms. What is really at stake is our doctrine of God. The historic preference for the Sermon on the Mount highlights that the church has rarely doubted the love of God. The difficulty is in assessing how much justice, judgment, or even hate can coexist with love.

---

5. 1 John 5:13
6. Heb 6:4
7. Chapter 7, section D, guideline 7

A Theology of God in the Imprecatory Psalms

Christ prayed imprecatory psalms. Some commentators have pointed out that the imprecatory prayers are messianic. This approach is examined in detail in chapter 2, but it is important to note here that even if this is not the best or only reading of every imprecatory psalm, some of the imprecations are messianic. Furthermore, Jesus even prayed some of these psalms himself. Jesus cited Psalm 41:8–10 as an imprecation against Judas. Jesus partially cites Psalm 8:2, "Through the praise of children and infants you have established a stronghold against your enemies."[8] In each of the Synoptic Gospels Jesus cites Psalm 110:1: "The LORD says to my lord: 'Sit at my right hand until I make your enemies a footstool for your feet.'" Though Jesus did not quote it, the psalm continues, "The Lord is at your right hand he will crush kings on the day of his wrath. He will judge the nations, heaping up the dead and crushing the rulers of the whole earth." When Jesus died, he cited Psalm 31:5 "Into your hands I commit my spirit." Psalm 35 contains these imprecatory elements: "I hate those who cling to worthless idols" (v. 6); and "let the wicked be put to shame" (v. 17). Twice Jesus invokes Psalm 69: when he said "zeal for your house consumes me" and on the cross when he said "I thirst" and was given wine with vinegar. Psalm 69 is thoroughly imprecatory: "May the table set before them become a snare; may it become retribution and a trap. May their eyes be darkened so they cannot see, and their backs be bent forever. Pour out your wrath on them; let your fierce anger overtake them" (vv. 22–24).

These passages show that Jesus prayed some portions of the imprecatory psalms, and that the authors of the New Testament regarded some of these Psalms as messianic. Clearly neither Jesus nor his disciples saw imprecation as inherently inconsistent with the nature of the Messiah. The biblical authors were able to maintain at the same time the severity of Christ's judgment and the limitless nature of his love. The fact that Jesus prayed these psalms and that some of them are messianic illustrates two important things: First, the psalms are more than "allowable;" they are also modeled. Second, imprecation is a compatible with God's nature. We must conclude, therefore, that imprecation is not contrary to love.

Curses are revocable. Another reason that imprecation is compatible with love is that the curses are revocable. Brueggemann explains, "We may note that this settlement of the question of vengeance is provisional."[9] Jonah's message to the Ninevites was, "Forty more days and Nineveh will be overthrown."[10] Yet the people of Nineveh rightly discerned that the Lord

---

8. Matt 21:16
9. Brueggemann, *Praying the Psalms*, 76.
10 Jonah 3.4

may relent, if they were contrite. And Jonah's curse upon Nineveh was indeed revoked, after the people repented. In this case, God's threat to the Ninevites was loving. Jonah's warning led to repentance, blessing, and the favor of God. Similarly, God spoke through Jeremiah that if at any time he announced he would uproot a nation, and if that nation repented of their sin, then he would not bring upon them the disaster that he had intended (Jer 18). Imprecation is a function of love as it warns people about the results of their failure to repent. Imprecation sometimes functions as an offer for a second chance. Interestingly, we even see this theme carried out through Revelation. Four times during the judgments poured out during the apocalypse, John laments that despite judgment people still did not repent (Rev 9:20, 21; 16:9, 11). This implies that there was some opportunity to repent, indicating that God's temporal judgments are never divorced from his mercy and love.

God's character is both loving and severe. Our understanding of the imprecatory psalms requires an understanding of God's character. We are uncomfortable with the severity of the Psalms, because we are uncomfortable with the severity of God. The apostle Paul understood that God exercised both attributes. He warned and marveled: "Behold then the kindness and severity of God."[11] We often see kindness and severity (wrath) as incompatible, so we see the imprecatory psalms and the Sermon on the Mount as incompatible. Grudem explains that the severity of God is essential to God's love:

> God's wrath means that he intensely hates all sin. . . . It is helpful for us to ask what God would be like if he were a God that did not hate sin. He would then be a God who either delighted in sin or at least was not troubled by it. Such a God would not be worthy of our worship, for sin is hateful and it is worthy of being hated. Sin ought not to be. It is in fact a virtue to hate evil and sin, and we rightly imitate this attribute of God when we feel hatred against great evil, injustice, and sin.[12]

While it may seem that the imprecations in the psalms are inconsistent with the Sermon on the Mount, neither imprecation of enemies nor love of enemies is inconsistent with God's character. The Bible tells us that all God's ways are justice,[13] that the Lord whose name is Jealous is a Jealous God,[14] and that the wrath of God is revealed from heaven against all ungodliness

---

11. Rom 11:22
12. Grudem, *Systematic Theology*, 206.
13. Deut 32:4
14. Exod 34:14

A Theology of God in the Imprecatory Psalms

and wickedness.[15] Mysteriously, the Bible portrays a God who is at the same time loving and judging. Ironically, judgment is consistent with (or even a form of) love. Brueggemann explains, "This is not a soft, romantic God who only tolerates and forgives, but one who takes seriously his own rule and the wellbeing of his partners."[16] The love and severity of God coexist, because severity is sometimes required to express love. Milne writes:

> God's wrath arises from his eternal self-consistency. His revealed character is an unalterable expression of his nature. All that opposes him he resists with a total and final commitment. "Wrath is the holy revulsion of God's being against that which is the contradiction of his holiness" (J. Murray). God's wrath is not, as is often alleged, a crude piece of anthropomorphism. It is rather the response of the normative Person in his personal quality of holiness towards the presence of sin in his universe.[17]

God's Character in the Psalms

God is holy. The holiness of God means that God is neither capable of committing sin, nor dwelling in the midst of it. We read, "For you are not a God who is pleased with wickedness; with you, evil people are not welcome."[18] Given the holiness of God, it is no wonder that the psalmist was able to pray with confidence that God would hear his case.

God is righteous and just. The justice of God means that God will not tolerate sin forever (balanced with his patience), nor let it go unpunished (balanced with his mercy). We read, "On the wicked he will rain fiery coals and burning sulfur; a scorching wind will be their lot."[19] And elsewhere, "But you, God, will bring down the wicked into the pit of decay; the bloodthirsty and deceitful will not live out half their days."[20] The psalmist takes solace in the thought that, "You reward everyone according to what they have done"[21] and that, "The LORD is a God who avenges. O God who avenges, shine forth."[22] The justice of God is not always apparent, and God's

---

15. Rom 1:18
16. Brueggemann, *Message of the Psalms*, 85.
17. Milne, *Know the Truth*, 86.
18. Ps 5:4
19. Ps 11:6
20. Ps 55:23
21. Ps 62:12
22. Ps 94:1

patience (with others) is longer than our liking. Sometimes the justice of God seems altogether lacking, and we begin to believe that "nice guys finish last." This was what the psalmist felt when he said, "But as for me, my feet had almost slipped; I had nearly lost my foothold. For I envied the arrogant when I saw the prosperity of the wicked."[23] He began to wonder whether righteousness paid off, given the apparent absence of God's justice. But later in the same psalm he affirms, "Those who are far from you will perish; you destroy all who are unfaithful to you."[24] The justice of God is part of the psalmist's eschatological hope. We read, "Then people will say, 'Surely the righteous still are rewarded; surely there is a God who judges the earth.'"[25] The goodness of God requires his justice. For God to be good and loving, he must do loving things. To withhold loving action when it is within his power to act would be unloving. For that reason, love requires actions of justice. A. A. Hodge explains,

> Goodness and justice are the several aspects of one unchangeable, infinitely wise and sovereign moral perfection. God is not sometimes merciful and sometimes just, nor so far merciful and so far just, but he is eternally infinitely merciful and just. Relatively to the creature this infinite perfection of nature presents different aspects, as is determined by the judgment which infinite wisdom delivers in each individual case. Even in our experience these attributes of our moral nature are found not to be inconsistent in principle, though our want both of wisdom and knowledge, a sense of our own unworthiness, and a mere physical sympathy, often sadly distract our judgments as well as our hearts in adjusting these principles to the individual cases of life.[26]

God is patient and compassionate. God's justice is tempered with and coincides with his compassion. We read, "Glorious and majestic are his deeds, and his righteousness endures forever. He has caused his wonders to be remembered; the LORD is gracious and compassionate."[27] The compassion of God is a consistent theme in the Psalms, and undeniably always on the psalmist's mind. Three times we read the phrase: "But you, Lord, are a compassionate and gracious God, slow to anger, abounding in love and faithfulness."[28] That God is slow to anger attests to his patience. The pa-

23. Ps 73:2–3
24. Ps 73:27
25. Ps 58:11
26. Hodge, *Outlines of Theology*, 161.
27. Ps 111:2–3
28. Pss 86:15; 103:8; 145:8

A Theology of God in the Imprecatory Psalms

tience of God is at times frustrating, when experienced as silence in regard to dealing with our enemies. On the other hand, mindful of our own sin, the patience of God is experienced as a blessing.

God can seem silent. At times the patience of God seems like silence. The psalmist asks, "Why, LORD, do you stand far off? Why do you hide yourself in times of trouble?"[29] It is no wonder that the psalmist directs his imprecatory prayers toward God. He knows that God is able to help (given his power), expects that God should help (given his love), and knows that inevitably God will help (given his justice). Yet, the help is not soon enough. He prays, "O God, why have you rejected us forever? Why does your anger smolder against the sheep of your pasture?"[30]

God is sovereign. The silence of God can only be understood alongside the sovereignty of God. Were we able to be God's counselors, we would "speak with him about his justice."[31] But in light of God's sovereignty, his silence is more tolerable. Perhaps part of our modern aversion to the imprecatory psalms is that modern theologians are less mindful of the sovereignty of God than were the ancient psalmists. The hatred the ancient author harbored toward his enemy was always tempered with a conviction that the enemy never did anything God did not allow. Similarly, the ancient author never believed that somehow he could "mess things up" by praying an imprecatory prayer. Both victory and defeat were completely determined by God's design. We read, "Through you we push back our enemies; through your name we trample our foes. I put no trust in my bow, my sword does not bring me victory; but you give us victory over our enemies, you put our adversaries to shame."[32] The modern reader has an aversion to the imprecatory psalms because they seem prideful. But the psalmist knows that there is no pride in any victory, since it only comes through the sovereign will of God. Similarly, the modern reader assumes that anger toward the enemy is also prideful. But in the very same psalm we read, "But now you have rejected and humbled us; you no longer go out with our armies."[33] Anger in the psalms is never wholly directed at the enemy, since God is "partly to blame." Anger at God, in fact, is every bit as much a theme in the psalms as anger at enemies.

God is love. The enduring beauty of the Psalter derives much in part because of the praise of God's love. We read, "Your love, LORD, reaches to

---

29. Ps 10:1
30. Ps 74:1
31. Jer 12:1
32. Ps 44:5–7
33. Ps 44:9

the heavens, your faithfulness to the skies. Your righteousness is like the highest mountains, your justice like the great deep. You, LORD, preserve both people and animals. How priceless is your unfailing love, O God! People take refuge in the shadow of your wings."[34] The love of God overshadows and more than counter-balances the themes of the justice, righteousness and silence of God in the Psalter. The psalmist declares, "Let them give thanks to the LORD for his unfailing love and his wonderful deeds for mankind, for he satisfies the thirsty and fills the hungry with good things."[35]

God is helpful. Given that God is sovereign, loving, and just, it follows that God is able to help, should help, and will help those in need.[36] Most psalms contain a plea for help. For instance, "But you, LORD, are a shield around me, my glory, the One who lifts my head high."[37] Similarly, the psalmist declares, "A father to the fatherless, a defender of widows, is God in his holy dwelling."[38] One of the greatest contributions a study of the imprecatory psalms offers the modern reader is a call to dependence upon God for help. For, "God is our refuge and strength, an ever-present help in trouble."[39] Because God is helpful, these imprecations are prayers. There are petitions to God that he would intervene, aid, and change the course of events. The have the expectation that God will act not because he is obligated, but because he is faithful to his covenant promises.

God has anger. That God in the Psalms has anger is undeniable. We read, "Arise, LORD, in your anger; rise up against the rage of my enemies. Awake, my God; decree justice."[40] This verse connotes an important relationship between love and anger. If God truly loves, we would expect him to be angry when the people he loves are harmed, threatened, or mistreated. For God not to be angry would be unloving. In fact, anger is not enough, but action (guided by his wisdom) is also required for God to be loving. Loving people do loving things. These things include deliverance, protection, and rescue. Brueggemann explains,

---

34. Ps 36:5–7
35. Ps 107:8–9
36. I do not mean that God is always obligated to help in every instance of suffering, as atheists often argue in their objections regarding theodicy. God's wisdom and love will always compel him to act, but he may not act in the way that we expect or see fit.
37. Ps 3:3
38. Ps 68:5
39. Ps 46:1
40. Ps 7:6

A Theology of God in the Imprecatory Psalms

The vengeance of God is understood as the other side of his compassion—the sovereign redress of a wrong. That is, in the Old Testament, two motifs belong together. God cannot act to liberate his people without at the same time judging and punishing the oppressors who have perverted a just ordering of life.[41]

In the Psalms we read, "God is a righteous judge, a God who displays his wrath every day."[42] The display of God's wrath is vital to the evidence of God's love. That display need not be explicitly supernatural (as in a lightning bolt from heaven). In light of the sovereignty of God, any way that causes the injustice to stop is God's action and is sufficient. God's anger is not only directed at others, but even at Israel. We read, "When God heard them, he was furious; he rejected Israel completely."[43] The "completely" here may be utterly felt, but not permanent. In fact, we read, "For his anger lasts only a moment, but his favor lasts a lifetime; weeping may stay for the night, but rejoicing comes in the morning."[44]

The Psalms address the unity of God's character: "Loving-kindness and truth have met together; Righteousness and peace have kissed each other."[45] Righteousness is the demand for all that is good, true, and just. Peace is the condition with no strife or pain. It is a mystery how these two could co-exist. In a world where the unjust deserve to be punished, how can we expect them to be dealt loving-kindness and peace? Erickson tries to explain the mystery:

> If we begin with the assumptions that God is an integrated being and the divine attributes are harmonious, we will define the attributes in the light of one another. Thus, justice is loving justice and the love is just love. The idea that they conflict may have resulted from defining these attributes in isolation from one another.[46]

F. Some Notable Differences

To say that the imprecatory psalms are consistent with the nature of God does not mean that they are consistent in every way. There are some

---

41. Brueggemann, *Praying the Psalms*, 70–71.
42. Ps 7:11
43. Ps 78:59
44. Ps 30:5
45. Ps 85:10 (not an imprecatory psalm)
46. Erickson, *Christian Theology*, 298.

Part Two: Theology

notable differences between the expressions of imprecation in the psalms, and in the words of Jesus.

In the Gospel of Mark Jesus curses a fig tree.[47] One could say that based on this passage, Jesus was not beyond cursing. It must be admitted, however, that the fig tree is not a person. In addition, the act was symbolic. One could argue that the symbolism actually accentuates the fact that Jesus cursed a *person*: for the fig tree represents the nation of Israel. On the other hand, because the act is symbolic, we must also admit that the cursing was also symbolic to some extent. This event does not have the same characteristics as the imprecatory psalms. But in defense of the psalms, they too are indirect to the enemies. It would be misleading to say that Jesus did not directly curse his enemies when he cursed the fig tree, because that would imply that the psalms do directly curse the enemy. But the psalms are directed toward God, and it is unlikely the enemies ever hear the words of imprecation.

There are also notable differences when Jesus curses the cities: "Woe to you, Chorazin! Woe to you, Bethsaida! For if the miracles had been performed in Tyre and Sidon which occurred in you, they would have repented long ago, sitting in sackcloth and ashes."[48] This phrase employs the word "woe" (*ouai*) which may be seen as a curse. But from the context, it is fair to assume that this utterance from Jesus is more of a lament. Jesus expresses sorrow, regret, and hopelessness. But the voice of anger and hatred is either subtle or non-existent.

Similarly, the eight woes to the Pharisees[49] are curses that employ the same Greek word. But these charges against the Pharisees also contain an element of grief and sadness. The anger is less subtle in this text. Jesus calls the Pharisees hypocrites seven times. He says they are blind guides, fools, whitewashed tombs full of hypocrisy and lawlessness, serpents, and a brood of vipers. Lastly, he says that they should not think they will escape the sentence of hell. Though this section is closer to the imprecatory psalms, there is still a notable difference. It could be stated that Jesus is prophesying the future (as some interpreters of the imprecatory psalms have insisted). There is more validity to that claim here than in the psalms, where the destruction is clearly *desirable*. It is not clear from any text in the gospels that Jesus *desired* retribution. A second obvious difference is that Jesus has the right to declare people guilty without implicating himself, whereas the psalmist does not. Jesus has the right to judge because he is the judge.

---

47. Mark 11:12–13, 21
48. Matt 11:21, Luke 10:13
49. Matt 23

A Theology of God in the Imprecatory Psalms

A significant difference between the Psalter and the teachings of the New Testament is that God's wrath was satisfied in the death of Christ. The messianic interpretation of the Psalms[50] (held by Luther, Bonhoeffer, Mays, Adams) has many pitfalls. In many cases it forces the text too much, and the interpretive model is unreflective of human nature, as well as of the initial context. That being said, the messianic interpretation makes a valuable contribution to this discussion about the wrath of God. Bonhoeffer explains this radical truth:

> God's vengeance did not strike the sinners, but the one sinless man who stood in the sinner's place, namely God's own son. Jesus Christ bore the wrath of God, for the execution of which the psalm prays. He stilled God's wrath toward sin and prayed in the hour of the execution of the divine judgment: "Father, forgive them, for they do not know what they do." No other than he, who himself bore the wrath of God, could pray in this way.[51]

While I do not think this is the best interpretive model of the imprecatory psalms, Bonhoeffer's understanding of the wrath of God satisfied in Christ is biblical, and vital for understanding the doctrine of God's wrath. The imprecatory psalms may not have arisen out of a context of Christological thinking, and it would be simplistic to assume that the sole voice of the Psalms is Christ. But nevertheless, Bonhoeffer is right when he says, "I pray the imprecatory psalms in the certainty of their marvelous fulfillment."[52] The death of Christ marks a change not in the nature of God, but in the way that God's people have understood the means by which God's wrath will be poured out. We know that we were former enemies of God, but that Christ has destroyed the enmity by bearing our curse himself.

G. Conclusion

The emotion in the imprecatory psalms seems to contradict the ethic of the Sermon on the Mount. I have argued here that perhaps this is too simplistic of a comparison. Instead, I suggest using the character of God as a standard of comparison. Rather than asking, "Are the imprecatory psalms consistent with Jesus' sermon on the Mount?" I have offered the question, "What are the imprecatory psalms consistent with?" There are several answers to the latter question. The imprecations in the psalms are consistent with covenant

---

50. Examined in chapter 2, section H, and also in chapter 3, section I.
51. Bonhoeffer, *Psalms*, 58.
52. Ibid., 59.

promises, they are consistent with imprecatory prophecy, and with the warnings in Scripture. They are also consistent with the practice of imprecation in the New Testament. Finally, the imprecatory psalms are (with some qualifications) consistent with a biblical doctrine of God. This is evidenced by the fact that Jesus prayed these psalms and uttered his own imprecations. God's use of imprecation is mitigated by the fact that his curses are revocable. God's character is both loving and severe. For God to be loving, he must commit himself to loving action. Since God is powerful, such action would include rescuing people from oppression. That rescue is seen as an act of judgment in Scripture, no matter how it comes to fruition. I state that the imprecatory psalms are consistent with God's character, given some qualifications. Those qualifications include the fact that judgment is not the only way God metes out justice. Sometimes God's justice is obtained by converting the enemy into a friend.[53] God's justice was also satisfied in Christ's sacrifice. But this is not to say that no expression of God's justice remains in the future. For Scripture teaches that judgment is the prerogative of the *eschaton*.

---

53. Rom 5:10

6

Human Nature in the Imprecatory Psalms

A. Introduction

THIS CHAPTER WILL EXAMINE the theology of human nature contained in the Psalms, to give a background for the larger context of the preaching and therapeutic value of the imprecatory psalms. Perhaps the greatest reason that the imprecatory psalms are problematic for contemporary interpreters is that we often fail to understand their anthropology. The modern Western reader often comes to the text with incorrect assumptions about such crucial concepts as: *enemy, innocent, self*, etc. Often we see in these psalms a level of individuality that was not envisioned by the ancient community. Reading these psalms from an individualistic perspective heightens their offensiveness. It is therefore necessary to understand the basic anthropology and other associated theological concepts in order to preach and teach these psalms for all that they are worth.

The psalms are a deep well from which to draw an anthropology of the Old Testament. The basic question, in fact, "What is man?" is explicitly asked and answered in Psalm 8, as well as implicitly answered throughout the Psalter. Furthermore, the Psalms are brutally honest; willing to evoke every emotion and thought experienced by humankind. The theology of humankind is therefore widely varied on a spectrum from positive to negative perspectives on human nature. The psalms take as their subject both friends, enemies, and friends turned enemies; meaning that the anthropology is wide enough to answer not only "Who am I?" but "Who are my enemies?" and "Who are my people?"

This chapter will examine fifteen characteristics of human nature which arise out of the Psalter. The Psalter has a rich theology about a person's relationship to God, oneself, and others. True, the psalter was written over time by a variety of authors, and does not exhibit a univocal theology on the subject, but rather evinces a wide spectrum. Here I list fifteen theological propositions found in the Psalms. The list is not exhaustive, but representative of the theologizing that the psalms employ regarding humanity's relationship to God, others and oneself. Regarding one's relationship to God, we are known by God, loved by God, judged as depraved by God, in need of redemption by God, used as an instrument of God to carry out punishment with others, and are destined for eternal life with God (or eternal separation from him). In relationship to oneself, people are frustrated in their quest for holiness, blind to their own faults, and experience severe angst at times. In relationship to others, the psalter says that humanity is collectively organized in nations, polarized as either good or evil, exerts dominion, and is in need of humility. Our lives are fleeting, and we are capable of either loving our neighbors, becoming oppressed by them, or becoming oppressors ourselves.

A people's theology is often expressed by their liturgy. The words they speak to God when they gather together express what is central in their beliefs and hearts. The songs they sing show what is essential to their faith. The Psalter, along with the citations of it in the New Testament, presents a definitive statement about God's relationship with his people. The notions of anthropology presented there answer the questions about who is God's enemy, and how does God deal with his enemies. This is a vital interpretive framework for understanding the imprecations in the psalms, because it helps us rightly understand the concepts of innocence, guilt, enemy, anger, etc.

B. Humans are Organized in Nations

The psalms do not treat human nature as a purely individual concept. People are organized in nations and, as with individuals, these nations have an underlying character: righteous or wicked. As with individuals, so this classification of nations as either righteous or wicked is not marked by any specific sin, or having reached a threshold of sin. Instead nations are evaluated solely on their relationship to the one true God; the LORD[1] God of Israel. If a nation identifies its God as the LORD, and cries out to the LORD, then it is righteous. But if the nation scoffs at the LORD, it is wicked. The psalmist asks, "Why do the nations conspire and the peoples plot in vain?"[2] Later we read, "You have rebuked the nations and destroyed the wicked; you have

---

1. The word LORD in caps signifies the Hebrew word Yahweh
2. Ps 2:1

blotted out their name forever and ever."[3] And elsewhere we are promised that the Lord "will judge the nations, heaping up the dead and crushing the rulers of the whole earth."[4] The collection of people into nations magnifies their depravity and sin.

Niebuhr speaks of this amplified effect in his discussion of collective egoism or national pride.

> Strictly speaking, only individuals are moral agents, and group pride is therefore merely an aspect of the pride and arrogance of individuals. Nevertheless some distinctions must be made between the collective behavior of men and their individual attitudes. This is necessary in part because group pride, though having its source in individual attitudes, actually achieves a certain authority over the individual and results in unconditioned demand by the group upon the individual.[5]

Nations are therefore accountable to God for their actions. Nations are not viewed merely as a large collection of individuals, but take on a quality of their own. This quality is seen primarily as a polarity between evil nations and righteous ones. Whether the nation is evil or good is expressed not in terms of the psalmist's perspective, but whether the writer sees the nation as a friend of God or an enemy to him.

In reading and interpreting the Psalms, it is vital to keep in mind that the words "I" and "we" speak for the community of Israel. These psalms were publicly read and sung, as part of community worship. Furthermore, the authors had in mind their covenant relationship with God. The declarations of innocence may seem repulsive to the modern reader who forgets the national and communal setting. But we must remember that in general the psalms do not express anger toward the injury that one person has suffered because of another. Instead, they express the anger that a nation has due to the suffering inflicted by another nation.

C. Humans are Polarized

One troubling aspect of human nature is the intense polarization expressed in the psalms. The first psalm begins with a contrast between the wicked and

3. Ps 9:5
4. Ps 110:6
5. Niebhur, *The Nature and Destiny of Man*, 208. It must be recognized here that the concept of "nation" in the ancient Near Eastern environment is different from the nation-states which emerged in the eighteenth century and provide the background for Niebuhr's comments.

the righteous. It states that the one who delights in the law of the Lord will be planted and prosper, but the wicked will be blown away like chaff. Clearly the author believes that the distinction between these two groups is identifiable, and the difference between them is great. Throughout the Psalter, the "us" and "them" motif is strong and pervasive. The author of Psalm 3 laments "how many are my foes!"[6] And he petitions, "Strike all my enemies on the jaw."[7] Not only is this distinction between victims and foes mentioned; it is exalted. We read, "Lord who may dwell in your sanctuary? [He] who despises a vile man."[8] The author states, "With you [God] the wicked cannot dwell."[9] It is noteworthy, however, that the division between the wicked and the righteous is based on more criteria than one's trespasses. The psalmist on several occasions admits his own sin, and the sins of his own country, which he still also views as righteous. Nor is the classification made by one individual having reached a threshold of intolerable sin so as to make him wicked. Instead, the distinction between the righteous and the wicked is the God with whom the person is allied. The wicked scoff at the LORD, worship idols, disregard the Law, are prideful, and are blind to their own errors. But the righteous, though also under the same curse of invariable depravity, cry out to the Lord. They love the law, humble themselves in light of their sin, and acknowledge their faults. Niebuhr discusses our tendency to treat human nature as a polarization between the good and the bad. He summarizes Pascal, "There are only two kinds of men, the righteous who believe themselves sinners; the rest, sinners, who believe themselves righteous."[10]

Niebuhr speaks of this polarity by drawing a distinction between the equality of sin and inequality of guilt. The psalmist is conscious that everyone has sinned, and as we will see below all are morally corrupt. But Niebuhr warns, "Theologies which threaten to destroy all relative moral judgments by their exclusive emphasis upon the ultimate religious fact of the sinfulness of all men, are rightly suspected of imperiling the relative moral achievements of history."[11] In other words, Niebuhr is concerned that if we are unwilling ever to draw a distinction among the types, consequences, or extent of sins that people commit we will be unable to point to heroes and reformers. Within such a relative moral framework, we will not

---

6. Ps 3:1
7. Ps 3:7
8. Ps 15:1, 4
9. Ps 5:4
10. Niebuhr, *Nature and Destiny of Man*, 257.
11. Ibid., 220.

have ground for any talk of moral progress if we cannot point to "a person who stood out."

The contemporary Western reader sees this polarity as prideful, contemptible, unchristian, etc. Perhaps that is because we tend to take this polarity to mean that there are good individuals and bad individuals (and obviously, I am one of the good kind, and my enemy is one of the bad kind). This individualistic reading understandably leads to an aversion to the imprecatory psalms. But the ancient worshipers sang these songs together, and they did so with an understanding that God made a covenant with their whole community. The polarity in the Psalms, therefore, expresses that the worshipers are part of the covenant community, while non-worshipers are not.

D. Humans are Invariably Depraved

The authors of the psalms were thoroughly convinced of the total depravity of humankind. Not only did they decry the baseness of their enemies, but they assumed a universal depraved condition. The psalmist writes, "Everyone lies to his neighbor,"[12] and, "Everyone has turned away, they have together become corrupt; there is no one who does good, not even one."[13] And there is of course the section Paul echoes in his treatise on the debased human condition, "All have turned aside, they have together become corrupt; there is no one who does good, not even one."[14] The depraved condition is also expressed (though not in the same universal tone) of people who not only practice evil, but who love it, or who practice malice unprovoked or without cause. Such people are said to be "blood thirsty and deceitful"[15] "enemies without cause,"[16] and people who "love war."[17] Finally, we read in Psalm 51: "Surely I was sinful at birth, sinful from the time my mother conceived me."[18] It is clear that the psalms do not reserve ascription of depravity only to one's enemies. Even the writer himself acknowledges his own thorough propensity to sin.

This depravity in some ways embraces the historic doctrine of original sin. Of this fallen state Niebuhr says, "Man does not know himself truly except as he knows himself confronted by God. Only in that confrontation

12. Ps 12:2
13. Ps 53:3
14. Ps 14:3
15. Ps 5:6
16. Ps 69:4
17. Ps 120:7
18. Ps 51:5

does he become aware of his full stature and freedom and of the evil in him."[19] This is not to say that God bears the responsibility for humanity's condition of total depravity, or that sinfulness is a necessary quality to being human.[20] Niebuhr explains, "Original sin, by definition an inherited corruption, or at least an inevitable one, is nevertheless not to be regarded as belonging to [man's] essential nature and therefore is not outside the realm of his responsibility. Sin is natural for man in the sense that it is universal but not in the sense that it is necessary. . . . Sin is to be regarded neither as a necessity of man's nature nor yet as a pure caprice of his will."[21]

Given the polarity within the psalms between the righteous and the wicked, it is natural for one to suspect that the depravity described within the Psalter applies only to the enemies. But the psalmist writes, "Look upon my affliction and my distress and take away all my sins,"[22] indicating that he is mindful of his own sin, and even anxious about the remedy or his standing with God. That being said, there is admittedly a greater focus on the depravity of one's enemies than of oneself. I do not mean to imply here that the psalms are primarily self-deprecating, or that there is even balance between the view of one's sin and the sin of others. But since the psalms of innocence are closely related to the imprecatory psalms, we must understand that the term "innocent" does not mean for the psalmist what it means for the contemporary Western reader. We take the word innocent to mean "completely free from any wrong-doing." We might argue that the psalmist knows he is not innocent in this sense, but that our modern Western definition of innocence is not even on the psalmist's mind. Innocence for the psalmist is defined by the community's covenant relationship with God. The people who remain faithful to their covenant with God are innocent. From a New Testament perspective we understand this concept as imputed righteousness. From ancient Israel's perspective the innocence was a statement of assurance that God shows solidarity with his people.

E. Humans can be God's Instrument of Punishment

The psalmist understood that God could rebuke the wicked using any or all means.[23] When natural disasters are mentioned in Scripture, for instance, they

---

19. Niebuhr, *Nature and Destiny of Man*, 131.

20. Christ was fully human, and not sinful, proving that sinfulness is not an inherent quality to humanness.

21. Niebuhr, *Nature and Destiny of Man*, 242.

22. Ps 25:18

23. I do not imply here that all or even most disasters are God's means of punishment.

Human Nature in the Imprecatory Psalms

are nearly always interpreted as a means of punishment. With the prominent exception of Job, diseases are also seen to fulfill this purpose. (We are told in Job that his diseases were not a punishment or the result of his sin, but rather Job's disease came upon him as a result of the hidden prerogative of God.) The psalmist asks God in dealing with his enemy to "appoint an evil man to oppose him."[24] In other words, the writer assumes that God's method of punishing his enemy will be the use of another enemy. The invasion of neighboring nations was also interpreted as God's instrument of punishment. This concept of one's enemies being used by God as a means of executing justice pervades the prophets' announcement of both the Assyrian invasion and later the Babylonian exile In each of these cases, the prophets' central messages were that neighboring nations would be used to punish Israel for idolatry and unfaithfulness. But after the time of punishment ended, God would forgive and restore his people. Hosea, Amos, and Isaiah were clear that the nation of Assyria would be used by God to punish the nation of Israel for its idolatry. Likewise, Jeremiah and Ezekiel were clear that God would use the nation of Babylon to punish Judah for its idolatry. The prophecies regarding the Babylonian exile and destruction were limited to a period of time, after which restoration of the nation was promised. This was Jeremiah's message:

> "Because you have not listened to my words, I will summon all the peoples of the north and my servant Nebuchadnezzar king of Babylon," declares the LORD, "and I will bring them against this land and its inhabitants and against all the surrounding nations. I will completely destroy them and make them an object of horror and scorn, and an everlasting ruin. I will banish from them the sounds of joy and gladness, the voices of bride and bridegroom, the sound of millstones and the light of the lamp. This whole country will become a desolate wasteland, and these nations will serve the king of Babylon seventy years. But when the seventy years are fulfilled, I will punish the king of Babylon and his nation, the land of the Babylonians, for their guilt," declares the LORD, "and will make it desolate forever."[25]

Interestingly, even though Babylon was used as God's instrument of punishment, the nation was also condemned for its actions.[26] The time of

---

The book of Job confirms this. Yet, there are some catastrophes during which God reveals his work. There are numerous problems with a theology that assumes divine retribution in all cases of suffering, as outlined in Richard Rubenstein's *After Auschwitz*.

24. Ps 109:6

25. Jer 25:8–12

26. This is the same message in Isaiah 10, especially verses 5–6: "Woe to the Assyrian, the rod of my anger, in whose hand is the club of my wrath! I send him against a

punishment is limited to seventy years, indicating that God is completely in control of the events, and he is using the invasion not for the purpose of destruction, but instruction. Jeremiah's perspective on punishment is shared by the psalmist who prayed, "If I have done evil to him who is at peace with me or without cause have robbed my foe then let my enemy pursue and overtake me; let him trample my life to the ground and make me sleep in the dust."[27] Lind makes this observation about warfare between Israel and her neighbors: "As Israel became like Near Eastern states, Yahweh's war was also directed against Israel herself."[28]

F. Humans are in Need of Redemption

The need for redemption and the desperate cry for it often resound in the Psalms. We read, "Redeem me and be merciful to me"[29] and "redeem us because of your unfailing love."[30] The psalmist is assured, "God will redeem my life from the grave"[31] and sings, "Blessed is the man whose sin is not counted against him." Clearly there is within the Psalms a need for a solution to the problems we face. The psalmist asks God to intervene and redeem. From a Christian perspective, we often think of "redemption" in terms of forgiveness of sin and the gift of eternal life. The psalmists and other Old Testament authors used the term to mean rescue from misfortune, as well as an eschatological hope for the restoration of the whole community.

It is appropriate for the modern Christian reader to see in the Psalms a cry for both kinds of redemption, extending to both parties in the conflict. But, as Augsburger warns, "To be true to the psalmist we must resist any attempts to 'tidy up' the psalms, to interpret away the hatred and rage and improve their piety."[32] Admittedly, the Psalms do not explicitly state that the writer primarily wishes for his enemies to covet and be redeemed, as if violent retribution is second-best. Today we may interpret these psalms with the implicit prayer, "Lord, convert the wicked . . . but if not . . . destroy them." But is this implicit in the Psalms? Although this is a difficult question to answer, the book of Jonah provides pertinent information. Jonah's

---

godless nation, I dispatch him against a people who anger me, to seize loot and snatch plunder, and to trample them down like mud in the streets."

27. Ps 7:5
28. Lind, *Yahweh is a Warrior*, 34.
29. Ps 26:11
30. Ps 44:26
31. Ps 49:15
32. Augsburger, *Hate-Work*, 205.

Human Nature in the Imprecatory Psalms

message to the Ninevites was exclusively imprecatory. His message was unilaterally condemnatory: "Forty more days and Nineveh will be overturned." Yet Nineveh was not destroyed because the people repented. Nevertheless, we may say that the redemption of Nineveh was God's prerogative but was not implicit in Jonah's prayer. Yet Jonah said, "O LORD, is this not what I said when I was still at home? That is why I was so quick to flee to Tarshish. I knew that you are a gracious and compassionate God, slow to anger and abounding in love, a God who relents from sending calamity."[33] So Jonah was aware before he went to Nineveh that even behind his imprecatory oracle there was in implicit preference (at least from God's perspective) for Nineveh's repentance rather than her destruction.[34]

Augsburger writes, "The book of Psalms addresses this God of violence and compassion with a wideness of emotion and expression and a great range of frank requests of God's violent support as a means of both safety and salvation."[35] Interpreting the imprecatory psalms against the entire Psalter, we can see that God's primary agenda is to redeem the whole earth, and to establish justice and loving-kindness. When the psalmist appeals to God's violence, he does so with God's ultimate plan for redemption in mind.

G. Humans are in a Frustrated Quest for Holiness

The psalmist admits sufficiently that even though he has enemies, he is not perfect. Occasionally in the midst of these vindictive psalms we get a glimpse of humility. Yet this concession of imperfection is expressed with anxiety. The psalmist sings, "Who may live on your holy hill? He whose walk is blameless and who does what is righteous."[36] Because the writers are so convinced of the polarity between the good and the righteous, they are clear that they want to be on the side of the righteous. No doubt in this particular psalm the author assumed he was one such righteous person who would dwell on God's holy mountain, yet there is a clear motivation and expectation that one lives a blameless life. Regarding this frustrated quest Niebuhr says, "Anxiety about perfection and about insecurity are thus inexorably bound together in human actions and the errors which are made in the search for perfection are never due merely to the ignorance of not

---

33. Jonah 4.2
34. God's readiness to relent is based in Leviticus 26 and Deuteronomy 28, and is summarized in Jeremiah 18.
35. Augsburger, *Hate-Work*, 207.
36. Ps 15:1

knowing the limits of conditioned values. They always exhibit some tendency of the agent to hide his own limits, which he knows only too well."[37]

The psalmist knows that God commanded "be holy, because I am holy."[38] He therefore says with conviction, "I will be careful to lead a blameless life—when will you come to me? I will walk in my house with a blameless heart."[39]

H. Humans Reap What They Sow

There is in the psalms a naturally retributive aspect of human nature that teaches, "What goes around comes around." This sentiment seems to describe a mutual relationship between the way the universe was designed and the way humans were designed such that their plans for evil fall upon themselves. The psalmist says, "He who digs a hole and scoops it out falls into the pit he has made. The trouble he causes recoils on himself; his violence comes down on his own head."[40] And elsewhere he writes, "Let the wicked fall into their own nets, while I pass by in safety."[41] And again, "The nations have fallen into the pit they have dug."[42] Not only is the retribution for negative actions, but also for positive. We read, "Surely you will reward each person according to what he has done."[43] Sometimes the retribution is due to the direct actions of God. But equally the retribution is stated as a proverb or a truism; an inevitable reality about to be realized not only because of the nature of humans, but the nature of the universe's design. God has created a universe where his laws lead to safety but departing from them leads to destruction.

The proverbs are also replete with this retributive theme. But a significant difference between psalms and proverbs must be noted. Attention to the genre is crucial to understanding the theme of "reaping what one sows." The proverbs are a distinct genre; they are not prophecy, proposition, or historical narrative. So when the proverbs promise that the foolish will reap what they sow, this is not a promise that it will absolutely be true in every instance. It is not a prophecy of the fate of the fool. Instead, the proverbs are an observation of the natural design of the universe. They describe the way

37. Niebuhr, *Nature and Destiny of Man*, 185.
38. Lev 11:45
39. Ps 101:2
40. Ps 7:15, 16
41. Ps 141:10
42. Ps 9:15
43. Ps 62:12

things are supposed to work. And when the fool reaps according to his folly, it is not often in the proverbs the result of some divine intervention, but a reflection of the design inherent in natural law. The psalms, on the other hand, recognize that the world is often not as it should be. The wicked often do not reap what they sow. The fact that the psalmist is crying out to God for justice indicates that he is aware that the retributive principle is often breached. A further difference between this theme in the psalms and proverbs is that when the wicked reap what they sow, it is expected to be a result of God's action. God is asked in prayer to right a situation that did not fare as one would have expected the retributive design of the universe to yield.

I. Humans are Known and Loved by God

The ultimate exaltation of the status of humans before God is contained in Psalm 8 which says, "What is man that you are mindful of him, the son of man that you care for him? You made him a little lower than the heavenly beings and crowned him with glory and honor."[44] Niebuhr speaks of this psalm regarding the paradox of human value and human insignificance. He says, "The obvious fact is that man is a child of nature, subject to its vicissitudes, compelled by its necessities, driven by its impulses, and confined within the brevity of the years which nature permits its varied organic form, allowing them to some, but not too much latitude. The other less obvious fact is that man is a spirit who stands outside of nature, life, himself, his reason, and the world."[45]

Keeping with this celebration of human value the psalmist sings with extraordinary self-confidence, "Keep me as the apple of your eye."[46] Not only are humans valued and loved by God, but they are completely known by him. We read, "O righteous God who searches minds and hearts."[47] In addition to knowing, loving, and valuing humans, we read that God listens to them. In several instances the psalmist says, "I cried and he answered."[48]

Similarly, the central theme of Psalm 139 is God's knowledge of people, even before they were born, and subsequently no matter where they are. The psalmist sings, "O LORD, you have searched me and you know me."[49] Niebuhr says of this psalm, "The psalmist exults in this relation between

---

44. Ps 8:4–5
45. Niebuhr, *Nature and Destiny of Man*, 3.
46. Ps 17:8
47. Ps 7:9
48. Pss 18:6; 81:7
49. Ps 139:1

God and man and rightly discerns that the greatness and uniqueness of man is as necessary as the greatness of God for such a relationship." He adds, "An important characteristic of the experience of God is the sense of being seen, commanded, judged, and known from beyond ourselves."[50]

Though the phrase "image of God" does not explicitly appear in Psalm 8 or Psalm 139, both of these songs speak of the valued place of humans within God's creation, thus harkening the biblical concept of *imago dei*. Elsewhere in Scripture there may be other rationales for defining the *imago dei* in terms of metaphysical substance or function, but in these psalms the unique exalted position of humankind is their capacity for a relationship with God, and God's desire to have such a relationship. Niebuhr explains, "Man is understood primarily from the standpoint of God, rather than the uniqueness of his rational faculties or his relation to nature."[51] He further explains that this relationship is sustained despite human depravity. Niebuhr writes, "The high estimate of human stature implied in the concept of the 'image of God' stands in paradoxical juxtaposition to the low estimate of human virtue in Christian thought."[52] The contention that humans are seen as the "apple of God's eye" is not exclusive to the community of Israel, but extends to all people. Despite the hateful language often directed at enemies, these very psalms also express God's tenderness, mindfulness, and loving-kindness expressed to *all* people.

J. Humans Can Be Oppressors

An unfortunate reality of which the psalms are mindful is that humans can be ruthless oppressors. In Psalm 10 we read, "In his arrogance the wicked man hunts down the weak."[53] It continues, "He lies in wait near the villages; from ambush he murders the innocent, watching in secret for his victims he lies in wait like a lion in cover; he lies in wait to catch the helpless."[54] Though we have already looked at the total and universal depravity of humankind in the psalms, here the senseless and debased nature of that depravity is expressed. And it is significant that this depravity is stated not only in private relation to God, but in external relationships to both the neighbor and the foreigner.

50. Niebuhr, *Nature and Destiny of Man*, 128.
51. Ibid., 13.
52. Ibid., 16.
53. Ps 10:2
54. Ps 10:8–9

Human Nature in the Imprecatory Psalms

It is this element of human nature and the imprecatory psalms that is often overlooked, and which leads to the feeling that these vengeful prayers have no appropriate place in our modern worship services. In this sense, the exclusion of this portion of the Psalter is ethnocentric as it negates the suffering of a mass of humanity still present today. As Augsburger explains, "To recite them in public, communal prayer seems incongruent to the liturgical event but their appropriateness becomes more understandable when seen in the context of abuse or atrocity."[55] Perhaps the reason we see these psalms as incongruent with modern worship services is that we are privileged to be little acquainted with suffering and oppression. But to deny these psalms is to deny the daily suffering and oppression many others endure.

K. Humans are Capable of Love

Implicit in the psalms is the conviction that human beings are capable of love and of keeping their promises. There would be no condemnation of enemies if there were no capacity for these neighboring nations to do justly, love mercy, or walk humbly with God. There would be no validity behind a complaint of injustice or oppression if human beings were not capable of keeping their covenants with one another. The psalmist praises this condition of peace among humankind. He says, "How good and pleasant it is when brothers live together in unity!"[56] The eschatological expectation of the psalmist is that this peace will extend throughout the world. We read, "May the nations be glad and sing for joy, for you rule the peoples justly and guide the nations of the earth."[57] Psalm 15 explains in several details some expectations of human goodness. It says,

> LORD, who may dwell in your sanctuary?
> Who may live on your holy hill?
> He whose walk is blameless
> and who does what is righteous,
> who speaks the truth from his heart
> and has no slander on his tongue,
> who does his neighbor no wrong
> and casts no slur on his fellowman,
> who despises a vile man
> but honors those who fear the LORD,
> who keeps his oath

---

55. Augsburger, *Hate-Work*, 209.
56. Ps 133:1
57. Ps 67:4

> even when it hurts,
> who lends his money without usury
> and does not accept a bribe against the innocent.
> He who does these things
> will never be shaken.[58]

L. Humans are in Need of Humility

The polarity between the righteous and the wicked is hard to miss in the imprecatory psalms. But the justification for distinguishing between the two groups is a little more subtle. One prominent theme does emerge, however, and it is the juxtaposition of pride and humility. The psalmist sings, "Let not the nations triumph, let them know they are but men."[59] And later, "You save the humble but bring low those whose eyes are haughty."[60] Psalm 49 speaks of, "the fate of those who trust in themselves."[61] Niebuhr says of this psalm, "The catastrophes of history by which God punishes this pride, it must be observed, are the natural and inevitable consequences of men's effort to transcend their mortal and insecure existence and to establish a security to which man has no right."[62] Niebuhr agrees that the sin of pride has a prominent position if there is such a hierarchy. He says, "Biblical and Christian thought has maintained with a fair degree of consistency that pride is more basic than sensuality and that the latter is, in some way, derived from the former."[63] Why pride should be so particularly offensive to God is a fair question. Niebuhr explains, "Man is tempted by the basic insecurity of human existence to make himself doubly secure and by the insignificance of his place in the total scheme of life to prove his significance. The will-to-power is in short both a direct form and an indirect instrument of the pride which Christianity regards as sin in its quintessential form."[64] So one of the defining marks that polarizes humans is pride. The wicked are proud, while the righteous are humble. This is not to say that the righteous are perfect, but that they are aware of their sin. But the wicked deny any wrong-doing. Pride and humility speak of the status of the human heart before (or in relation to God) and are not just abstract concepts.

58. Ps 15
59. Ps 9:19
60. Ps 18:27
61. Ps 49:13
62. Niebuhr, *Nature and Destiny of Man*, 139.
63. Ibid., 186.
64. Ibid., 192.

Human Nature in the Imprecatory Psalms

In Psalm 51 David is seen practicing this attitude of humility, while at the same time recognizing his own sin. His prayer of confession (after adultery with Bathsheba and the murder of Uriah) expresses how a person can commit evil acts and yet still be considered a man after God's own heart. David affirmed, "The sacrifices of God are a broken spirit; a broken and contrite heart, O God, you will not despise."[65]

M. Humans are Blind to Their Own Faults

The psalmist asks, "Who can discern his errors? Forgive my hidden faults."[66] We have already looked at the concept of universal and total human depravity, yet the psalmist is aware that his sin can even be hidden from himself. The psalmist allows God to look and, "see if there is any offensive way in me."[67] This angst over subconscious or inadvertent sin is reminiscent of the Levitical sacrifice for unknown sin. Moses wrote, "If the whole Israelite community sins unintentionally and does what is forbidden in any of the LORD's commands, even though the community is unaware of the matter, they are guilty."[68] So there is in the ancient Jewish worldview an awareness of unintentional or hidden sin.

Niebuhr speaks of this blindness as self-deception. He says, "Our analysis of man's sin of pride and self-love has consistently assumed that an element of deceit is involved in this self-glorification. Man loves himself inordinately. Since his determinate existence does not deserve the devotion lavished upon it, it is obviously necessary to practice some deception in order to justify such excessive devotion."[69]

N. Human Life is Fleeting

Pervasive in the psalms is the expression of angst regarding the temporality of human life. The psalmist reflects, "You have made my days a mere handbreadth; the span of my years is as nothing before you. Each man's life is but a breath."[70] Interestingly, though the development of eternal life in heaven is admittedly incomplete in the Old Testament, a contrast between the fleeting

---

65. Ps 51:17
66. Ps 19:12–13
67. Ps 139:24
68. Lev 4:13
69. Niebuhr, *Nature and Destiny of Man*, 203.
70. Ps 39:5

Part Two: Theology

life of the wicked and the eternal life of the righteous is expressed. We read, "Like sheep they are destined for the grave and death will feed on them. The upright will rule over them in the morning; But God will redeem my life from the grave; he will surely take me to himself."[71]

Acknowledgement of mortality can have both healthy and unhealthy expressions. As Niebuhr notes, "In this view mortality, insecurity, and dependence are not of themselves evil but become the occasion of evil when man seeks in his pride to hide his mortality, to overcome his insecurity by his own power and to establish his independence."[72] Within the psalms there is an anxious recognition of life's brevity, yet this angst is meant to conjure humility and thus inspire dependence upon God, "For he knows how we are formed, he remembers that we are dust."[73]

O. Humans are in Severe Angst

A severe angst pervades the Psalms, as endemic to the human condition. Repeated four times is the phrase, "Why are you downcast, O my soul?"[74] The author sings, "give me relief from my distress."[75] "I am worn out from groaning; all night long I flood my bed with weeping and drench my couch with tears."[76]

Niebuhr speaks of this angst. He says, "Man, being both free and bound, both limited and limitless, is anxious. Anxiety is the inevitable concomitant of the paradox of freedom and finiteness in which man is involved. Anxiety is the internal precondition of sin. It is the inevitable spiritual state of man, standing in the paradoxical situation of freedom and finiteness."[77] Indeed, the presence of anxiety does emerge as inevitable in the psalms, as a result of sin at large: sin by one's enemies, and even one's personal sin.

The sources of anxiety listed in the Psalms are many. As stated above, there is the anxiety about life's brevity. We have also looked at the anxiety over the quest for holiness. And there is the anxiety about the world not being as it should, in that the wicked prosper but the righteous suffer. We see anxiety over the schemes of an enemy. Immediately noticeable in the imprecatory psalms is the helplessness of humankind, which also fosters

71. Ps 49:14–15
72. Niebuhr, *Nature and Destiny of Man*, 174.
73. Ps 103:14
74. Pss 42:5; 42:6; 42:11; 43:5
75. Ps 4:1
76. Ps 6:6
77. Niebuhr, *Nature and Destiny of Man*, 182.

anxiety. In a case of such helplessness the psalmist cries, "Save me from bloodthirsty men."[78] And also, "In my distress I called to the Lord, I cried to my God for help, from his temple he heard my voice, my cry came before him into his ears."[79]

A fair question to ask when reading of the anxiety over one's foes is, "Does the angst match the threat?" If David,[80] for instance, had a real enemy crouching at the door or pursuing him to take his life, then the anxiety is understandable with a straightforward interpretation. But if this is the case, then the application of these verses is more difficult for us today, for it would mean that in order for us truly to relate to the concept we must also be facing an imminent threat to our life. But if David did not face such an imminent threat at the time of writing these psalms then perhaps he suffered from paranoia. If this is the case, then we are not necessarily meant to gain from reading these psalms some example of healing catharsis. Or perhaps David was not paranoid but the foe is more symbolic. If this is the case, then the complaints of these psalms appear as gross exaggerations. The threat is disproportionate to the angst. It is best, therefore, to assume that the threat was proportionate to the anxiety, and that David was not paranoid. Given that presumption, many modern readers may be able to relate to the same type of persecution, but not the scale or type that David faced. This is of course only true for the fortunate among us, for there are millions throughout the world who do face a threat as imminent and lethal as described in the psalms. If the psalmist trusted God in far worse circumstances than mine, then I can trust God in my relatively good circumstances.

Hefner sees such anxiety in Psalm 90 which reads, "You turn men back to dust, saying, 'Return to dust, O sons of men.' For a thousand years in your sight are like a day that has just gone by, or like a watch in the night. You sweep men away in the sleep of death; they are like the new grass of the morning." Hefner says, "In the psalmist's context, this naturalness of the human is cause for puzzlement and anxiety."[81] Miller says of Psalm 8, "To be human is to experience a kind of fundamental anxiety in the face of the universe. That is something that distinguishes human beings from other sensate beings. The psalm reveals that this is not a modern phenomenon."[82]

78. Ps 59:2

79. Ps 18:6

80. I use the term David here in keeping with the text and context. I recognize that the Psalms serve a communal liturgical function, and that long after David's death the Psalms were recited by the people. In this case, even after David's enemies were gone, the nation continued to experience threats from thugs, kings, and nations.

81. Hefner, *The Human Factor*, 71.

82. Green, *What about the Soul?* 68.

Part Two: Theology

Similarly, Miller says of Psalm 144, "Like Psalm 8, there is an awareness of our insignificance, but here it is not so much finitude as the sense that we are really almost nothing, and especially that we are so briefly around that we are no more than a quick breath of air."[83]

P. Humans are Destined for Eternal Life

Whether or not the Psalms explicitly teach or even hint at eternal life is debated.[84] Moreland argues,

> Life in Sheol is often depicted as lethargic, inactive, and resembling an unconscious coma (Psalm 88.10–12; 115.17–18). However the dead in Sheol are also described as being with family and as awake and active on occasion. We have already seen that *nephesh* [soul] departs to God upon death (Psalm 49.15). The Old Testament clearly teaches the hope of the resurrection beyond the grave (Psalm 73.2).[85]

Cooper also notes the development of resurrection in the Psalms. Arguing against Wolff, he says,

> So talk of *nephesh* departing at death or being located in Sheol is not to be taken literally about something which exists in the afterlife, at least according to Wolff. But does this really account for Psalms 16.10, 139.8 and especially 49.15, the latter unquestionable about the literal end of life?[86]

In Psalm 49:15 we read, "But God will ransom my soul from the power of the underworld; for he will release me." Cooper argues that this "signifies rescue from out of the realm of death, not mere restoration to health during life. The same is true of Psalm 73.26. 'My heart and flesh may fail, but God is the strength of my heart and my portion forever.' The writer has hope beyond death which the wicked do not have." As evidence of the afterlife we can look to Psalm 16:10 which reads, "Because you will not abandon me to the grave, nor will you let your Holy One see decay." Regarding this psalm, Cooper says, "Peter applies that verse to the resurrection of Jesus

---

83. Ibid., 69.

84. Rather than try to settle the debate, I will assume that the integrity of God's revelation allows the Christian to read the Psalms with an understanding of eternal life as taught in the New Testament.

85. Moreland. *Body and Soul*, 32.

86. Cooper, *Body, Soul and Life Everlasting*, 61.

Christ. But even for the psalmist himself it is a clear expression of hope beyond the grave."[87]

The doctrine of eternal life, whether explicitly taught in the Old Testament, or whether read back into the Psalms by the New Testament believer, has a profound impact on the justice of God and the ethics of imprecatory prayer. If it is for this life alone that we have hope, then God's justice seems more questionable. How could God allow the innocent to perish, and the guilty to go unpunished? Liberation theologians are mindful of this problem, and they recognize that the justice of God is upheld only through eschatological hope. In the same way, the permissibility of imprecatory prayer is also upheld with eschatological hope.

Q. Conclusion

Difficulty in understanding, applying, or even accepting the canonicity or inspiration of the imprecatory psalms arises from misunderstandings of their theology and anthropology. The psalmist's view of human nature may seem simplistic at first glance, since the polarization between the wicked and the righteous is so pervasive. But upon closer examination the anthropology is more involved. Even the righteous are plagued with sin: enough sin that they recognize much of their offenses are hidden and unknown. Furthermore, the righteous are anxious about their sin and its effect upon their standing with God. Further informing the psalmist's view of human nature is the realization that we were given a task of caring for the world; yet we have failed at this task. In light of the recognition of one's own sin, and the obvious sin of others, as well as the failure of humans to carry out our mandate, the picture of human nature that arises from the psalms is one of people in need. There is the immediate need of rescue, the larger need of justice in the world, and the eschatological need of eternal life. Humans are in need of God's action, love, and redemption.

87. Ibid., 63.

7

A Practical Theology of the Imprecatory Psalms

A. Introduction

Our church recently staged an event for Halloween which was intended to draw children from the surrounding community. Many of the volunteers donned costumes and worked carnival type booths for the kids. Kelly, our church's pastoral intern, offered something creative and innovative. She said that instead of being a palm reader, she would be a psalm reader. She would dress in a costume like a palm reader, and set up a booth, but when kids came she would read them a psalm and pray a prayer of encouragement. She would ask the children for their birthdate, and read a psalm that corresponds in some way to that number. For instance, if a child was born on May 5, she would read Psalm 5:5. It wasn't always so tidy; for someone born on December 28, she would have to either read a verse from Psalm 12 or Psalm 28 (since Psalm 12 only has 8 verses). Since I have devoted a great deal of time studying the Psalms, I was intrigued to find out what she would do should she land upon a psalm with an element of imprecation (which I'd say she had a 30 percent chance of doing so).

I asked Kelly how she was going to handle the imprecatory psalms. She was not caught unaware and had already worked out a solution. She preselected about a hundred verses and highlighted them in her Bible. These were verses that she deemed appropriate for children, and for bestowing a blessing. Each of these verses was either in Psalms 1–31, or had verse numbers 1–31. In other words, Kelly took great care to prevent an awkward moment.

A Practical Theology of the Imprecatory Psalms

Kelly's painstaking preparation illustrates a theological dilemma. We want to practice and preach "the whole counsel of God" (Acts 20:27) yet we do not want uncomfortable verses popping up out of the Bible and creating awkward moments. If these psalms belong to the word of God, then are they ever inappropriate? Do they have less value than other parts of Scripture? Must children, or worshipers of any age, be sheltered from them?

Kelly is not alone in her decision to censor the Psalter. As shown below, the imprecatory psalms occupy a disproportionately small section of the Psalter in mainline lectionaries or books of worship.

The purpose of this chapter is to develop a practical theology of the imprecatory psalms, following Thomas Groome's general approach to practical theology in *Sharing Faith*. Groome's methodology calls for five "movements" through which a community works together to discover its current praxis[1] and arrive at a plan for future action. This chapter deals specifically with the matters of practical church life. I will confront the problems of using the imprecatory psalms in preaching as I examine why and in what way the imprecatory psalms should be addressed in sermons. I will also deal with the question of how Christians ought to pray these psalms in their own devotional life.

B. Movement 1: Naming the Present Action.

Groome's first step (or movement) in developing a practical theological approach to a problem is "Naming the Present Action." I suggest that the present action is neglect of the imprecatory psalms in modern Western culture. This is in part evidenced in the mainline Psalters.

The *United Methodist Hymnal* contains 100 psalms. The Psalter includes six "unedited" imprecatory psalms, but omits sixteen of them. And most poignant is that the Psalter includes eight other imprecatory psalms, but the verses of imprecation have been omitted, leaving a "tidied up" version.

---

1. Readers may wonder why I use the word "praxis" instead of "practice." Though the words are similar, many authors in the field of practical theology prefer praxis because it conveys a technical nuance of "feedback loop." Practice often refers to what happens after theory. Praxis, on the other hand, refers to a continuous process of practice-theory-practice.

Part Two: Theology

Figure 7.1: Imprecatory Psalms[2] in the United Methodist Hymnal

Imprecatory Psalms not included	Imprecatory psalms included	Psalms where imprecatory verses have been omitted
6, 7, 35, 54, 55, 56, 58, 59, 69, 74, 79, 83, 94, 109, 129, 140	5, 10, 28, 70, 137, 139	17, 25, 31, 40, 68, 71, 119, 143

A similar trend can be seen in the *Revised Common Lectionary*. Below is a table of imprecatory psalms that are either included, excluded, or where selected imprecatory verses have been omitted.

Figure 7.2: Imprecatory Psalms in the Revised Common Lectionary

Imprecatory psalms not included	Imprecatory psalms included	Psalms where imprecatory verses have been omitted
6, 7, 10, 28, 35, 55, 56, 58, 59, 74, 83, 94, 109, 129, 140, 141	54, 70, 71, 137, 143	5, 17, 31, 40, 68, 69, 79, 119, 139

A final example should suffice to show the trend in worship with regard to the imprecatory Psalms. Below is a similar table for the *Episcopal Sunday Lectionary*.

Figure 7.3: Episcopal Sunday Lectionary

Imprecatory psalms not included	Imprecatory psalms included	Psalms where imprecatory verses have been omitted
5, 6, 10, 28, 35, 55, 56, 58, 59, 74, 79, 83, 94, 137	17, 31, 40, 54, 70, 71, 143	7, 68, 69, 119, 139

It would be unfair to say that the *United Methodist Hymnal*, the *Revised Common Lectionary*, or the *Episcopal Sunday Lectionary* have eradicated imprecation from the Psalter. Each of these includes some imprecatory psalms, and two of the sources above include the most notorious of imprecations in Psalm 137. Yet evidently the compilers took intentional steps to remove imprecation from many of the psalms included, and the vast majority of imprecatory psalms are not included.

---

2. The selection of psalms to include in these charts is somewhat subjective. Not all of the psalms in these charts are strictly imprecatory, but they all contain a significant element of imprecation.

A Practical Theology of the Imprecatory Psalms

In order to begin developing a practical theology of the imprecatory psalms, Christians living in the developed world must come to grips with the fact that many of us neglect a major biblical practice and theme. Such neglect ought to be disturbing to Christians who take the Word of God seriously. When those of us who do not practice imprecation, but who do hold to a high view of Scripture read the imprecatory psalms, we ought to ask, "Why do we not do this anymore?" But this question is not likely to emerge until Christians have an accurate view of the present praxis. It is too soon to delve into questions such as "What is the place of these psalms in the canon? In what way are they inspired? Are they normative or merely descriptive?" According to Groome, these questions are premature to the "Way of shared praxis," and they presuppose a theory-praxis method of theology. Groome's method, however, insists on a praxis-theory-praxis structure. Before answering any theoretical questions, Christians must be able to identify the present praxis. Groome states,

> Participants in every struggle for emancipation and social transformation are empowered by naming reality as they see it and testing their expressions in a community of dialogue; from this, the critical consciousness needed for emancipatory action is likely to emerge.[3]

Groome's practical theology is thoroughly participatory. Each step is inherently dialogical (thus his title, *Shared Praxis*). This shared method includes naming the present action. Groome suggests that a congregation come to its own conclusion, rather than have the pastor shortcut the process by announcing her/his own findings. Below I offer a participatory activity where a congregation may be able to discover the disparity between an ancient biblical practice of imprecation and the present praxis.

A pastor or educator can start with these discussion questions in a group:

1. When I say "enemy," what comes to mind?
2. Do you think of yourself as having any enemies?
3. How do you usually pray for your enemies?
4. What response do sermons about enemies usually elicit?
5. What response do books about enemies usually elicit?
6. Why do you suppose there are more books about forgiving enemies than cursing them?

---

3. Groome, *Sharing Faith*, 180.

Part Two: Theology

7. What is your reaction to reading the imprecatory psalms?
8. Do you see any instances of imprecation in our culture today?
9. What would it be like, if I asked you to picture an enemy of yours, and pray one of the imprecatory psalms with that person in mind?
10. If you were to write an imprecatory prayer, what would it say? How would it be different or similar to the imprecatory prayers in Scripture?

These questions focus exclusively on the present praxis. A variety of other questions could have been included here but have intentionally been omitted. I have not listed questions such as "Why have these prayers fallen out of practice?" "Why are they included in the Bible?" "What should be the role of these prayers in our church today?" Each of these questions jumps too quickly to theory, and neglect the importance of how our culture and present church practice shape our theory. These questions require an objectivity that a congregation is not able to develop until worshipers have reflected deeply on their current practice.

C. Movement 2: Critical Reflection on Present Action.

In the second movement Groome brings Christians to reflect critically on the present praxis. He lists six different types of critical reflection: critical and social reasoning, analytical and social remembering, and creative and social imagining. "Rather than accepting uncritically what first appears to be as what 'is' and 'ought' to be, critical reflection can uncover the personal and social biases, ideologies, and so on in present praxis."[4] Such critical reflection is obviously needed, since a variety of responses to the imprecatory psalms are mutually exclusive or culturally conditioned.

For instance, Christian fundamentalist groups understand every verse in Scripture to be normative unless proven otherwise. It is assumed not only that all portions of Scripture are inspired by God, but they are also exemplary and prescriptive. They reason, for example, that since David was a man of God, and inspired by God, then we ought to do as David did. They do not, however, commit adultery as David did, because adultery is explicitly forbidden in the Bible. When a fundamentalist sees imprecatory psalms in Scripture, he most likely immediately assumes that these prayers are a model for how we too ought to pray. And while he may come to that conclusion after critical reflection, Groome points out that it is more likely an assumption preconditioned by his fundamentalist social environment. That

4. Ibid., 189.

social environment holds to a certain hermeneutic about Scripture which is pervasively propositional and prescriptive. In other words, this social group assumes that the Bible's primary function is to make statements about how we ought to live, act, and believe.

On the other hand, in other Christian contexts we will see a radically different approach. There is an assumption in theological liberal contexts that Scripture is primarily descriptive. Even if the imprecatory psalms are inspired, that revelation is personal (rather than propositional) in nature. Readers with this bias are not immediately confronted with difficulty when they become aware of the disparity between present praxis and the imprecatory prayers. They do not see the psalms as presenting them with a decision: whether to imitate these prayers or to reject them. When these psalms are seen as descriptive, liberals are comfortable with noting that they no longer describe our culture. Many liberal Christians reason that the imprecatory psalms are merely a cultural expression. If the cultural situation has radically changed, then it is appropriate for prayers to change as well.

The immediate task here is not to decide who has a better hermeneutic, but to point out that decision making regarding how to deal with the imprecatory psalms is premature at this point. One needs to become aware of his or her own ideology, bias, hermeneutic, and assumptions about Scripture before one is able to move on to questions of theory or future praxis. Christians of all backgrounds must be aware that their construction of theory is informed and determined by their hermeneutical bias (which is an element of present praxis).

For this second movement of reflecting on present action, Groome suggests a critical, creative hermeneutic. He explains. "It is hermeneutical in that people interpret and explain to themselves and one another the meaning and value of some aspect of what they are 'doing' or what is being done in their context. It is critical in that they attempt to see what to affirm, question, or refuse in present praxis, it is creative in that they envision the historical possibilities and ethic of a new praxis."[5]

Groome has practical theological reasons for insisting that Christians think critically about their current praxis. From a pragmatic standpoint, Groome observes that handing down beliefs from atop the hierarchy does not allow people to appropriate them as articles of faith. But from a theological standpoint, Groome sees the Holy Spirit engaged in the process of critical reflection. He writes, "The second and more theological reason for

---

5. Ibid., 191.

the critical reflection of movement 2 is to enhance the revelatory possibilities of present praxis."[6]

As mentioned above, Groome delineates six different (though related) types of critical reflection. In the remainder of this section on Movement 2, I offer comments on each of Groome's six categories of critical reflection.

Critical personal reasoning. Groome begins his critical exercise of current praxis by asking, "Why are things this way, and why do I see them as I do?"[7] Underlying the personal psyche of most Christians is the golden rule: "Do to others as you would have them do to you."[8] Many of us reason that to pray imprecations against someone else would violate this golden rule. Failure to forgive an enemy, and continued identification of another person as an enemy also violate the way we would wish others to treat us. The imprecations of the Psalter may strike us as barbaric, and inherently unloving. Perhaps the strongest personal reason many of us do not practice imprecatory prayer is that we have not seen it modeled. If we have not heard these prayers prayed in church, or in small groups, or by our parents, we have no personal experience with which to appropriate them when we read them in the Bible.

Critical social reasoning. In reflecting on our current social praxis, Groome suggests that we ask, "What are the social structures and the cultural ethos that shape present praxis of this theme or symbol to be as it is?"[9] Within the church culture there is an obvious answer to this question as it relates to our understanding of enemies. The cultural ethos that shapes our present praxis with enemies is the Sermon on the Mount. Jesus said, "You have heard that it was said, 'Love your neighbor and hate your enemy.' But I tell you, love your enemies and pray for those who persecute you."[10] For many people, this verse shapes and controls the way we speak about our enemies. Inwardly there may be personal dissent, variation, or varied interpretation of this aphorism, but it is the sole expression of our publicly stated ethic of enemies within the church.

The secular culture is also greatly affected by the Sermon on the Mount as a means of dealing with enemies. Americans tolerated imprecatory language directed at Osama bin Laden and Saddam Hussein, but these are perhaps the only two examples in recent history. When Hugo Chavez waxes imprecatory against the United States, he is regarded by some people as insane

---

6. Ibid., 196.
7. Ibid., 199.
8. Luke 6:31
9. Groome, *Sharing Faith*, 200.
10. Matt 5:43, 44

A Practical Theology of the Imprecatory Psalms

(presumably because sane people do not utter imprecations). When Representative Joe Wilson blurted on the House floor "You lie" during President Obama's address on health care, he was charged with an unacceptable breach of decorum. Scandal erupted when the treatment of prisoners at Abu Grebe became known, and this led to a nationwide debate on whether torture is occurring, or should ever occur. The wars in Iraq and Afghanistan illustrate that Americans go to war apologizing at the same time. As congress or the president speak about war plans, it is always within the same breath that we are assured of the plans for reconstruction. We will not bomb anything that we do not intend to rebuild. All this is to say that at least in our public discourse, we are expected to speak and treat enemies with respect and discretion. We are expected to treat our enemy with "civility." We are expected to take no pleasure in his demise, even if it is a result of our plan or effort. These are all legitimate biblical ideas, but they are not "the whole story."

Analytical personal remembering. "How have our own biographies shaped our present praxis . . . and our perspective on what is 'going on' around us?"[11] Most Americans in recent decades have escaped the threat of a wartime enemy. Though we all watched the horrific events on September 11, 2001, few of us were actually personally violated. Though violent deaths are tragic, they are by far the least common cause of death. Many Americans never experience physical harm intentionally caused by an enemy. It seems, therefore, that most Americans lack a personal memory evoked by reading about the enemies in the imprecatory psalms. Or to put that statement in the positive form, most Americans have memories of rather benign enemies. When we read the imprecatory psalms, to the extent that we try to remember our own enemies, many of us think "No one has done anything quite that bad to me. No one deserves this kind of punishment. I do not know anyone as evil as the person the psalmist is describing."

Analytical social archaeology. In addition to reflecting on personal experiences, Groome suggests that we look at cultural experiences which shape our praxis. He asks, "What are the historical influences, traditions, and customs behind society's praxis of this theme?"[12] One of the social influences pertaining to the imprecatory psalms is the real presence of enemies. Judging by the content of these psalms, the authors lived among enemies who posed a constant threat of taunts, war, death, and torture. Most Americans, on the other hand, do not live in such a threatening situation. Among those Americans who have faced enemies, few have had to endure them for a long period of time. Fortunately, most of us in the modern developed world

---

11. Groome, *Sharing Faith*, 203.
12. Ibid., 204.

live without constant threats to our safety. We need the news to remind us of enemies, and many of us are oblivious to how national enemies affect us except when occasional large scale tragedies occur. The relative safety which we enjoy is a sociological condition that shapes our understanding of who enemies are and how we should treat them. This has two opposite but related effects. As long as the enemy is unknown, he is un-hated. It is difficult to harbor the type of hatred expressed in the psalms for an unknown enemy. On the other hand, as long as the enemy is unknown it is also easier to turn a blind eye when someone is abusing him or annihilating his kind.

Creative imagination for the person. Groome states that the next step of reflecting on present praxis is to imagine the possibilities of change.[13] We go on to ask, "What if . . . ? How can we . . . ? What will be . . . ?" This is where the prospect of incorporating imprecatory prayers into Christian life can be quite disturbing or outright terrifying. What if I were to pray for the death of my enemy? What would that say about me? Perhaps I am being disobedient to Christ's teaching in the Sermon on the Mount. Perhaps it would make me unloving. I might be disregarding the biblical command to "Be kind and compassionate to one another, forgiving each other, just as in Christ God forgave you."[14] Certainly it would mean that I am violating my community's norms about how to speak of enemies. Would this make me barbaric? Will fellow Christians regard me as unchristlike? It is hard to imagine a positive outcome of altering the current praxis. It is difficult to envision good coming of praying the imprecatory psalms. But that is the purpose of this exercise.

Here are some of the possibilities where good can emerge from imprecatory prayer. As we meditate upon these psalms, what if God's reputation became our primary concern, rather than our own reputation? How would or actions change if we place God's passions above our own? How would being convinced of the absolute sovereignty of God—just as the psalmists were—affect our propensity to worry and plan for the future? What if we were able to have a fuller sense of ourselves as former enemies of God who are now reconciled? How would this new sense of gratitude change us?

Creative Imagination toward Society. Groome finishes the exercise of reflecting on present praxis with this question, "What will our society be like?" Many of the questions above deal with how we would be changed if we prayed these imprecatory prayers. But what if many Christians prayed these prayers? Or to put it more radically, What if these prayers were answered? What if we prayed for the plans of the wicked to fail, and the wicked

---

13. Ibid., 205.
14. Eph 4:32

did indeed fail? Is this not a desirable outcome? And what if the reason the wicked failed is not because we took matters into our own hands, but because the world became more under submission to the reign of God?

D. Movement 3: Making Accessible Christian Story and Vision

According to Groome, the purpose of Movement 3 is to "make the Christian Story/Vision accessible and to prompt participants to critically appropriate its meaning and truth to their lives."[15] In the first movement, we named the problem. In this case, the problem is that the Bible contains prayers that curse enemies, but in our present praxis we tend to eschew that practice. In the second movement we reflected critically upon our current praxis, and the sociological and personal reasons that explain it. In this third movement we reflect critically on the Christian tradition (including Scripture and its interpretation over time) with respect to the imprecatory psalms.

In Movement 3, Groome recommends the discovery of Christian norms. He explains, "By normativity I *do* mean that the symbolic expressions of the Christian Story/Vision are sources of trustworthy guidance for people in the present to discern together who their God is and how they are to live as a people of God."[16] In the task of making the Christian Story accessible, Groome outlines nine hermeneutical principles. In what follows, I apply these principles to the imprecatory psalms.

Guideline 1. "The 'first criterion' for the hermeneutics of Movement 3 of shared Christian praxis is the reign of God."[17] Since Groome's theology begins with praxis, and is action-focused, his first question is partially future-oriented. Rather than begin with theory, or past interpretation, he begins with an eschatological vision. We know from the teaching of Jesus that God is interested in establishing his reign on earth. God's plan for the future is to bring all things under his rule. Correct theological practice, therefore, will always conform to this purpose. Ray Anderson addresses this point. He writes,

> Theological discernment as a form of ministry requires two things. First, one must have insight into God's revealed purpose for the outcome of a situation. Second, theological discernment must be open to the direction of the Holy Spirit in order to interpret any given situation in terms of the eschatological

---

15. Groome, *Sharing Faith*, 215.
16. Ibid., 219.
17. Ibid., 227.

Part Two: Theology

preference of God rather than merely conform to historical precedence and principle.[18]

Our task, therefore, is to see how the practice of the imprecatory psalms contributes to the reign of God. Fortunately, the imprecatory psalms make this task quite easy. That "first criterion" is also the primary concern of the psalms of cursing. In the midst of all the cries of the downfall of one's enemies we find the consistent affirmation that God's glory and reign is of paramount importance. This point is well illustrated in Psalm 83:13–18,

> Make them like tumbleweed, my God,
> like chaff before the wind.
> As fire consumes the forest
> or a flame sets the mountains ablaze,
> so pursue them with your tempest
> and terrify them with your storm.
> Cover their faces with shame, LORD,
> so that they will seek your name.
> May they ever be ashamed and dismayed;
> may they perish in disgrace.
> Let them know that you, whose name is the LORD—
> that you alone are the Most High over all the earth.

Clearly the psalmist desires the downfall of his foe. He prays that they become like chaff, are set on fire, are terrified with God's storm, and covered with shame. Yet amazingly, there is a selfless tone in this prayer. The destruction of the enemy is not for the sake of the worshiper, but for God's sake. The psalmist is praying on behalf of God's reputation. Why does he want his enemies covered with shame? So that they seek God's name. Why does he pray that they are ashamed and dismayed? So that they know that the LORD alone is the Most High over all the earth. The imprecation is kingdom-oriented. It is theocentric, rather than anthropocentric.

Though the Psalter is replete with this desire for the reign of God, one additional example should suffice here. We read in Psalm 109:21–27,

> But you, Sovereign LORD,
> help me for your name's sake;
> out of the goodness of your love, deliver me.
> For I am poor and needy,
> and my heart is wounded within me.
> I fade away like an evening shadow;
> I am shaken off like a locust.

---

18. Anderson, *The Soul of Ministry*, 14.

A Practical Theology of the Imprecatory Psalms

> My knees give way from fasting;
> my body is thin and gaunt.
> I am an object of scorn to my accusers;
> when they see me, they shake their heads.
> Help me, LORD my God;
> save me according to your unfailing love.
> Let them know that it is your hand,
> that you, LORD, have done it.

Twice in this psalm the author expresses his concern for God's reputation. In verse 21 he prays for deliverance not for his own sake, but for the sake of God's name. And in verse 27 he prays that when God saves him, his enemy may know that it was by God's hand.

Some readers may suspect that Groome's reason for his future focus is somehow to nullify historical precedence. But in our ancient record of the imprecatory psalms we see the same eschatological preoccupation. These psalms share our desire that above all else the reign of God will be established. Though many Christians today seem to think Jesus had little in common with those who prayed imprecations in the Psalter, we see one strong common thread: "Yet not my will, but yours be done."[19]

Ray Anderson captures the importance of this driving concept in his own practical theology. He contends that Christians do not serve the Father on behalf of the world, but instead we serve the world on behalf of the Father. Anderson writes,

> Many have confused the serving with the sending, resulting in a ministry that makes human need the criterion and motivation for turning toward the world. The reconciliation of the world to God does not occur through solidarity with the world alone, but in the bringing of the world into the reality of God's love and grace through Christ's ministry to the Father on behalf of the world.[20]

Guideline 2. In guideline 2 Groom says, "Religious educators are to remember the interests and perspectives they bring to every text of Christian Story/Vision from their own 'life' in place and time."[21] The story that I bring to the imprecatory psalms is ambivalent. On the one hand, I (like many of my peers) have little personal experience with threatening, violent, or national enemies. Most of my experience with enemies is trivial, so I am inclined to think that an imprecatory prayer against them is unwarranted.

---

19. Luke 22:42
20. Anderson, *The Soul of Ministry*, 88.
21. Groome, *Sharing Faith*, 229.

Part Two: Theology

No one has done anything deserving the type of retribution described in the Psalter. I am mindful, however, that my experience does not speak for the world, so neither should my preconceptions about imprecation speak for the world. Nevertheless, if I were to make a ruling about imprecation based on my own experience, to pray these prayers against my *personal* enemies would amount to maniacal self-absorption if not megalomania.

On the other hand, I can identify national enemies for whom it would not be an exaggeration to say that they have taken innocent life and they deserve punishment. I must admit, I do not want my enemies to prosper. I do not want their plans to succeed. It would be naïve to think that the psalmist did not actually desire his enemies' destruction when many of us do have this experience. Since his threat was greater than mine, why should not his desire for destruction be even greater?

In the midst of this desire that my enemies fail, I am also constantly mindful of Jesus' teaching to love our enemies. Furthermore, I recognize our commission to, "go and make disciples of all nations, baptizing them in the name of the Father and of the Son and of the Holy Spirit."[22] The annihilation of my enemy and his conversion are incompatible. My desire for his conversion therefore, must precede any hope for his defeat or demise. Yet these two incongruent desires are both biblical and honest. My personal story that I bring to the imprecatory psalms, therefore, is a "but if not" attitude. I first pray for my enemies' conversion (change of heart and behavior). This would bring to God the greatest pleasure. But God knows the future. And if conversion is not forthcoming, I pray that the threat will cease. God also knows by what possible means that threat will cease. "God, convert my enemy . . . but if not . . ."

Guideline 3. Groome says that in guideline 3, "Religious educators are to remember what they bring to the texts of the tradition from the stories and visions of participants."[23] Perhaps one of the reasons that the imprecatory psalms feel incongruent with modern worship is that most modern worshipers lack life experience with the type of enemies described in the Psalter. To nullify the value of these psalms in contemporary worship, however is both parochial and myopic. That sentiment implies that "since I do not have enemies, no one else does." This attitude is ignorant of our true global situation. In reality, a great number of the world's inhabitants live under the same looming threat of violent enemies that we find in the Psalter. The stories of these participants must be included in the conversation of how to incorporate the imprecatory psalms in modern worship. Christians

---

22. Matt 28:19
23. Groome, *Sharing Faith*, 230.

living in Darfur immediately see the relevance of imprecatory prayers, as they face persecution, annihilation, and slavery at the hands of national rebels. Though Americans may vaguely feel the threat of Muslim extremists, the real threat of terrorism faces Muslims and Christians in their own neighborhoods in the Middle East. These people see the relevance of the imprecatory prayers, and give that part of the Psalter serious consideration. These stories must be included as part of a global conversation regarding the imprecations in the Psalter. We cannot let our treatment of the imprecatory psalms reflect a small view of the world that negates the immense suffering which a large part of humanity endures daily.

Furthermore, whether any of us has violent enemies is irrelevant to whether God has enemies. The enemy addressed in the imprecatory psalms is not any violent person or nation, but wicked people who oppose God's covenant. So we cannot assume from our own personal situations who are God's enemies. The sight of relative peace outside our window does not set us at ease with respect to the global situation, because violence is not the only indication of enmity. Instead, godlessness is a more apt indication, and it is ubiquitous.

Guideline 4. Groome says of guideline four, "The educator employs a 'hermeneutic of retrieval' to reclaim and make accessible the truths and values symbolically mediated in the texts of Christian Story/Vision."[24] The Psalms offer a rich trove from which we can retrieve valuable insight. One such insight is an unrelenting concern for God's reputation, as shown above in guideline 1. Another is the absolute conviction that God will take care of our problems. Expressive of all the imprecatory psalms, we find in Psalm 35:1–3,

> Contend, LORD, with those who contend with me;
> fight against those who fight against me.
> Take up shield and armor;
> arise and come to my aid.
> Brandish spear and javelin
> against those who pursue me.

The author has no intention of solving his problem on his own. He has no other resource but to rely on God for help, and he fully expects God to do so. Either his own efforts have failed, or he has learned by experience that they are futile. In either case, he prays that God will do the contending. The psalmist has a peaceful assurance in the midst of troublesome circumstances because he knows there is a God who does the fighting. The contemporary church would do well to retrieve this peaceful confidence in God's sovereignty.

Another gem available for our retrieval is a change in the things about which we are passionate. The psalmist knows what is dear to the heart of

---

24. Ibid., 231.

God. He appeals to the Lord as, "A father to the fatherless, a defender of widows."[25] And in praying against his enemies he reminds God: "You rescue the poor from those too strong for them, the poor and needy from those who rob them."[26] If we take the imprecatory psalms seriously, they are likely to realign our passions with God's, because it is in these psalms that we are constantly reminded of what God cares about. We read in Psalm 10:17–18,

> You, LORD, hear the desire of the afflicted;
> you encourage them, and you listen to their cry,
> defending the fatherless and the oppressed,
> so that mere earthly mortals
> will never again strike terror.

From these psalms are able to retrieve a fuller understanding of what God cares about, and therefore what we should care about. A hermeneutic of retrieval in the imprecatory psalms leads us to a realignment of priorities. Another gem available for retrieval is worth noting, and more subtle. In these psalms we are constantly confronted with how evil our enemies can be, but we also have occasional reminders that we too sin. These psalms offer us an opportunity to take responsibility for our own sin. In Psalm 7:4–5 we have this double-edged prayer,

> Those who hate me without reason
> outnumber the hairs of my head;
> many are my enemies without cause,
> those who seek to destroy me.
> I am forced to restore
> what I did not steal.
> You, God, know my folly;
> my guilt is not hidden from you.

In verse 4 the psalmist contends that he has been accused falsely, and prays that God takes note. But in verse 5, he admits his own folly and gives God permission to take note of that as well. The Psalter's way of dealing with enemies does not completely ignore our own guilt. And this fact is available for retrieval as we study its imprecatory prayers.

Guideline 5. "The educator," Groome states, "employs a hermeneutic of suspicion to uncover mystifications and distortions in the dominant interpretations of Christian Story/Vision and to reclaim its 'dangerous memories.'"[27]

---

25. Ps 68:5
26. Ps 35:10
27. Groome, *Sharing Faith*, 232.

A Practical Theology of the Imprecatory Psalms

This hermeneutic of suspicion is multi-faceted. On the one hand, we must be suspicious of our own preconceived interpretation of these psalms. On the other hand, we must also be critical of the various interpretations throughout history. Finally, we must also be suspicious of our new developing interpretation. The dangerous memories to which Groome refers also have a double meaning. The Christian tradition contains "dangerous memories" because they are actually harmful or wrong. But there are also "dangerous memories" which threaten our way of life much like the Civil Rights Movement threatened the way of life of many Americans in the 1960s and 1970s.

One of the distorted ways that the imprecatory psalms have been treated is to see them solely as allegorical (addressing a spiritual, but not physical enemy). This is dangerous, in that it keeps Christians in denial of the obvious fact that we all do have physical enemies. Why should the psalmist not have had physical enemies, when I have plenty? Nothing positive can be gained by denying the existence of real human enemies.

Treating the imprecatory psalms merely as an historical phenomenon is also dangerous. It implies that our current life situation is so radically different from that of the psalmist, that his ancient imprecations have no relevance to us today. Admittedly, much has changed. If this were not the case, we would not be trying to "recover" the value of these psalms. But interestingly, the key characters have not changed much. We still have enemies who pursue us, who defy God's reign. There are still some who are sympathetic to God's reign among us. And God is still listening to our prayers. The historical interpretation also leads to unhealthy denial: it assumes that ancient people harbored hatred for their enemies, but modern people do not.

The notion that the imprecations belong to a pre-New Testament dispensation is also a dangerous memory. It assumes that the ancient Jewish people were fundamentally less forgiving than modern Christians. Interpreters in this tradition see something inferior in this part of the canon, which means they inevitably see something inferior in the people who produced it.

The prophetic theory (which says the imprecatory psalms do not ask for destruction, but predict it) and quotation hypothesis (which says the imprecations were uttered by the enemy) are both dangerously naïve. These theories give the impression that godly people would never harbor anger or resentment, and would never wish the downfall of their enemies. Even if we were to determine that it is wrong to pray for the destruction of one's foe, it is still naïve to think that godly people never desire this. It would be more realistic to say that these prayers mean what they say, and the authors (whether right or wrong) were at least honest.

Guideline 6. Regarding the sixth guideline Groome writes, "The educator employs a 'hermeneutic of creative commitment' to construct more adequate understandings of Christian Story/Vision and to envision more faithful ways of living it with personal and social transformation."[28]

This is where the redemptive hope of the imprecatory psalms is reconciled with a holistic view of the Bible's ethic for one's enemies. We must dispel the notion that the command to love one's enemies originated with Jesus. As long as Christians are under this impression, they will fail to see the Old Testament's consistent "hermeneutic of creative commitment." It is true that Jesus said, "You have heard that it was said, 'Love your neighbor and hate your enemy.' But I tell you, love your enemies and pray for those who persecute you."[29] But where did Jesus' disciples hear it said that the godly man loves his neighbors and hates his enemies? This command is not in the Old Testament, but is a misguided teaching originating with the Pharisees. It is this mistaken teaching that Jesus corrects.

Love for one's enemies is not altogether absent in the Old Testament. Moses wrote, "Do not seek revenge or bear a grudge against anyone among your people, but love your neighbor as yourself. I am the LORD."[30] The story of Jonah also illustrates this point. Jonah clearly did not want his enemies to repent, and he was disappointed when it became evident that they were not going to be destroyed. Nevertheless, his attitude is portrayed as deplorable, and God rebukes him. The readers know that Jonah should have rejoiced in his enemies' conversion, for this is what God did.

Though a vehement imprecatory prayer, Psalm 35:11–14, contains a moving example of love for one's enemy. The psalmist prays for the downfall of his enemy, but he appeals to God concerning the way he has acted toward his foe in the past. He writes,

> Ruthless witnesses come forward;
> they question me on things I know nothing about.
> They repay me evil for good
> and leave me like one bereaved.
> Yet when they were ill, I put on sackcloth
> and humbled myself with fasting.
> When my prayers returned to me unanswered,
> I went about mourning
> as though for my friend or brother.
> I bowed my head in grief
> as though weeping for my mother.

---

28. Ibid., 234.
29. Matt 5:43–44
30. Lev 19:18

A Practical Theology of the Imprecatory Psalms

In verse 13 the author states that he prayed for his enemies when they were sick. And when they were still not healed, he prayed even more ardently. He covered himself with sackcloth and ashes, mourning for his enemies as he would for his family or friends. This Old Testament saint prayed both for and against his enemy. He acted out a "creative commitment" toward his foe. Looking again at Psalm 83:15–18, we read that while the worshiper desires shame to come upon his accusers, he also has a redemptive hope for his enemy. Admittedly, this is a quiet voice in the Psalter, but it is not altogether absent. We cannot neglect that the psalmist had a desire for his enemy to turn to God. He writes,

> so pursue them with your tempest
> and terrify them with your storm.
> Cover their faces with shame, LORD,
> so that they will seek your name.
> May they ever be ashamed and dismayed;
> may they perish in disgrace.
> Let them know that you, whose name is the LORD—
> that you alone are the Most High over all the earth.

In verse 16 the author writes that the purpose of God shaming his enemies is that they will seek God's name. And in verse 18 he prays that his enemy may come to know that the Lord is the Most High over all the earth. It would be unfair to say that concern for the well-being of an enemy began in the New Testament, or that the sense of "creative commitment" emerged after the teaching of Jesus. Though the explicit creative commitment expressed here is sparse in the Psalter, perhaps it is implicit whenever God's people pray against/for their enemies.

Guideline 7. Groome states in guideline 7, "Every authentic explanation of a particular text is in *continuity* with and appropriate to the constitutive truths and values of the whole Story/Vision."[31] I have demonstrated in the section above that there is some continuity between the Old Testament and New Testament regarding love for enemies. This point should be made, because if it were not true then the integrity of God's revelation is in question. We would be left with an impression that over time God changed his mind about how we should deal with our enemies. Furthermore, we ought to reconsider our interpretation if it has no precedence in the Old Testament. In general, we should be leery of theology that is totally new with no historical precedence. Ray Anderson speaks of the importance of this continuity and precedence. He writes, "For every instance of theological innovation there must be a theological antecedent. This will lay to rest,

---

31. Groome, *Sharing Faith*, 236.

Part Two: Theology

hopefully, the charge that theological innovation invents new options out of 'whole cloth.'"[32] Finally, if we do not point out that the Old Testament has continuity with the message to love enemies, we imply there was something inferior about the Jewish people who received it; as if they had a "lower" morality and Christianity presents a more highly evolved message.[33]

Continuity also exists among the testaments with regard to imprecations. A few are worth noting here.

Figure 7.4: Imprecation in the New Testament

Curse	Speaker
Matthew 11:21-24 Woe to you, Chorazin! Woe to you, Bethsaida! For if the miracles that were performed in you had been performed in Tyre and Sidon, they would have repented long ago in sackcloth and ashes. But I tell you, it will be more bearable for Tyre and Sidon on the day of judgment than for you. And you, Capernaum, will you be lifted to the heavens? No, you will go down to Hades. For if the miracles that were performed in you had been performed in Sodom, it would have remained to this day. But I tell you that it will be more bearable for Sodom on the day of judgment than for you.	Jesus
Matthew 12:34 You brood of vipers, how can you who are evil say anything good? For the mouth speaks what the heart is full of.	Jesus
Matthew 13:32 He replied, "Go tell that fox, 'I will keep on driving out demons and healing people today and tomorrow, and on the third day I will reach my goal.'"	Jesus
Matthew 23:33-35 You snakes! You brood of vipers! How will you escape being condemned to hell? Therefore I am sending you prophets and sages and teachers. Some of them you will kill and crucify; others you will flog in your synagogues and pursue from town to town. And so upon you will come all the righteous blood that has been shed on earth, from the blood of righteous Abel to the blood of Zechariah son of Berekiah, whom you murdered between the temple and the altar.	Jesus
Matthew 26:24 But woe to that man who betrays the Son of Man! It would be better for him if he had not been born.	Jesus

32. Anderson, *Soul of Ministry*, 21.

33. This would also imply that there is something inferior about the God who revealed the Old Testament to the God who revealed the New Testament.

Acts 23:3 God will strike you, you whitewashed wall! You sit there to judge me according to the law, yet you yourself violate the law by commanding that I be struck!	Paul
1 Corinthians 16:22 If anyone does not love the Lord, let that person be cursed!	Paul
Galatians 1:8–9 But even if we or an angel from heaven should preach a gospel other than the one we preached to you, let them be under God's curse! As we have already said, so now I say again: If anybody is preaching to you a gospel other than what you accepted, let them be under God's curse!	Paul
Galatians 5:12 As for those agitators, I wish they would go the whole way and emasculate themselves!	Paul
2 Timothy 4:14 Alexander the metalworker did me a great deal of harm. The Lord will repay him for what he has done.	Paul
James 5:1–6 Now listen, you rich people, weep and wail because of the misery that is coming on you. Your wealth has rotted, and moths have eaten your clothes. Your gold and silver are corroded. Their corrosion will testify against you and eat your flesh like fire. You have hoarded wealth in the last days. Look! The wages you failed to pay the workers who mowed your fields are crying out against you. The cries of the harvesters have reached the ears of the Lord Almighty. You have lived on earth in luxury and self-indulgence. You have fattened yourselves in the day of slaughter. You have condemned and murdered the innocent one, who was not opposing you.	James
Jude 11–13 Woe to them! They have taken the way of Cain; they have rushed for profit into Balaam's error; they have been destroyed in Korah's rebellion. These people are blemishes at your love feasts, eating with you without the slightest qualm—shepherds who feed only themselves. They are clouds without rain, blown along by the wind; autumn trees, without fruit and uprooted—twice dead. They are wild waves of the sea, foaming up their shame; wandering stars, for whom blackest darkness has been reserved forever.	Jude
Revelation 6:10 How long, Sovereign Lord, holy and true, until you judge the inhabitants of the earth and avenge our blood?	John

These New Testament verses illustrate that there is continuity between testaments with regard to loving and cursing enemies. Both testaments contain these teachings alongside each other. Our modern practice of the

Part Two: Theology

imprecatory psalms must preserve this tension. It must not be simplistic: either dismissing the practice of imprecations, or adopting it "as is" in the Psalter. A faithful biblical practice will preserve both of these traditions.

Guideline 8. Groome states that, "An authentic explanation of a particular text of Christian tradition promotes personal and social consequence creative of God's reign."[34] Several personal and social consequences emerge from a serious study and practice of the imprecatory psalms.

First, and most obviously, we will pray for the plans of the wicked to be foiled.

Second, we will take responsibility for our own sin. On many occasions the psalmist confidently declares that he has enemies without cause. He writes that they hate him "without reason,"[35] and that "there is no offense of mine."[36] He says they "attack me without cause,"[37] and "they question me on things I know nothing about."[38] Surely we all have enemies on occasion that we do not deserve. But sometimes we do bear some of the blame. Even the psalmist admits, "if I have done evil, or without cause have robbed my foe, let my enemies pursue and overtake me."[39] He writes, "My guilt is not hidden, you know my folly."[40] He offers, "Search me and know me, see if there is any offensive way in me."[41] The author of these psalms was willing to admit that he too has done evil. He gave God permission to convict him of sin, and appeared ready to repent. When we begin to pray against our enemies we must couple our complaint with humility.

Third, we will become more passionate for God's purposes. The language of the imprecatory psalms is unquestionably passionate. It evokes a level of anger which most of us spend our whole life suppressing. Perhaps the real lesson for modern readers from these psalms is that we can, and should, increase our level of passion for right and against wrong. The psalmist calls his enemies, "lions,"[42] "those who hate me,"[43] "bloodthirsty men,"[44] men

---

34. Groome, *Sharing Faith*, 236.
35. Ps 35:19
36. Ps 59:3
37. Ps 35:7
38. Ps 35:11
39. Ps 7:4, 5
40. Ps 69:5
41. Ps 139:23, 24
42. Ps 35:17
43. Ps 35:19
44. Ps 59:2

A Practical Theology of the Imprecatory Psalms

who "snarl like dogs,"[45] lions who "rip me to pieces,"[46] "wicked and deceitful men"[47] who "form an alliance against God."[48] The passion for God's glory in the psalms is well known, and cannot be overstated. The passion against evil in the psalms is less-known, but likewise cannot be overstated. I believe passion is not simply an unchangeable part of one's personality. Perhaps it is not accurate to say that passion can be taught, but I believe that it can be "caught" by those who meditate on these psalms and begin to adopt their language.

All the psalms, including imprecatory ones, increase our level of passion for the things that God cares about: they make us zealous for what is right, and for his holy name. Ray Anderson writes, "If there are two sides to humanity, Jesus will be found on the wrong side."[49] In other words, the heart of God is for the weak, oppressed, poor, alien, etc. These psalms give us passion against God's enemies and develop hatred for sin and injustice. When our passions match God's passions our worship becomes even more powerful and authentic.

Guideline 9. The last hermeneutical guideline Groome provides is the central place of the church. He explains, "Community is a guideline in that authentic explanation of a particular expression of Christian Story/vision is informed by the understanding of 'the church' and is adequate to the praxis of this community of participants."[50]

It is of paramount importance for Christians to keep in mind that the psalms do not address personal enemies.[51] The authors of the psalms were not saturated with the individualism that permeates modern life in the Western world. The enemies of the psalmist were *national* enemies, God's enemies, and enemies of God's people (whether Israel, or the righteous). The only reason the psalmist could pray with confidence was that he knew he was praying on behalf of God's people and in accordance with God's agenda.

---

45. Ps 59:14
46. Ps 7:2
47. Ps 109:2
48. Ps 83:5
49. Anderson, *Soul of Ministry*, 176.
50. Groome, *Sharing Faith*, 237.
51. By "personal" here, I do not mean that the psalmist did not personally know his enemy, or that he did not personally suffer, or that he did not have a specific person in mind. What I mean is that the offense was not merely a personal one, and that the desire for revenge was not a personal vendetta. Instead, the psalmist believes that his enemy is also an enemy of God. The enemy has assaulted God's covenant people, and has broken God's commands.

Part Two: Theology

E. Movement 4. Dialectical Hermeneutics to Appropriate Story/Vision to Participants' Stories and Visions

For Groome, the fourth movement is appropriation. He writes, "The most complete dynamic activity that undergirds [appropriation] is that of participants' placing in dialectical encounter their present praxis and the version of Christian Story/Vision made accessible in movement 3."[52] Beyond the communication of new elements of Christian praxis, educators must ensure that there are means for appropriating these elements. "Rather than an exercise in negativity," Groome writes, "it is a creative and hope-filled activity."[53]

One of the ways Christian educators offer to appropriate a new praxis is through sermons. In chapter 9 I offer a series of five sermons that tie together the central theme of the imprecatory Psalms (concern for God's reputation) with Groome's first criterion (the reign of God).

Undoubtedly, preaching alone is unlikely to effect widespread lasting change. That notion alone defeats Groome's concept articulated in *Shared Praxis*. I learned early in my ministry to stop being amazed when sin continued in our church despite the fact that "I preached on that last week." Of the wide spectrum of types of change that can be achieved within a community, the change expected in this preaching series is on the most basic level. It is hoped that this sermon series will give the congregation an awareness of the incongruity between our present culture and an ancient biblical practice. In other words, the level of change which is aimed for in teaching about imprecatory psalms to a congregation is that of *understanding*. Further levels of change may come with time and experience, such as lasting and profound appropriation of the practice of imprecatory prayer.

F. Movement 5. Decision/Response for Lived Christian Faith

The last movement for appropriating new elements of praxis includes decisions such as "who to become" and "what to do." From the previous movements, several specific questions regarding the imprecatory psalms emerge. Because this is a process of "shared praxis," the following questions can help the church community in a dialogue of response to these imprecatory psalms.

1. Will I make God's reputation my primary concern?
2. Will I trust in God's sovereignty and let him take care of my problems?

52. Groome, *Sharing Faith*, 251.
53. Ibid., 253.

A Practical Theology of the Imprecatory Psalms

3. Will I ask God to develop in me a concern for the things he cares about?
4. Can I identify my enemies? Will I make my complaint to God?
5. Can I pray an imprecatory prayer? Will I pray for the plans of the wicked to fail?
6. In the past, when has cursing been closest to our lips without us realizing it (i.e., actions that curse others?)
7. Have I identified my own sin against my enemies? Whom have we already damned or cursed by our actions (rather than our words)?
8. Have I asked God for a passion for righteousness and justice?

The final test of appropriation is what kind of imprecatory prayer a Christian is able to formulate. I suggest that a prayer will include the following characteristics, which are the contents of the next chapter:

1. Concern for God's reputation
2. Confidence in God's sovereignty
3. Care for the poor, oppressed, fatherless, foreigner, etc.
4. Clear identification of one's enemies
5. A prayer for the plans of that enemy to fail, and also for his/her conversion
6. Admission of one's own guilt; and
7. Passion for God's reign to flourish

I close with a suggested imprecatory prayer as an example. This prayer is prompted by the persecution of Christians, especially in Darfur.

> *Lord, we pray for the strength of persecuted Christians in Sudan. May they maintain their strength, their confession of you as their one and only Lord, and may they be assured of your presence and blessing. God we ask that our country would be able and willing to intervene and prevent this persecution, if it is your will. We confess our lack of concern for Christians living in persecuted regions, especially in Darfur. Our nation has failed to come to their aid, and we have failed to press the issue with our national leaders. We confess that we have been self-absorbed, fearful, and have often turned a blind eye. Lord, we pray that you would remove the dictators from power who carry out persecution on your saints. We pray specifically against the plans of the Janjaweed, and against Ali Kushayb, the leader of this persecution. We pray that their hearts would turn to you and they would repent. But if not, we pray that*

you would frustrate their plans, remove them from power, and let them fall in the pit they have dug for others. We trust that you are in control and that you deeply care for these persecuted believers. May your deliverance be great, and may your protection of these Christians serve to honor your name. We pray that people would look to you as the solution to this tragic problem. Amen.

Part Three

Application

8

The Therapeutic Value of the Imprecatory Psalms

A. Introduction

> From the lips of children and infants
> you have ordained praise
> because of your enemies,
> o silence the foe and the avenger.[1]

OF THIS PSALM, ERICH Zenger asks, "Who is not repelled by the warlike and aggressive mood?"[2] His point is well-noted; that many Christians find the cursing in the psalms problematic. Zenger assumes that all modern people, especially Christians, will be repelled by the thought of war and aggression. But there is an obvious answer to his question. Who is not repelled by the tone of these Psalms? The person who is suffering intensely at the hands of a vicious and unjust enemy. There is a long list of people not repelled by these curses, especially people in the midst of war. The list of those not repelled by this language also includes the victims of rape, religious persecution, genocide, ethnic cleansing, and the slave trade. In fact, the list includes all victims of unjust treatment from violent enemies.

For these victims of violence, the imprecatory psalms are a relevant friend. That is because their enemies are,

> [n]ot occasional transgressors who harmed out of ignorance
> or whose abuses were casual rather than premeditated and

1. Ps 8:2
2. Zenger, *A God of Vengeance?* 10.

Part Three: Application

repetitive but on those who chronically and violently flaunted their position contrary to Gods' righteousness. They held positions of governing, legislative, or judicial authority, and they exploited their power for evil and their own ends.[3]

Though the empathetic task of understanding both the ancient psalmist and the contemporary victim may be a difficult one, it is necessary to do just that in order to discern the preaching and therapeutic value of the imprecatory psalms. I suggest that the task is achievable by considering the following seven steps. To gain maximum value from the imprecatory psalms, first we concern ourselves with God's reputation (rather than our own). Second, let God take care of our problems (rather than do it ourselves). Third, we appeal to the things God cares about. Fourth, we make our complaint clear. Fifth, we pray for the plans of the wicked to be foiled. Sixth, we take responsibility for our own sin. Seventh, we overcome apathy and adopt the passionate language of the psalms. After examining these seven steps I will outline the biblical and therapeutic cases for and against anger.

B. Concern Yourself with God's Reputation

The thought of praying for someone to fail is understandably repulsive to Christian teaching. While it might seem that praying a curse on someone should raise concern, the psalmist clearly does not share our aversion to asking God to repay God's enemies with calamity. This is most likely because we have a propensity not to concern ourselves with God's reputation, but with our own. We assume that it is arrogant to say, "God's enemies are my enemies." But this is only arrogant if it is not true. As a matter of fact, God and the ancient psalmists actually had the same enemies. The psalmist, unlike us, made it his passion to see the name of God lifted up. In each of the imprecatory psalms the author's primary concern is the fame and greatness of God's name. The psalmist prays that his enemies will be laid low in the hope that, "the Lord will be exalted by all who delight in my vindication,"[4] and "men will say, 'surely there is a God who judges the earth,'"[5] and, "then it will be known to the end of the earth that God rules over Jacob."[6] He prays that his enemy's plans will fail so that, "heaven and earth will praise him,"[7]

3. Day, "The Imprecatory Psalms and Christian Ethics," 170.
4. Ps 35:27
5. Ps 58:11
6. Ps 59:13
7. Ps 69:36

and, "men will seek your name,"[8] and "they will know that you are the most high."[9] He asks God, "Deal well with me for your name's sake."[10] It is important to consider that perhaps our aversion to these psalms indicates that God's reputation is not our highest concern. The more we are concerned with God's reputation, the more we can relate to the passion in these psalms.

There are legitimate causes for anger. But often anger is aroused when we feel personally violated, rather than when we are sympathetic to an act that offends God. We become angry when we do not get our way, or even when selfish desires are not served. In this sense, as Lester comments, "Anger can serve as an idol detector."[11] Are we angry because God's reputation has been defamed, or because our own interests are threatened? If we can confidently affirm that our cause for anger is an assault on the image of God, or that image imparted to humans, then our anger may be righteous. But if our anger is rooted in our own will or concerns, it has taken a more subjective form.

Augsburger speaks of the need for righteous anger to be rooted in something objective. He asserts that there needs to be a transforming moment when hatred goes from being subjective to objective.[12] When this occurs, the plaintiff makes the first step from "retributive hatred" to "principled hatred." This moment of transformation is not complete, however. We will see below that healthy hatred must also include an empathic view of the enemy in order to become "just hatred."

Healthy anger, however, is not self-directed or self-motivated. It is focused on the nature and glory of God. Basset explains, "Holy anger is above all not that appropriation of God's anger that makes us believe in a divine mission against others."[13] In other words, we cannot assume the right to utter an imprecatory prayer simply because we are offended or angry. The health of such a complaint depends upon the object and objectivity of the anger. The enemy is not the object of the imprecatory psalms, and thus these psalms are not a "divine mission *against* others." Instead, the focus of the psalms is God's reputation, consequently, these psalms become a divine mission *for* God's glory.

---

8. Ps 83:16
9. Ps 83:18
10. Ps 109:21
11. Lester, *The Angry Christian*, 201.
12. Augsburger, *Hate-Work*, 46.
13. Basset, *Holy Anger*, 210.

Part Three: Application

C. Let God Take Care of Your Problem

Writing of Psalm 137, Basset points out, "The Bible gives a realistic illustration of our desire to reproduce the violence that we have first endured ourselves, a desire that is exacerbated by the lack of empathy around us."[14] The desire for vengeance seems imbedded in human nature. Yet that desire quickly proves self-destructive; an observation equally embedded in human nature. The church has long held that personal vengeance must concede to divine vengeance, both as a matter of health and justice. In her discussion of the history of forgiveness, Basset, while specifically commenting on the preaching of Lactantius (230–325), aptly summarizes this position: "It is indisputable that fundamentally, he is preaching the expectation of divine vengeance as a substitute for personal vengeance."[15]

Not only is the yielding of vengeance to God an historical Christian practice, we are told three times in the Bible that, "to avenge is mine, I will repay."[16] Shriver points out that the first murder in the Bible (where Cain killed Abel) goes un-avenged. Instead of retribution, whether human or divine, God shows mercy and allows Cain to live with a seal of protection. Shriver concludes, "God alone is the custodian of vengeance."[17] The authors of the imprecatory psalms appear to have had reverence for this certainty. The psalmist was keenly aware that it would be presumptuous to take vengeance himself. We have all sinned, so none of us is able to cast a stone without implicating ourselves. Besides, if our passion is for God's reputation, then he is more concerned with his enemies than we are! Knowing that God must have taken more offense than the psalmist, he says, "contend with me, fight with me"[18] and "arise to my defense,"[19] and "I take refuge in you."[20] The call of the psalmist to God indicates that he will not take matters into his own hands. Basset explains that this appeal to God is central to a healthy expression of anger. She writes, "Holy anger is that, without ever denying itself, still does not claim control over vengeance. Because it does not decide to leave the human community, it delegates to [God] the right to impose [God's] law."[21]

---

14. Ibid., 29.
15. Ibid., 31.
16. Deut 32:35; Rom 12:19; Heb 10:30
17. Shriver, *An Ethic for Enemies*, 23.
18. Ps 35:1
19. Ps 35:2
20. Ps 7:1
21. Basset, *Holy Anger*, 215.

The Therapeutic Value of the Imprecatory Psalms

One obvious reason for appealing to God, of course, is that we are incapable of defeating our enemies. There may be a sense of this in the psalms. Because the lamenter is unable and unauthorized to solve the problem, he appeals to a powerful God. From a therapeutic perspective, there is great value in appealing one's case to God. Failure to transfer the responsibility of righting the universe, in fact, leads to despair, depression, anxiety, as well as pathological self-importance. Sittser observed this decline into anxiety and depression occurring in himself after a tragic auto accident claimed the lives of his mother, wife, and daughter. He writes,

> It eventually occurred to me that this preoccupation was poisoning me. It signaled that I wanted more than justice. I wanted revenge. I was beginning to harbor hatred in my heart. The thought of forgiveness seemed abhorrent to me. I realized at that moment that I had to forgive. If not, I would be consumed by my own unforgiveness.[22]

Sittser was incensed that the accused drunk driver who killed his family was acquitted since the defense claimed that the man's wife was driving. Both the man and his wife were ejected from the vehicle, making it impossible to prove beyond all doubt who was driving. One can imagine the imprecatory prayers and curses Sittser may have uttered after the acquittal. Yet these fantasies of revenge proved self-destructive. Sittser observed, "The real problem however is not revenge itself but the unforgiving heart behind revenge. Unforgiveness is like fire that smolders in the belly, like smoke that smothers the soul. It is destructive because it is insidious."[23]

The counselor's task in dealing with anger and desire for revenge is to help the client transfer the role of vengeance to God. LaMothe calls this process "containment" and argues that since people inevitably and understandably feel anger, it must give rise to verbal expression. The counselor must be willing to receive angry complaints, and demonstrate that the relationship will survive these expressions. In his discussion of a case study he concludes, "The counselor's intervention was one of the first steps toward the client's learning to recognize and contain his hate and hostility in more constructive ways."[24] This particular client had become reluctant to express anger, because "When he had acted this way in other situations, the other person would become frightened and eventually leave him."[25] We know

---

22. Sittser, *A Grace Disguised*, 119.

23. Ibid., 120.

24. LaMothe, "A Psychodynamic Perspective and Theological Implications of Hate and Hostility in Pastoral Counseling," 39.

25. Ibid., 39.

from Scripture, however, that God will not leave us.[26] With God there is security in expressing our anger. In this sense, like the therapist, God contains our anger when we make a verbal complaint and appeal to him.

This is what the imprecatory psalms do. The psalmist said, "Rouse yourself to punish the nations"[27] and "let them know that it was your hand, that you have done this."[28] The author knew that even though evil men were coming against him, they were more God's enemies than his. He prayed, "Let them know that it was your hand, that you, O Lord, have done it."[29] A repeated characteristic of these psalms of anger is that they transfer personal vengeance to divine vengeance. They shift the responsibility for executing justice from the individual to God.

But when we appeal our case to God, we may not always be satisfied with the results. The fact that the Psalms are replete with complaints against enemies indicates that the Israelites had become accustomed to living in a world that was not right (though they knew God would make things right in the end). Depending on the sovereignty of God, therefore, does not mean assuming that the all-powerful God will make things go our way. Instead, this dependence affirms the "but if not" attitude of Shadrach, Meshach, and Abednego, who knew that God could rescue them from the furnace, but even if he did not, they would still praise him.[30] Basset iterates the importance of this type of dependence on the sovereignty of God. She says, "Leaving the mystery of God's anger to God is perhaps the first step on the way of holy anger."[31]

In the Wisdom literature we have a prime example of the importance of trusting God's sovereignty through suffering. Job's friends were certain that they had the answers for why he suffered, but Job remained uncertain. He appealed his case to God, but also maintained a strong conviction of the goodness of God. Basset writes, "Job would reply, I do not know everything about the unjust evil I endured, but I know that you know, and that is enough for me, for I trust you."[32] The sovereignty of God brought Job great

---

26. Heb 13:5
27. Ps 59:5
28. Ps 109:27
29. Ps 109:27
30. According to Daniel 3:17–18, these men were convinced that God not only *could*, but *would* deliver them. But whether the deliverance would come through the furnace or through some other future judgment was uncertain.
31. Basset, *Holy Anger*, 211.
32. Ibid., 92.

peace. Basset continues, "This, no doubt, is why Job is willing to renounce being judge in God's stead."[33]

D. Appeal to the Things God Cares About

Like any plaintiff, the psalmist wants the judge (God) on his side. But God does not waver in allegiance, so it is easier to get on God's side. There is no easier way to enlist someone's help than to start doing what he is doing. The psalmist knew which things are dear to God's heart. He knew that God has a special place in his heart for the poor, the needy, and the oppressed. He knew which things make God angry. The Lord hates dishonest scales. He hates false testimony and false accusations. He does not tolerate the oppression of the foreigner, the homeless, the orphan, or the poor. So when the psalmist wanted to get God's ear, those are the things he mentioned. He knew he was on God's side when he prayed, "you rescue the poor, needy, and the robbed,"[34] and he reminded God that his enemies were, "false witnesses"[35] who make, "false accusations."[36] He knew God would come to his aid so he said, "arise in your anger."[37]

"Why does God get angry?" Andrew Lester asks.

> Anger is an arousal pattern that occurs in response to a perceived threat to the self and is characterized by the desires to attack or defend. Can God be threatened? God has values and desire to which God is committed. These values are expressed in covenants that direct God's desires, plans and hopes for the creation and explain God's actions.[38]

In other words, the things that make God angry are not isolated acts or violations of a list of prohibitions, but assaults on God's character or his image. According to Genesis 1, human beings are the image of God, so God's anger is also aroused when people are threatened. Lester continues, "Because of God's investment in us and our well-being, behaviors that demean, dehumanize, oppress, and cause physical and emotional suffering threaten God.

---

33. Ibid., 93.
34. Ps 35:10
35. Ps 35:11
36. Ps 35:20
37. Ps 7:6
38. Lester, *The Angry Christian*, 158.

Part Three: Application

In response to this threat, God feels and expresses anger. This capacity for anger is activated only as an expression of God's love."[39]

Augsburger provides a more specific answer to what angers God. "Just hatred is profound antipathy to all that works evil, that creates systems that impoverish, devalue or destroy persons."[40] The psalmist knew God would pay attention to his complaint about these evil works. We read, "They plot against those you cherish"[41] and "they hound to death the poor, needy, and broken hearted."[42] When we read the psalms of cursing, we will find more relevance, and more confidence to echo their prayers, if we become more familiar with the issues about which God is passionate. Augsburger explains, "The moral person who fears God, according to the Psalmist, hates those who threaten the safety and security of loved ones and of the community that provides their safety and security, but even more fundamental, evildoers are hated because they threaten the divinely established order of justice and seek its destruction."[43] The psalmist has achieved a degree of objectivity in his complaint. In this sense, "The psalms of outrage are not only cries against specific evil acts, they are also a passionate struggle against oppression, structural violence, and systematic evil."[44]

Augsburger asserts that unlike other ancient religions, the biblical account rejects,

> The immortal lie of sacred violence, a revelation of the true nature of evil. And this is the Christian gospel. Its roots lie in the Hebrew Scripture, where for the first time in human history God is seen as identified with the victims of violence. All other religious myths are written from the point of view of the victimizers (see Isaiah 19.19–25, Isaiah 53, Micah 4.2–4, Psalm 5.)[45]

In other words, a natural consequence of God's character and nature is sympathy toward humans. That sympathy translates to anger when God finds his people, made in his image, victims of injustice. God takes this injustice personally, because an assault on those made in his image is an assault against him. Armed with this theological truth, Basset expresses holy anger in this

---

39. Ibid., 167.
40. Augsburger, *Hate-Work*, 15.
41. Ps 83:3
42. Ps 109:16
43. Augsburger, *Hate-Work*, 208.
44. Ibid., 209.
45. Augsburger, *Helping People Forgive*, 133.

The Therapeutic Value of the Imprecatory Psalms

way: "I admit, I accept that I have enemies. . . . I turn myself over to him who takes and will always take my side in the injustices that I experience."[46]

If God is thus offended by injustice, then we have the right also to be offended (when our anger is rooted in something objective, like a true understanding of God's character), and indeed we ought to be angry. Lester observes, "Walter Brueggemann reminds us that within the covenant we have with God 'it is a faithful human action to rage and protest.'"[47] By raging against the things that enrage God, we are faithful to him. Making the move from saying that we have the right to be angry to saying that we ought to be angry implies that anger has a positive aspect or nature. Numerous authors have made a case for anger's redemptive qualities. Citing Beverly Wildung Harrison, Lester writes, "We must never lose touch with the fact that all serious human moral activity, especially action for social change, takes its bearing from the rising power of human anger."[48] Righteous anger can be a catalyst for social change, and thus it would be wrong to suppress it. As Basset argues, "Holy anger, if we are to believe the entire Bible, is anything but a renunciation of the truth by means of flight, retreat, or breaking of the relationship."[49] Instead, holy anger engages with injustice and motivates us to right what is wrong in the world (without losing our dependence upon God).

E. Make Your Complaint Clear

The psalmist had a clear and specific complaint. He saw an injustice and named it to God. He says his enemies "seek my life,"[50] or "plot my ruin."[51] He complains that his enemies have "hid their net for me"[52] or "dug a pit."[53] He laments that they are "ruthless witnesses"[54] and they have "gathered in glee when I stumbled."[55] Passion can only truly grow when it is focused. And we can see that as the writer of these songs was able to call out a specific complaint; he was able to build his passion for righteousness, his frustration

---

46. Basset, *Holy Anger*, 197.
47. Lester, *The Angry Christian*, 200.
48. Ibid., 207. Harrison's assertion is a bit of an overstatement. Mother Theresa engaged in serious moral action, but there is no indication that she was angry.
49. Basset, *Holy Anger*, 208.
50. Ps 35:4
51. Ps 35:4
52. Ps 35:7
53. Ps 35:7
54. Ps 35:11
55. Ps 35:15

with evil, and his confidence in God. Similarly today, a generalized prayer for world peace is typically uttered with less passion than an informed prayer for the end of the tyranny of the Janjaweed in Darfur, Sudan. The imprecatory psalms will continue to be irrelevant to us if every time we hear the word "enemy" we are unable to conjure an image. To capture the depth of these psalms we must be willing to consider, meditate, and even use the word "enemy."

Why do many of us have such a strong aversion to making our complaint clear to God? We may doubt the legitimacy of the threat: is there a real enemy? We may lack confidence that our complaint resonates with God's passions. Yet, as LaMothe points out, we may fear that God does not allow or approve of such expression of anger. LaMothe's approach in pastoral counseling is to provide a safe place to vent anger. He reasons that once the client realizes that his relationship with the counselor survives an outburst of anger, (as most relationships do survive these outbursts), then so will his relationship with God survive such an outburst.[56]

Basset argues that not only does God allow, and even encourage our complaints, but they have an eschatological necessity. She writes, "The first obstacle to the divine relational life within us and among us— to the reign of God, as the texts put it—is this censorship of complaint which, while leaving the wound intact, prevents healing and poisons all relationships."[57] Job's friends attempted to censor his complaints to God, yet in the end he was commended for his response. We read, "In all this, Job did not sin by charging God with wrongdoing."[58] But the friends who censored Job's complaints were rebuked.

The verbal expression of complaint in these psalms has the therapeutic effect of *remembering*. And remembering is central to survivors of injustice as they seek to forgive and reconcile. Augsburger speaks of the importance of verbally remembering acts of injustice:

> History, indeed the social memory of humankind, would be rewritten by the victors, since history becomes the property of the winning generals. How can we foil this plot? *By remembering*. "Isn't there a danger that memory may perpetuate hatred?" Elie Wiesel asks. "No, there is no such danger. Memory and hatred are incompatible; memory may serve as a powerful remedy against hatred."[59]

---

56. LaMothe, "A Psychodynamic Perspective and Theological Implications of Hate and Hostility in Pastoral Counseling," 27.

57. Basset, *Holy Anger*, 26.

58. Job 1:22

59. Augsburger, *Hate-Work*, 83.

The Therapeutic Value of the Imprecatory Psalms

In Wiesenthal's book *The Sunflower*, the holocaust survivor asks the question, "You are a prisoner in a concentration camp. A dying Nazi soldier asks for your forgiveness. What would you do?" Wiesenthal includes responses from fifty-three scholars, politicians, or celebrities. Though the answers are varied, they share at least one unanimous sentiment: The atrocities ought to be remembered. The story must be told and re-told, and the only hope for reconciliation, forgiveness, or health is in "making the complaint clear."

As stated earlier, the verbal expression of complaint can have a containment effect. By finding words to describe the sense of our powerlessness, we prevent ourselves from acting out in violent, retributive, or self-destructive ways. In addition, finding in God a safe place to express anger has the effect of a healing catharsis. Basset laments, "We have not been taught to face God as we are, and to tell him what we think of him when pain and anger are ravaging us."[60] But telling God the truth of what we feel and how we see the world about us is central to our own health and therapy. Rather than eschew our complaint, God allows it, and in fact offers help. Basset explains, "We could say that the biblical God offers himself as a punching bag (to use a colloquial term) to the fury of human beings, in religious terms as a scapegoat, and in prophetic terms as the suffering servant."[61] Basset confidently concludes,

> It does not seem to me that the biblical texts ask us to cut off or stifle anything. On the contrary, to act on our anger as belonging to us, to name it in the encounter with an OTHER, thus to welcome it with benevolence instead of banishing it, allow us to let it clarify itself, to cleanse itself of all that was not yet holy anger, in a fair fight for the life of the other and our own life.[62]

In other words, when we make our complaint clear to God, we benefit. We grow and mature. And we increase the chances of turning our experience of injustice into redemptive action.

The Therapeutic Limits of Catharsis

The notion that the imprecatory psalms are best interpreted as a catharsis was examined in chapter 2. This model has many strengths, and was judged compatible with other interpretive frameworks of the psalms. In this section on the therapeutic value of the imprecatory psalms, the idea of catharsis must be revisited. Even if the psalms were best understood as a catharsis, the

---

60. Basset, *Holy Anger*, 81.
61. Ibid., 85.
62. Ibid., 222.

therapeutic value of this model should be critically understood. Catharsis means cleansing. It often implies a release of pent-up emotion. With regard to the imprecatory psalms, the idea is that the psalmist had a reservoir of rage which he released when he prayed. The theory is that his anger reached a boiling point, and he exploded. But the explosion left him in a better place: with less anger, and more at peace.

The assertion that catharsis is necessary or beneficial has been debated for thousands of years. Plato condemned the tragic playwrights for inciting crowds. He said the tragedies provoked a catharsis, thus undermining the authority of the state over the mobs. In recent time the notion that catharsis has value, or that it is a beneficial metaphor for emotion, has also been controversial. Freud's own position on catharsis evolved over time. Initially, he believed that a vigorous expression of prolonged subconscious anger was necessary. But he later argued that the catharsis did not produce any long-term change. Berkiwitz argued that catharsis was not helpful because it only encouraged people to become more angry, which was what they were trying to avoid. On the other hand, Lowen argued that catharsis was helpful and he sparked a host of therapeutic strategies that are still used today.[63]

If there is any value to the idea that the psalms provide a catharsis, it is that imprecatory prayer helps us overcome denial of our anger. But this concept is insufficient to explain prayer in general, and the presence of imprecatory prayer in the Psalter. The word catharsis implies a hydraulic model.[64] One problem with the hydraulic model is it raises the question: "Once released, where do the emotions go?" The idea of catharsis does not deal with future action. It does not confront the client with a decision of how to act, once the emotion has been expressed. On the contrary, it assumes that no further action is necessary, since the emotion has not "disappeared." It is no wonder that Freud eventually abandoned the concept as "not effective." There is some promise to the idea of catharsis that it helps the client escape denial. But that promise is unfulfilled by the hydraulic metaphor, since it does not require the client to consider future action.

Another problem with the hydraulic model is that it perpetuates the false dichotomy between inner and outer space. It assumes that emotions can be held "inside." Actions, on the other hand, are supposedly "outside." This dichotomy assumes that emotions come from some external force and overwhelm a person. But in reality, emotions are never truly "inside." And they do not "come upon us." Our actions create emotions. Our emotions

63. I am indebted to *Catharsis in Psychotherapy* by Michael Nichols and Melvin Zax for this brief listing of authors who critique catharsis.

64. Hydraulic refers to emotions as water, and our dealing with them in ways that water is stored, released, pressurized, and exhausted.

influence actions. And our emotions have public consequences because they lead to actions. In this sense, the hydraulic model neglects the complex relationship between thoughts, actions, and emotions.

Furthermore, the hydraulic model neglects the idea that catharsis can actually be addictive, rather than relieving. Consider sexual behavior, for example. The catharsis model assumes that a person has building sexual drive and pressure, and this pressure needs to be relieved on a regular basis (or else!). The traditional assumption within the catharsis metaphor is that a sexual act relieves the pressure, and the client is then in a healthier state for some period of time. But in actuality, the sexual act creates more need, drive, and addiction to the behavior. Perhaps a momentary relief has been gained, but the overall sexual drive of the person has been heightened. What if we consider anger as catharsis instead? Berkiwitz argued that the "angry act" actually heightened the angry drive, so the catharsis makes things worse. Specifically in regard to the imprecatory psalms, Brueggemann agrees that venomous imagination heightens feelings. He says, "Such imagination . . . is no doubt cathartic. We need not flinch from the therapeutic value of the psalms. But it is more than cathartic, more than simply giving expression to what we have felt and known all along. In genuine rage, words do not simply follow feelings. They lead them."[65]

Modern critics of the concept of catharsis argue that the hydraulic model advocates "letting go" without telling the client what to "take hold of." This is the key difference between catharsis, and the "just hatred," for instance, in Augsburger's *Hate-Work*. Beyond catharsis, the therapeutic goal of anger is to help the client decide what to embrace.

Finally, the hydraulic model assumes that one can have an "ejaculation" of anger. But in reality, we are more likely to experience an "exercise" of anger. When we exercise, we become more proficient, and we have more endurance. We need to decide whether we really want to help clients become more proficient at expressing anger, and to have more endurance in doing so. If this is the case, then that exercise will take a more redemptive shape than mere ventilation.

F. Pray for the Plans of the Wicked to be Foiled

In these imprecatory psalms the author repeatedly prays for the plans of his enemies to fail. He asks God to "put to shame,"[66] his enemies so that

---

65. Brueggemann, *Praying the Psalms*, 66.
66. Ps 35:4

they will "be turned back in dismay."[67] He prays that they will "fall in their own pit,"[68] and be "entrapped by their own net."[69] He asks God to "pursue them like tempests,"[70] and "cover their faces with shame."[71] If we consider the power of prayer and the promises in Scripture that God hears us, then it would be irresponsible for us not to pray that the plans of the wicked will fail. Surely we are to pray according to God's will. In the case of God's enemies, we can be confident of what is God's will. For instance, if we pray for the end of human trafficking in Thailand, we do not need to pray a benign prayer like, "may your will be done among the slaves." Instead we can pray for the downfall of the slave traders, the industry, the regimes that support them, and that God will remove the demand for such an industry. We can do this, because we know it is God's will. A prayer for the downfall of God's enemies will surely increase our passion in prayer, and unleash our passion and involvement in the issue as well.

A recurrent theme in literature that deals with enemies is an admonition of empathy. In praying for (or against) our enemies, we must remember the humanity of those who perpetrate injustice. Regarding this empathy for enemies Shriver states: "This combination of moral judgment upon the wrong with empathy of wrongdoers may be rare in human affairs, but in fact acknowledgement of fellow humanity lays a groundwork for both construction and the repair of any human community."[72] Apparently, developing this empathy is so successful at achieving reconciliation, that in efforts to sustain war, empathy must be averted. Shriver writes, "Indeed it may be impossible for any wartime population to maintain an image of consciousness of the enemy as fully human, for under that image, the enemy is psychologically more difficult to kill."[73] Citing Capra, Lester comments on World War II training videos: "The war department insisted that the script must not 'portray the Japanese as ordinary humans victimized by their leaders.'"[74] It is tempting to dehumanize the enemy, which makes hatred seem more justified. But as seen earlier in the discussion about making complaints that resonate with God's concerns, we do not need to justify our anger by demonizing our enemy; it is enough that the enemy's actions threaten God's values.

67. Ps 35:4
68. Ps 35:8
69. Ps 35:8
70. Ps 83:15
71. Ps 83:16
72. Shriver, *An Ethic for Enemies*, 8.
73. Ibid., 122.
74. Ibid., 123.

The Therapeutic Value of the Imprecatory Psalms

Wiesenthal echoes this tendency to dehumanize the perpetrator in *The Sunflower*. Arthur, a fellow prisoner in a concentration camp states, "I am prepared to believe that God created a Jew out of this tear-soaked clod of earth, but do you expect me to believe he also made our camp commandant?"[75] Denial of empathy, however, does not have a positive healing effect. It not only perpetuates feelings of anger and resentment, but these feelings are misplaced. Rather than directed at actions which offend God, these complaints focus upon one's personal offense. Basset explains, "We will never be able to differentiate ourselves from those who behave monstrously if we imagine that making them out to be monsters protects us from them."[76] The monster motif does not promote a healthy view of injustice. The truth is that no enemy is wholly evil, nor is any plaintiff wholly good. Shriver notes this tendency to place people in "good" and "bad" categories. Speaking of the public outcry against reconciliatory speeches marking the fiftieth anniversary of the bombing of Pearl Harbor, he writes, "In the standoff, leaders were playing to roles of descendants of victims, not descendants of people who inflicted mixtures of good and evil on each other."[77]

Not only is it tempting to dehumanize the enemy, we also have the tendency to impute the sins of one generation to another, resulting in patterns of prejudice and racism. Speaking of the World War II conflict between Americans and Japanese, Shriver observes, "Each side experienced its conflict with the ancestors of the other."[78] When such a projection of anger at the sins of a nation's ancestors is present, it is clear that hatred has taken a subjective focus, rather than an objective focus on injustices that resonate with God's passions. Prayers against the plans of the wicked must therefore be distinguished from prayers against the wicked. Shriver offers this definition of an ethic for enemies: "the willingness to count oneself as neighbor and fellow citizen with enemies in spite of the latter's continuing resistance to reciprocating."[79] Though the New Testament unequivocally calls us to love our enemies, the Old Testament's model of praying against injustice remains equally valid. Shriver illustrates the difference, "It is an old Christian principle that one must seek always to 'hate the sin and love the sinner,' which might have suggested to more theologians that we are called to forgive sinners more fundamentally than their sins."[80] Augsburger

---

75. Wiesenthal, *The Sunflower*, 6.
76. Basset, *Holy Anger*, 224.
77. Shriver, *An Ethic for Enemies*, 137.
78. Ibid., 127.
79. Ibid., 173.
80. Ibid., 231.

explains how the evil actions of the enemy can be distinguished from the enemy himself: "A theology of justice, reconciliation, and peacemaking does not deny hate; instead, it metamorphoses hate into empathy, compassion, and commitment to seek what is truly good for friend and enemy alike."[81] Augsburger challenges that the goal of just hatred is to focus on the causes of injustice which rouse God's anger, rather than the person who commits these acts. He writes, "as long as the other [person] is hated as an enemy, there is little likelihood of our experiencing truly just hate."[82]

G. Take Responsibility for Your Part

On many occasions the psalmist confidently declares that he has enemies without cause. He writes that they hate him "without reason,"[83] and that "there is no offense of mine."[84] He says they "attack me without cause,"[85] and "they question me on things I know nothing about."[86] Surely we all have enemies on occasion that we do not deserve. But sometimes we do bear some of the blame. Even the psalmist admits, "if I have done evil, or without cause have robbed my foe, let my enemies pursue and overtake me."[87] He writes, "my guilt is not hidden, you know my folly."[88] He offers, "search me and know me, see if there is any offensive way in me."[89] The author of these psalms was willing to admit that he too has done evil. He gave God permission to convict him of sin, and appeared ready to repent. When we begin to pray against our enemies we must couple our complaint with humility.

Key to appropriating the preaching or therapeutic value of the imprecatory psalms is an attitude of humility. Scholars who deal with reconciliation continuously give admonitions to self-reflection. Gerald Sittser, whose family was killed in a drunk-driving accident, came to develop this attitude himself. He asserts that people who forgive, "Define the role they play in

81. Augsburger, *Hate-Work*, 194.
82. Ibid., 164.
83. Ps 35:19
84. Ps 59:3
85. Ps 35:7
86. Ps 35:11
87. Ps 7:4, 5
88. Ps 69:5
89. Ps 139:23, 24. I recognize that many scholars deem Psalm 139 to be a "psalm of innocence." In this case, perhaps the original context of this verse was not exactly a call to self-examination. But there is no reason why this psalm cannot be used in this way today.

The Therapeutic Value of the Imprecatory Psalms

life modestly."[90] Through tragedy he came to see his limited place within the universe, and more importantly, the limited power he has to change it. Adopting such humility in the face of enemies is rare and difficult. We may have a legitimate case against our enemies, but we should not allow the glaring guilt of others to completely blind us from any guilt in ourselves.

Many people exhaust every effort to avoid personal responsibility. This is odd, since even when we are passive we often bear some measure of blame. Shriver points out that during the Japanese internment camps of World War II, even "Ordinary [American] voters had their large part in concocting the injustice."[91] The same could certainly be said of those who committed no overt crime against Jews during the holocaust, yet committed sins of omission. When Simon Wiesenthal visited the mother of a Nazi soldier, he remarked,

> Without doubt she must often have shown sympathy for the oppressed, but the happiness of her own family was of paramount importance to her. There were millions of such families anxious only for peace and quiet in their own little nests. These were the mounting blocks by which the criminals climbed to power and kept it.[92]

From the most egregious to the most passive, there seems to be room for finding fault with all. Yet despite ample availability for guilt, many resist the occasion for self-examination. Mark Goulden believed he saw that sentiment in Germany where, "we are reminded always that it was the Nazis—a mythical horde of subhumans from outer space—who did it all. Apparently no living German was ever a Nazi, very few even saw one, and whatever atrocities did happen, took place during what is known as the 'Hitler era.'"[93] Though he unfairly exaggerates the German response, Goulden touches on a fair point that we are often hesitant to bear our own guilt when there is always a "guiltier person" close at hand. Americans are equally capable of resisting self-reflection. As Shriver points out, in common political speech we hear, "the China war 'was caused,' Pearl Harbor 'was bombed,' and the atomic bomb 'was dropped.'"[94] The passive verbs used by politicians and reporters to describe such horrific events may indicate a reluctance on their part to assign blame for the atrocities to any actual person.

---

90. Sittser, *A Grace Disguised*, 128.
91. Shriver, *An Ethic for Enemies*, 159.
92. Wiesenthal, *The Sunflower*, 91.
93. Ibid., 157.
94. Shriver, *An Ethic for Enemies*, 153.

Part Three: Application

Some heroes, on the other hand, welcome the opportunity for self-reflection. As examples, Shriver offers Dietrich Bonhoeffer and Willy Brandt who because of their overt actions to curb Nazi efforts, could have been exempt from collective guilt, but they were even more overwhelmed by it.[95] These men understood that adoption of personal responsibility, provided that it is legitimate and sincere, is liberating rather than frightening.

Augsburger notes that the empathy required for praying for/against enemies leads to such humility. He says, "It is compassion that allows us to realize the cohumanity of another and the humility to affirm our cofallibiltiy with her."[96] Not only is our enemy human like we are; we are imperfect like our enemy. Augsburger contends that lack of humility can have violent consequences: "When reason has claimed an absolute authority, we can act with confidence that our mandate is infallible, claim knowledge of truth that is incontrovertible, and make decisions that need no review or reparation."[97] We may have legitimate reason to accuse our enemy of injustice, but coupled with pride that sense of injustice could arm us with the justification for evil as well.

Speaking of Psalm 139, Augsburger states, "Here is the crucial sign of moral hate becoming just hate, the psalmist recognizes the precariousness, the arrogance, the fatal ambiguity of hate."[98] The ambiguity of this psalm is striking. We read in verses 21–22,

> Do I not hate those who hate you, LORD,
> and abhor those who are in rebellion against you?
> I have nothing but hatred for them;
> I count them my enemies.

But immediately following we see a more self-reflective tone in verses 23–24,

> Search me, O God, and know my heart;
> test me and know my anxious thoughts.
> See if there is any offensive way in me,
> and lead me in the way everlasting.[99]

In this imprecatory psalm, the author gives God permission to test his own heart and thoughts, and to point out an offensive way. The psalm admittedly contains an element of anger and hatred, yet the author retains

---

95. Ibid., 114.
96. Augsburger, *Hate-Work*, 50.
97. Ibid., 118.
98. Ibid., 212.
99. Admittedly, this psalm may be a psalm of innocence. With this caveat, readers can understand the original context, and still open their hearts to God for examination.

enough humility to acknowledge not only his own imperfection, but his dependence upon God to know where that sin lay.

H. Get Passionate

The language of the imprecatory psalms is unquestionably passionate. It evokes a level of anger which most of us spend our whole life suppressing. Perhaps the real lesson for modern readers of these psalms is that we can, and should, increase our level of passion for right and against wrong. The psalmist calls his enemies, "lions,"[100] "those who hate me,"[101] "bloodthirsty men,"[102] men who "snarl like dogs,"[103] lions who "rip me to pieces,"[104] "wicked and deceitful men"[105] who "form an alliance against God."[106] The passion for God's glory in the psalms is well known, and cannot be overstated. The passion against evil in the psalms is less-known, but likewise cannot be overstated. Passion is not simply an unchangeable part of one's personality. Perhaps it is not accurate to say that passion can be taught, but it can be "caught" by those who meditate on these psalms and begin to adopt their language.

The Case against Anger

The anger and hatred of the imprecatory psalms is evident from the language above. Yet to many modern readers it seems inappropriate, or at least, irrelevant in a church setting. Below I offer several reasons for why the imprecatory psalms have become distasteful or irrelevant.

#1. Lack of Life Experience

Writing of the imprecatory psalms, Zenger asks, "Who is not repelled by the warlike and aggressive mood?"[107] To the modern reader in a peaceful country, it may seem that everyone would be repelled, but this assumption reveals a narrow view of both the world and history. Much of the world lives

100. Ps 35:17
101. Ps 35:19
102. Ps 59:2
103. Ps 59:14
104. Ps 7:2
105. Ps 109:2
106. Ps 83:5
107. Zenger, *A God of Vengeance?* 10.

in a state of constant war, and the "warlike mood" does not exist merely in an ancient text, but also in daily life. It is probably a fair assumption that most modern pastors in peaceful countries find the imprecatory psalms irrelevant and distasteful. But aversion to these psalms is due less to their violent and angry nature, and more to the reader's lack of life experience. On the other hand, we are surrounded by survivors of traumatic experiences with whom the passion of these psalms resonates strongly. Wiesenthal notes that immediately after World War II altruists who were uninvolved in the conflict began speaking about reconciliation and forgiveness. He claims, "Most of these altruists had probably never even had their ears boxed, but nevertheless found compassion for the murderers of innocent millions."[108] Wiesenthal's book is evidence of his willingness to consider forgiveness, yet his criticism illustrates that lack of personal experience of suffering makes it easier to dismiss the angry tone of the psalms.

A fundamental reason why people are hesitant to appropriate the language of the imprecatory psalms is that they cannot identify an enemy. As stated above, this could be due to a lack of life experience. Ignorance and apathy could also be factors. Some may have such a myopic worldview that they are unaware of global instances of injustice and violence, occasions for true anger. Others may know of these oppressive situations, but because they are distant geographically they become distant emotionally, and rather than angry find themselves apathetic. There could also be a sense of triviality that leads some to eschew the imprecatory psalms. They might be thinking to themselves, "Sure, I may be angry at the person who cut me off on the freeway, but I wouldn't call him my enemy."

Regarding this lack of an identified enemy, Zenger says "The book of Psalms as a whole appears rather unattractive because of its obsession with enemies and violence."[109] On the other hand, these psalms are attractive to those surrounded by enemies. They are a place of comfort, solace, and dependence on God who is more passionate, more able, and more benevolent than any other place of appeal in times of crisis. Those who identify their enemies will not be repulsed by these psalms, but drawn to them.

#2. Anger is Assumed to be Ungodly

The Bible does indeed say, "Get rid of all bitterness, rage and anger, brawling and slander, along with every form of malice."[110] For that reason, it is

---

108. Wiesenthal, *The Sunflower*, 85.
109. Zenger, *A God of Vengeance?* 9.
110. Eph 4:31

understandable that some Christians believe anger is always wrong. There is some justification, therefore, to assume that, "Good Christians would not express anger and the best would not even feel it."[111] Jesus commanded that we love our enemies, and many assume that it is impossible to love someone and be angry at the same time. But in addition to the biblical prohibition of anger, theologians have drawn more fundamental conclusions about the nature of God and of humans. "Early Christian theologians," Lester explains, "influenced by stoicism, also needed to show a more transcendent God than the pagan one, and thus gave emotions an inferior status to God and to man."[112] These early Christian theologians assumed that God is incapable of any emotions. This is assumed to be the logical consequence of the doctrine of the immutability of God. Calvin, Aquinas, and Cassian, for instance, assumed that if God does not change, then his emotions do not change.[113] He is therefore, emotionless. Whenever the Bible does attribute emotions to God, according to Augustine, these anthropomorphisms are merely accommodations of language. Lester quotes Augustine: "Ordinary language ascribes to God and angels also these mental emotions, because, though they have none of our weaknesses, their acts resemble the actions to which these emotions move us."[114]

This theology of emotions developed to the point that, "by the Middle Ages anger had become one of the seven deadly sins."[115] If God is emotionless, then perfect people will also achieve that state. Our susceptibility to emotions is a sign of our immaturity and weakness in controlling them. Citing James and Evelyn Whitehead, Lester demonstrates that Christian theologians have often assumed that, "Emotions are unruly instincts erupting with blind and selfish force."[116] If it is the case, then emotions are automatically suspect and must be tamed.

Most modern Christian theologians, however, solve the apparent contradiction between the immutability of God and the appearance of God's emotions by saying that immutability refers to his incommunicable attributes. In other words, God will always be omniscient, omnipresent, omnipotent, etc. But as a personal being (not the mere force of logic), God also has thoughts, will, and emotions. These personal characteristics by nature are mutable. Yet even if one accepts that God has emotions and the human

---

111. Lester, *The Angry Christian*, 1.
112. Ibid., 40.
113. Ibid.,.42.
114. Ibid., 42.
115. Ibid., 2.
116. Ibid., 35.

presence of emotions is value-neutral, it still seems that the Bible prohibits anger. There are several lists in the New Testament, as well as in the proverbs, of negative character traits, and these lists often include anger. Lester observes, "When one reads enough of these [biblical prohibition] lists, it would be easy to conclude that anger is always negative. The casual reader could easily assume that all anger is destructive, like the conflictual, alienating ways of behaving with which it is listed. However, that very context is our clue that the anger being described here is anger that is expressed in ways that are life-destroying to both individuals and community."[117]

The central thrust of Lester's *Angry Christian* is that the Bible does not support the "anger-is-sin" concept.[118] He justifies this claim with two verses. In Ephesians Paul at least allows if not commands anger: "In your anger do not sin."[119] And in James we read, "My dear brothers, take note of this: Everyone should be quick to listen, slow to speak and slow to become angry."[120] From this verse it is apparent that the Bible does not expect Christians to eradicate anger, but to control it. In practicing allowable anger, Christians must learn self-control.

Sometimes, admittedly, there is not a legitimate cause for anger. When God made a vine grow to shade Jonah, it withered the next day and Jonah became very angry. Yet God told Jonah he had no right to become angry. Jacob was angry with Rachel when she complained of her barren womb, yet he did not sin in his anger. Moses became angry on repeated occasions, and his anger seems justified, for God did not rebuke him, but instead promised to rectify the problem and remain faithful to his people.

#3. Jesus Told Us to Love Our Enemies

Undeniably a persistent reason that Christians eschew anger is that Jesus said, "But I tell you who hear me: Love your enemies, do good to those who hate you, bless those who curse you, pray for those who mistreat you."[121] Many Christians have therefore drawn the conclusion that it is impossible to love and be angry at the same time. Dennis Prager, in his contribution in *The Sunflower*, states, "I believe that . . . the Christian doctrine of forgiveness has blunted Christian anger at those who oppress them; the notion that one should pray for one's enemies has been taken to mean 'pray

---

117. Ibid., 146.
118. Ibid., 148.
119. Eph 4:26
120. Jas 1:19
121. Luke 6:26–27

for them, do not fight them."[122] Prager explains that though he sees many similarities between the Christian and Jewish worldviews, one of the fundamental differences is the traditional approach toward forgiveness. Prager argues explicitly (though the sentiment is ubiquitous in *The Sunflower*) that Christians feel compelled to extend forgiveness in all situations, whereas the Jewish tradition is more comfortable refusing forgiveness in some instances, especially murder. I suggest, however, that these two worlds are not far apart, but what gives the appearance of disunity is actually a confusion of terms. When a Nazi soldier on his deathbed asks for forgiveness, we must consider what he is exactly requesting. If it is absolution of guilt, then neither the Christian nor the Jew would be in a position to offer it. This would be God's prerogative alone. If it is acquittal from legal guilt that he desires, I suppose neither the Jew nor the Christian would offer this either. I suspect that what the Nazi soldier is really asking is "Will you remain in a relationship with me, rather than dismiss me?" He is, in a fundamental sense, asking, "Will you love me?" It is possible to seek legal justice for such a person, and to hate and remember his actions, while at the same time offering communion (friendship). Since the word forgiveness is so difficult to define or understand in this context, it would have been clearer if the Nazi soldier had asked instead, "Will you offer me an opportunity for reconciliation?" Had this been his question, I suspect that the Jewish and Christian responses would have aligned more closely.

The Case for Anger
#1. There is Reason to be Angry

As stated earlier, one reason modern readers are reluctant to identify or appropriate these psalms with their own prayers is the lack of an identified enemy. Those of us fortunate enough to live in peaceful lands have little experience with any significant enemy. This leads to an assumption that there really is no legitimate cause for anger. There is not enough evil going on to be as upset as the psalmist was. Today we are so insulated, in fact, that some commentators believe the threat to the psalmist could not have been as great as he perceived. He must have exaggerated. He must have an allegorical enemy. We know, though, from the experience of people living in other lands and other times that real enemies have often defied imagination and description. Wiesenthal describes one of the Nazis who was in charge of a concentration camp as a "man, who daily slaughtered prisoners from

---

122. Wiesenthal, *The Sunflower*, 229.

sheer lust for killing."[123] He describes a Jewish ghetto where a boy named Eli lived. The Nazis wanted to relocate all the children to a concentration camp, but they had difficulty convincing the children to come out of hiding. So the soldiers promised to set up a kindergarten in the ghetto, as a pretense for earning the trust of the families. The kindergarten was set up with suitable rooms, rations of food, and an international inspection before opening. According to Wiesenthal, "The Jews, as eternal and incorrigible optimists, took this as a sign of a more humane attitude."[124] But when the children arrived, three SS trucks took the children to the gas chambers. Stories like this are quickly forgotten, and as a result we see that "eternal and incorrigible optimists" abound. People who are only slightly removed from these situations quickly forget the existence of a real enemy.

Lester explains that there is ample opportunity for legitimate anger. He writes, "Becoming angry means that a particular life situation has been perceived through one of our core narratives as a threat so the self's values, beliefs, and meanings."[125] We can have assurance that anger is justified because there is reason to be angry. When we see that our core values are threatened or that the world is drastically opposite to how we believe it ought to be we can, should, and indeed will become angry.

#2. Some Expressions of Anger are Healthy

The expression of anger has a therapeutic effect. It gives voice to the powerless. If anger is truly felt, then denial only has a negative effect. Lester writes, "Chronically angry people pay a physical price for their unresolved anger."[126] This does not mean that we should avoid being angry. On the contrary, it means that we should avoid being chronically angry. But denial is no way to avoid chronic anger. Denial actually perpetuates it, whereas giving expression to anger is the only way to overcome it. Anger can have the effect of a healthy catharsis. Lester writes, "When anger at God is claimed and spoken, according to Brueggemann, it seems to evoke a change in the palmist. Toward the end of the psalm, she or he is then able once again to claim the promises of God."[127] This catharsis is healthy for the plaintiff, and making God the object of the catharsis is healthy for one's relationship with God. The relationship can survive such an outburst of real and legitimate

---

123. Ibid., 12.
124. Ibid., 46.
125. Lester, *The Angry Christian*, 98.
126. Ibid., 5.
127. Ibid., 141.

pain. Denial of anger, therefore, prevents healing. "The church continues to suffer," Lester believes, "from the historical theological constructs that led early church theologians to move from the Hebraic traditions open acceptance of anger to a negative, suppressive stance."[128]

In addition to anger at times being healthy and allowable, Lester makes a case for anger as inherent to human nature. "Our capacity for anger," says Lester, "is one of God's good gifts, intentionally rooted in creation and serving important purposes in life."[129]

#3. Emotions are Value Neutral

Historically philosophers have placed a higher value on reason than on emotion. Perhaps one reason for the inferior status of emotions is that they are fickle and apparently unreasonable in nature. This suspicion has granted to (primarily negative) emotions a demon-like quality, as if they possess us. But, "Emotions are neither impulses that come over us unwillingly (they do not 'have a life of their own'), nor inherently wrong or worth less than reason."[130]

Lester also makes a case for the value neutrality of emotions based on our physical makeup. He states that we are physiologically wired to have emotions and even anger. In this sense, emotions are rational, for many of our emotional responses are logical in light of the interactions between our bodies and our environment.[131] In other words, "The temptation to divide emotions into good and bad overlooks both the scientific theory and the experiential reality that all emotions have as their basic purpose the promotion of life, not its destruction."[132] Just as we cannot "turn off" our thoughts, we cannot "turn off" our emotions. Lester explains, "Aggression is expressed through initiative, activity, searching, exploring, testing, working and so forth; it is deeply rooted in our physiology and biological history. Without this motivating life force, our ancestors would not have survived."[133]

To expect people to escape emotions would be as absurd as overcoming any other activity endemic to human life. We are always fully emotional; but these emotions change, vary in intensity, and we may not always be aware how we are feeling. The presence of emotions is inherent to our brain activity. Lester writes, "Some people in the Christian tradition have suggested

128. Ibid., 8.
129. Ibid., .3.
130. Ibid., 20.
131. Ibid., 28.
132. Ibid., 59.
133. Ibid., 74.

that the most mature response to anger is eradication. But what we learn from the neurosciences about this capacity's neurological rootedness communicates the reality that anger cannot be removed from our physiology."[134]

As we have seen above, the presence of our emotions is a result of our likeness in the image of God. The inevitability of emotions includes the inevitability of anger. This emotion, like others, is value-neutral. The goal is not to eradicate it, therefore, but to conform this emotion into the likeness of Christ.

#4. Anger Evokes Positive Action

The Bible is replete with references to God's anger. In fact, Basset argues, "Anger is one of the most frequently mentioned divine emotions in the Hebrew Bible, making it much more a feature of God than of human beings."[135] When anger is legitimate, it is focused on injustice. As such, anger can be a motivating force for positive change. We read on several occasions that Jesus became angry. He repeatedly called the Pharisees hypocrites, and compared them to "white washed tombs." Jesus made a whip and overturned the tables of the money changers. When speaking of Herod, Jesus told the Pharisees to, "Go tell that fox, 'I will drive out demons and heal people today and tomorrow, and on the third day I will reach my goal.'"[136] Paul was angry enough with the legalists in Galatia that he wished they would emasculate themselves. In each of these cases, the anger was legitimate. There was a real threat. And in each of these cases, the anger led to positive action. When Jesus was angry with the money changers, he drove them out of the temple. When Paul was angry with the Judaizers, he suppressed their movement and placed a lighter burden on new converts. Because of the positive action that anger provokes, Basset writes, "It would be better to regard anger as an engine capable of transforming a potentially devastating energy into the violent life force that accompanies every birthing process."[137]

Once a person identifies the cause of his anger as a threat to his values, he is energized to act. This moment of transformation from a past grief to a future plan is a healthy catalyst for change. "When people finally allow themselves to fully feel their legitimate anger," Lester explains, "they often experience a rebirth of hope."[138]

---

134. Ibid., 87.
135. Basset, *Holy Anger*, 22.
136. Luke 13.32
137. Basset, *Holy Anger*, 16.
138. Lester, *The Angry Christian*, 192.

The Therapeutic Value of the Imprecatory Psalms

I. Conclusion

What we have seen in this chapter is that the imprecatory psalms have relevance and value for us as we concern ourselves with God's reputation, and trust that God will take care of our problems. Contemporary application of these psalms calls us to care about the things God cares about. As we practice this type of prayer, we make our complaints clear, we pray for the plans of the wicked to be foiled, we take responsibility for our own sin, and we become passionate about the struggle for justice. These psalms are not only relevant, but they become therapeutic agents of healing, dealing with anger, and preventing violence. They also are valuable for preaching as they help us address the fact that, "It is not these psalms that are provocative and outrageous, but human beings and their world."[139]

---

139. Zenger, *A God of Vengeance?* 85.

9

Preaching the Imprecatory Psalms

A. Sermon #1: Concern for God's Reputation.

WHAT IS YOUR REACTION to the reckless driver on the freeway who cuts you off, then speeds ahead to do the same to six others? Have you ever wished that you would see him two miles ahead, pulled over to the side of the road, receiving a traffic ticket? I have. And once my wish came true. I was vindicated, and I was elated. But while my wish (which may have been more of a hopeful prediction) came true, I didn't pray that he would get a ticket. Why not? Because I'm not in the habit of calling down curses from heaven. Also, I'm aware of my own shortfalls as a driver. And, I recognize my own immaturity in equating my enemies with God's enemies, as well as the triviality of my experience on the freeway in comparison to the things that grieve God.

King David had bigger problems. He prayed, "May all who gloat over my distress be put to shame and confusion; may all who exalt themselves over me be clothed with shame and disgrace."[1] Given that many of us are reluctant to pray that those who gloat over us be put to shame or clothed in disgrace, why was David willing to do so? Did he have a worse temper? Was it because he was pre-Jesus, and had an Old Testament worldview? I believe that since this passage of Scripture is no less inspired than the New Testament, there must be value to his prayer. And since David was "a man after God's heart," it's too simplistic to say that he had a bigger temper. I think the reason David had the confidence to pray for the shame and disgrace of his enemies is a sign of maturity. That maturity is manifest in several ways, including the assurance that his enemy was also God's enemy, and recognition of his own faults.

---

1. Ps 35:26

But the mark of maturity that eludes most of us is the psalmist's concern for the reputation of God. He continues "May those who delight in my vindication shout for joy and gladness; may they always say, "The LORD be exalted, who delights in the well-being of his servant."[2] David's prayer was primarily motivated by concern for the name of the Lord. It was his prayer that his enemies would be put to shame, so that men would say, "The Lord be exalted." When Elijah was on Mount Carmel contesting with the prophets of Baal, he prayed that the false prophets would be put to shame.[3] After taunting them, he built his altar of wood and prayed that God would consume the fire. His purpose was in no way selfish. He was not interested in vindication of his own reputation. Consider the immediate response of his audience when the fire was consumed. The men took a step back, fell to the ground, and shouted: "The Lord, he is God. The Lord, he is God. The Lord, he is God." The fruit of Elijah's prayer was that the Lord's reputation was upheld; his name was praised. Elijah prayed that fire would consume his altar, because concern for God's name consumed Elijah.

God's Unmistakable Work

Have you ever walked into a room and seen the unmistakable work of someone you know, even though he was absent? My wife and I returned from a three week vacation and when we walked into our home, it was evident that my sister-in-law, had been there. Every inch of the floor was clean. Our van was detailed. The grass was freshly cut (I suspect she talked her husband into doing that). The house bore the image of her work. In the same way, when God acts his work is unmistakable.

When David prayed for the downfall of his enemies, he knew that the aftermath would reveal the unmistakable work of God. He prayed, "For the sins of their mouths, for the words of their lips, let them be caught in their pride. For the curses and lies they utter, consume them in wrath, consume them till they are no more. Then it will be known to the ends of the earth that God rules over Jacob."[4] It may seem shocking that David prayed for God to consume his enemies till they were no more. But what motivated this prayer? Frustration? Anger? Undoubtedly he was angry and frustrated, but his primary motivation was that "it would be known to the ends of the earth that God rules over Jacob." After God dealt with his enemies, God's

---

2. Ps 35:27
3. 1 Kgs 18
4. Ps 59:12, 13

Part Three: Application

name would be well known and his reputation upheld, because his work would be unmistakable.

Concern for God's Name

When I was a youth pastor for about six years at a church in Southern California, each year I led the group on a summer retreat at Lake Havasu. Among the families at our church, the summer of 2000 has gone down in history as, "The Time Dan 'Lost It' at Havasu." For several days I listened to the kids say things like "God, it's hot" and "God, that boat went fast." They seemed oblivious to the fact that they were not only breaking the third commandment, but grieving the Lord by misusing his name. I asked them politely to stop using God's name in vain, but it didn't bring about much change, so I decided to use a more effective tactic. On the last day, I waited for someone to misuse his name, and when she did I said, "I'm getting F***ing tired of hearing you guys say 'God.'" They were stunned. They were silent. Then I told them that they should be more shocked and more grieved when they hear God's name misused than when they hear the "F word." Needless to say, the point was made very effectively, and unforgettably. Fortunately, the parents backed me up, too.

Similarly, King David had a similar passion for God's name. He prayed some fierce curses against his enemies. "May the table set before them become a snare; may it become retribution and a trap. May their eyes be darkened so they cannot see, and their backs be bent forever. Pour out your wrath on them; let your fierce anger overtake them. May their place be deserted; let there be no one to dwell in their tents. For they persecute those you wound and talk about the pain of those you hurt. Charge them with crime upon crime; do not let them share in your salvation. May they be blotted out of the book of life and not be listed with the righteous."[5] But the motivation for this passionate prayer was clearly stated. "Let heaven and earth praise him, the seas and all that move in them, for God will save Zion and rebuild the cities of Judah. Then people will settle there and possess it; the children of his servants will inherit it, and those who love his name will dwell there."[6] David was concerned about the name of the Lord. He was grieved that God's reputation was mocked, and he prayed for the downfall of God's enemies because he longed for the day when God's name would be praised.

My wife and I struggled with infertility for several years. We were prepared to bring children into our home through other means. In fact,

---

5. Ps 69:22–28
6. Ps 69:34–36

we have adopted two children. We were also making plans to try in-vitro fertilization. But we sensed that if we handled our struggle in our own strength, we would not give God an opportunity to magnify his reputation. We wanted to see God make his name known. So we prayed with a group of friends for a child, and pleaded with God that he would make his name great, and uphold his reputation as a great and awesome God. Within a month we conceived our first child (now we have three biological and two adopted children). We named our first son Micah, which means in Hebrew, "Who is like the Lord?" And the obvious answer to the question is "no one."

The king's record keeper and musician Asaph also wanted God to make his name great. He lamented of his enemies, "'Come,' they say, 'let us destroy them as a nation, that the name of Israel be remembered no more.'"[7] Asaph was concerned that the name of Israel would not be remembered. Israel in Hebrew means "He will be victorious," meaning of course that God will be victorious. And God's victory was manifest in the nation of Israel. It was assumed by the neighboring nations that if Israel was great, then their God must be great. So Asaph was concerned that if Israel suffered, God's reputation would suffer. Then he prayed this against his enemies, "Cover their faces with shame so that men will seek your name, O LORD. May they ever be ashamed and dismayed; may they perish in disgrace. Let them know that you, whose name is the LORD—that you alone are the Most High over all the earth."[8] Note that Asaph prayed for his enemies to be covered with shame, so that men would seek the name of the Lord. This was a selfless motive and a mature prayer: a prayer of passion so men would know that the Lord alone is the Most High.

Our Response to our Enemy's Downfall

When the polygamist compound in Texas was exposed on the media the nation responded with a variety of reactions, including curiosity and disgust. A mature response would be worship. Worship because the exposure proved that God would not allow his name to be maligned by those who pervert his design. Similarly, when Saddam Hussein was hanged the media reported reactions of relief and vindication. A mature response, however, would be worship. Worship because God brings justice to the guilty and sets the oppressed free. Our response to these events is a test of maturity. God does not provide for the fall of an enemy for your sake. Not for your

---

7. Ps 83:4
8. Ps 83:16–18

amusement. Not for your prosperity. And not for your relief. He does it for the sake of his name.

David prayed for the downfall of his enemy, but he knew why God would answer his prayer. He prayed that the curses of his enemy would instead by curses around his waist like a belt worn forever. He said, "May this be the LORD's payment to my accusers, to those who speak evil of me. But you, O Sovereign LORD, deal well with me for your name's sake; out of the goodness of your love, deliver me."[9]

Elsewhere David prayed, "The righteous will be glad when they are avenged, when they bathe their feet in the blood of the wicked. Then men will say, 'Surely the righteous still are rewarded; surely there is a God who judges the earth.'"[10] As surely as the Lord lives, one day his enemies will be defeated. Similarly, I pray for the end of legalized abortion in our country. I believe I will live to see that day. I am confident because, "Surely there is a God who judges the earth." I am confident because this judge is active, and he is not silent. His enemies will be avenged. But as I pray for that day, I reflect on what my future response will be. What will your response be? For some it will be a fleshly, self-centered satisfaction: "I knew I was right all along." Some will praise their own efforts, and the efforts of others who helped the cause. Some pray for the end of abortion because the practice outrages them. Others consider the golden rule, and recognize that babies are not treated the way any of us would want to be treated. While I agree with these thoughts, they are earth-centered. They are thoughts of low ambition. The psalmist said the righteous are glad when the wicked are avenged because God's reputation is upheld: "Surely there is a God who judges the earth."[11]

But what does it mean that God's judgment should lead us to worship? Worship means that we become lesser, and that he becomes greater.[12] The worshipful response in light of God's enemies begins with the question: "Is it I Lord?" Or, as the traditional spiritual affirms, "It's me Lord, standing in the need of prayer. Not my mother, not my father, not my brother, not my sister, not my elder, not my leader. But it's me Lord, standing in the need of prayer." Paul emphatically states, "While we were God's enemies, we were reconciled to him through the death of his Son."[13]

---

9. Ps 109:20–21
10. Ps 58:10–11
11. Ps 58:11
12. John 3:30
13. 1 Cor 5:10

Conclusion

The foundation for understanding these imprecatory psalms is the author's passion for God's name and reputation. "Hatred erupts with uncontrolled malevolence—yet the psalmist asks for God to destroy those hated, and does not claim the right to annihilate them himself."[14] Our reluctance to pray curses similar to those found in these psalms reveals an immaturity of which we are probably aware. We are only ready to understand and value the prayer modeled in these psalms when we can honestly admit that zeal for God's name and reputation consumes us. Until then, we are not ready to pray in this way. McKenzie explains, "Does it not appear possible that the imprecatory psalms are not a model, not because of their lower degree of perfection, but because they are too lofty for most of us to imitate them without danger?"[15]

B. Sermon #2: Let God Take Care of Your Problem

Three times in Scripture we are told not to take revenge, for vengeance belongs to the Lord. "It is mine to avenge; I will repay. In due time their foot will slip; their day of disaster is near and their doom rushes upon them."[16] We are assured that we need not take matters into our own hands, because God is already more concerned with our enemy than we are. And he has structured the world in such a way that the wicked will fall into their own trap. The examples of this truth are endless. The Roman Emperor Claudius was poisoned by Nero's mother, so that her son would become Emperor. When he did, he had his mother killed. Many who worked to put the revolutionaries in power during the French Revolution were among the first to die when they got their wish, as were many Russian revolutionaries. Two men who taunted a tiger at the San Francisco zoo were attacked by the tiger when it escaped. A drunk driver gets a DUI, loses his license, goes to jail and then loses his job. When released, he cannot get a job because he cannot get to work because he does not have a license. And he cannot get his license until he pays a fine and gets insurance, which he cannot afford because he does not have a job. In each of these cases, revenge is unnecessary because perpetrators of injustice eventually incurred the consequences of their sin.

Paul encouraged us, "Do not take revenge, my friends, but leave room for God's wrath, for it is written: 'It is mine to avenge; I will repay,' says the

---

14. Augburger, *Hate-Work*, 211.
15. McKenzie, *The Imprecations of the Psalter*, 96.
16. Deut 32:35

Part Three: Application

Lord."[17] You can let God handle your enemies. You can leave room for God's wrath, because it is his prerogative to avenge.

Convinced of the sovereignty of God, the psalmist prays his curses against his enemy with resignation to his own strength, and dependence on God. He was keenly aware that it would be presumptuous to take vengeance himself. We have all sinned, so none of us is able to cast a stone without implicating ourselves. Besides, if our passion is for God's reputation, then he is more concerned with his enemies than we are! The psalmist does not trust in his own strength, his own wisdom, nor in horses or chariots, nor in the power of money. Instead he prays, "O Lord my God, I take refuge in you; save and deliver me from all who pursue me."[18] Knowing that God must have taken more offense than the writer, he says, "rouse yourself to punish the nations"[19] and "let them know that it was your hand, that you have done this."[20] The author knew that even though evil men were coming against him, they were more God's enemies than his. He prayed, "Let them know that it was your hand, that you, O Lord, have done it."[21]

God Cares

For several years our nation's military has been involved in wars in Iraq and Afghanistan. Because many troops have been deployed to the Mideast three times in just a few years, the military has been aggressively recruiting to prevent burnout. The Navy, for instance, offers many new recruits a large signing bonus paid upon completion of boot camp. Despite these incentives, and the evident need to protect our country from terrorists, as of 2008, the number of men and women in the armed forces accounts for just 0.67 percent of our total population. Compare that to the situation during the Revolutionary War when America fought for independence from Great Britain when about 8 percent of the American population at some point served in the military. What is the difference? The obvious answer is passion. Because the war was in our own homeland, the Revolutionary War evoked a sense of urgency that foreign wars do not. People cared, so they took up their arms.

God cares, so he too takes up arms. The psalmist called out to God to "Contend, O LORD, with those who contend with me; fight against those who

17. Rom 12:19
18. Ps 7:1
19. Ps 59:5
20. Ps 109:27
21. Ps 109:27

fight against me. Take up shield and buckler; arise and come to my aid. Brandish spear and javelin against those who pursue me."[22] Why would God take up his shield and spear? What makes him arise and come to aid? The answer is that God cares for us. He sees our affliction, and he cares for us. He also cares for his own reputation and his name. He cares about justice. That's why the psalmist had the confidence to pray, "Arise O Lord, in your anger; rise up against the rage of my enemies. Awake, my God; decree justice."[23] You can let God take care of your enemies because he cares for you.

God is Able

Desmond Tutu was convinced of God's ability and willingness to end oppression. He wrote,

> The powers of evil, of injustice, of oppression, of exploitation, have done their worst and they have lost. They have lost because they are immoral and wrong, and our God, the God of Exodus, the liberation God, is a God of justice and righteousness, and he is on the side of justice and liberation and goodness. Our cause, the cause of justice and liberation, must triumph because it is moral and just and right. Many who support the present unjust system in this country know in their hearts that they are upholding a system that is evil and unjust and oppressive, which is utterly abhorrent and displeasing to God. Yes, there is no doubt whatsoever that freedom is coming.[24]

The psalmist was confident that God would do a better job of dealing with his enemies than he could. He prays, "O righteous God who searches minds and hearts, bring to an end the violence of the wicked and make the righteous secure."[25]

There is a proverb that says, "The wealth of the rich is their fortified city; they imagine it an unscalable wall."[26] Some people imagine themselves to be an unscalable wall. The psalmist knew that he was completely unable to handle his problems or to deal with his enemy. Consider how much a tiny ailment can render us completely debilitated. I fell when walking on ice several years ago. The scream must have been loud, because a neighbor down

---

22. Ps 35:1–3
23. Ps 7:6
24. Tutu, *Crying in the Wilderness*, 64.
25. Ps 7:9
26. Prov 18:11

the street came running to my aid. I walked on crutches for two months, and continued to limp for another two months. Even after six months I still felt pain when I walked. But amazingly, when I got my ankle X-rayed immediately after the injury, there was no visible break. An injury that was invisible left me unable to walk for months. So I am not an unscalable wall. I am not fit for the fight with my enemy. I agree with the psalmist who said, "The LORD is King for ever and ever; the nations will perish from his land. You hear, O LORD, the desire of the afflicted; you encourage them, and you listen to their cry, defending the fatherless and the oppressed, so that mere earthly mortals will never again strike terror."[27] I recognize that I am merely *of the earth*. I will perish from the land.

God, on the other hand, is able to take on any enemy. And this is not a faint or a future hope. It is certain, and it is both present and future. "The LORD reigns forever; he has established his throne for judgment. He will judge the world in righteousness; he will govern the peoples with justice."[28] You can let God take care of your enemies because he is able, and you are not.

God is Active

The psalmist prayed, "O LORD God Almighty, the God of Israel, rouse yourself to punish all the nations; show no mercy to wicked traitors."[29] How often do you think God *rouses himself* to punish the wicked? Once a year? Once a decade?

I used to think of God as a dormant volcano, but then again, I'm not very afraid of those either. Our family visited Mount Saint Helens in Washington in the summer of 2004. We watched a DVD of the previous eruption of 1980 before we got to the volcano. My son who was five at the time was quite disturbed, having seen the video and now standing before the giant. He kept asking me if it was going to erupt. I know I have no right as a mere mortal to say whether a volcano will erupt or not, but I felt the responsibility as a father to ease his worry. So I gave him a completely "unauthorized" assurance that the volcano was not going to erupt. We were only going to be there for one day! What were the chances? Well, my baseless promise worked in my favor, but less than two weeks later the volcano did erupt. Not on the magnitude of the 1980 eruption, but it led to an evacuation of the immediate area nonetheless.

27. Ps 10:16–18
28. Ps 9:7–8
29. Ps 59:5

Preaching the Imprecatory Psalms

When I read the psalmist's prayer that God "rouse himself" I reflect on God as a dormant volcano. What are the chances he will express his wrath today? The psalms give an answer to this question. "God is a righteous judge, a God who expresses his wrath every day."[30]

Instead of Mount Saint Helens, according to this verse, God is rather like Mount Yasur. My brother and his wife are Wycliffe Bible Translators who live on the island of Tanna, Vanuatu, in the South Pacific. Mount Yasur is in view of their front door. It is the most accessible, and one of the most active volcanoes in the world, erupting every few minutes.

When you think of God, are you more inclined to imagine Mt. Saint Helens, or Mt. Yasur? The Bible says he expresses his wrath daily. You can depend on God to handle your enemies, because he is active.

God Will Take Care of Your Enemies

In the book of Esther, we read of a villain named Haman. The man built gallows for a man he hated named Mordecai. He planned a holocaust for all the Jews. And he planned a parade for himself where he would be honored throughout the city. The beautifully written and intricate story ends with Haman being hanged on the gallows he built. The holocaust backfired on all who conspired with him. And the parade was given to honor Mordecai. Mordecai let God handle his enemies. The psalmist had the same sense of serenity and assurance. He sang, "He who is pregnant with evil and conceives trouble gives birth to disillusionment. He who digs a hole and scoops it out falls into the pit he has made. The trouble he causes recoils on himself; his violence comes down on his own head."[31]

You can let God take care of your enemies because he cares, he is able, he is active, and he will do it.

---

30. Ps 7:11
31. Ps 7:14–16

Part Three: Application

C. Sermon #3: Appeal to the Things God Cares About

When Joshua approached Jericho and saw an angel of the Lord whose sword was drawn, he asked the angel, "Whose side are you on?" "Neither," the angel said, "but as commander of the army of the LORD I have now come."[32] So if we are going to enlist God's help in our struggle with an enemy, it makes sense to ensure that we are on God's side. The most certain way to be sure we're on God's side is to appeal to the things that God cares about. The imprecatory psalms give a clear picture of what God cares about.

As we look though Psalm 10 we learn of the people for whom God weeps: the weak, oppressed, afflicted, and fatherless. These are the people over whom he keeps watch. He defends them. And he opposes their adversaries. If you want to be on God's side, care for these hurting people. If you want to be sure that he will fight for you, fight for them. If we have any confidence in our ability to pray an imprecatory prayer, it is because we know God takes sides, and we align ourselves with him. Desmond Tutu wrote, "Our freedom is an inalienable right bestowed on us by God. And the God whom we worship has always shown himself to be the one who takes sides."[33]

The Weak

The psalmist complains, "In his arrogance the wicked man hunts down the weak."[34] We know that God cares about the weak. The widow of Zaraphath is a prime example. She and her son lived during a famine in Israel. Widows in ancient Israel typically had no means of income, and often no inheritance or land. This widow was destitute, as she was left with only a little flour in a land experiencing famine for three years. But God provided for this woman and her son while the prophet Elijah lived with her. God daily provided oil and bread. At some point during the long stay, which perhaps lasted almost three years, the widow's son died. She asked Elijah if he came to bring her grief. But God allowed Elijah to bring the boy to life.[35] God performed this miracle to make his name great and to show his power. But God could have chosen any number of people to benefit from his sign. He chose the widow, because God defends the weak. He loves the broken hearted and downcast, and he opposes those who are strong in their own eyes.

---

32. Josh 5:14
33. Tutu, *Crying in the Wilderness*, 89.
34. Ps 10:2
35. 1 Kgs 17

Preaching the Imprecatory Psalms

The Humble

The singer also laments of the evildoer, "He boasts of the cravings of his heart; he blesses the greedy and reviles the LORD. In his pride the wicked does not seek him; in all his thoughts there is no room for God. His ways are always prosperous; he is haughty and your laws are far from him; he sneers at all his enemies. He says to himself, 'Nothing will shake me; I'll always be happy and never have trouble.'"[36] Clearly, God opposes the proud and gives grace to the humble. The wicked man in this psalm has seen prosperity, and now sees himself as unshakable, so he laughs at his enemies in his pride. The Babylonian king Nebuchadnezzar rose to a similar view of himself. He erected a statue and called people to pray to it. God saw his pride, but must have seen a ray of hope, because he saw fit to teach the king a lesson in humility. Nebuchadnezzar lived for seven years among wild animals eating grass, "as cattle." At the end of this peculiar sentence, the king had a change of heart. His son, however, was not as promising. God saw the pride in Belshazzar's heart, and didn't give him seven years to think about it. His kingdom was torn away in violence, because God opposes the proud, but gives grace to the humble. When Paul was in Caesarea, Herod was speaking to the crowd and the people began to shout that they were listening not to the voice of a man, but of a God. Because Herod loved the flattery, and did not give glory to the true God, he immediately fell dead and was eaten by worms.[37] God opposes the proud. As Mary sang when she learned of her expectation of the Messiah, "every valley shall be filled in, and every mountain laid low."[38] If you want to be on God's side, develop a humble attitude.

The Poor

Of this enemy, we read, "he blesses the greedy and reviles the LORD."[39] God opposes the greedy. But he defends the poor. The letter of James tells us of a tragic situation where the early church favored the rich and despised the poor. Depending on one's clothes or appearance, he was offered a better place to sit among the Christians. James had harsh words for the rich. He warned the rich (and that's most of us in America, in comparison to the rest of the world) that we have hoarded our wealth and have fattened ourselves in the day of slaughter. James threatens that the wages of the workers who

---

36. Ps 10:3–6
37. Acts 12:23
38. Luke 3:5
39. Ps 10:3

mowed our fields (sewed our clothes, assembled our shoes) cry out against us, for we have lived in luxury and self-indulgence.[40] Now James declares that our wealth, silver, and gold has corroded and testifies against us. God loves the poor and keeps watch over them. But he also keeps watch over their oppressors. If you want to be on God's side, make great sacrifices to defend the poor.

The Righteous

Regarding the wicked, the psalmist complains to God, "your laws are far from him."[41] God opposes the lawless, and defends the righteous. King David knew this to be true. Though he was destined, and even anointed to be the next king, he would never lay a hand on the Lord's anointed (who happened to be King Saul). So despite having three perfect opportunities to slay Saul, David resisted the urge. He would observe God's order. Unfortunately, David's example was not contagious. Two of David's sons attempted to steal the throne. Absalom was the first. He set up his own army to defeat his father, but his long hair was his undoing. He was caught by his coiffure in a tree, and then his pursuers ran him through with a sword. Adonijah also crafted a rebellion against Solomon, whom David had selected to succeed him. Solomon forgave the first attempt. But Adonijah again attempted to take the throne, and like his rebellious brother was killed. God opposes the lawless, but defends the righteous. If you want to be on God's side, keep God's law written dear in your heart.

The Honest

The psalmist charges the wicked that, "His mouth is full of curses and lies and threats."[42] God opposes liars, or as the writer previously called them, schemers. Jesus called the devil the father of lies. A lie was at the root of Adam and Eve's fall. Lies were also at the root of Judas' treachery. When Judas complained about the great expense of perfume poured on Jesus' feet, he said the money could have been given to the poor. But John assures us that Judas was not concerned about the poor, instead he kept the common purse and he used to steal from it. He was a bandit, thief, and liar. Consider

40. Jas 5:1–6
41. Ps 10:5
42. Ps 10:7

his fate. He hung himself, and his body fell with his guts gushing out.[43] God opposes schemers, liars, and the dishonest. He defends the honest. If you want to be on God's side, speak the truth at all costs.

The Helpless

Concerning the wicked man, we read that, "His mouth is full of curses and lies and threats; trouble and evil are under his tongue. He lies in wait near the villages; from ambush he murders the innocent, watching in secret for his victims. He lies in wait like a lion in cover; he lies in wait to catch the helpless; he catches the helpless and drags them off in his net."[44] The wicked man is a bully who makes threats against the helpless. This is why God opposed Goliath. Each day Goliath of Gath came out to the Israelite camp and made threats. He ridiculed the people of Israel, and he sneered at their God. David heard the threats, and knew that God opposed such a man. He was armed with confidence that God would not allow his own reputation to be defamed. And of course, with one stone Goliath fell. God opposes the threat-making bully. He defends the helpless. If you want to be on God's side, take risks to come to the aid of the helpless.

The Fatherless

In confidence the psalmist sang, "But you, O God, do see trouble and grief; you consider it to take it in hand. The victim commits himself to you; you are the helper of the fatherless."[45] God defends the fatherless, and opposes any who would take advantage of their weak state. Ruth was fatherless, and her mother-in-law was a widow. These two women had no means of income, no inheritance, no land for produce, and no hope. But Ruth learned to trust in Naomi's God, who defends the fatherless. Boaz was the kinsman redeemer who took compassion on the women. In a world where poverty and suffering was commonplace, Boaz noticed them. He married Ruth, who then was able to provide for Naomi. This man's provision is a clear type or image of God's compassion. As Boaz was a kinsman redeemer, so Jesus became a redeemer of all humanity, and also became kin of all humanity. Today God continues to spread the corner of his garment over the fatherless, the widow, and the helpless. He defends them. And he demands that we do the same.

43. Acts 1:18
44. Ps 10:7–9
45. Ps 10:14

Part Three: Application

The Old Testament law required that harvesters only work their fields over one time. To pass by the same spot a second time is stingy and selfish. Any leftover gleanings were for the poor, the widow, the fatherless. They were not to extract from the land every last drop of income for their own advantage. Ruth literally gleaned from Boaz' field. The destitute among us, both near and far, are worthy of the same. If you want to be on God's side, make provisions for the fatherless. Spread a corner of your garment over them.

The Oppressed

The psalmist appealed to God, "You hear, O LORD, the desire of the afflicted; you encourage them, and you listen to their cry, defending the fatherless and the oppressed, in order that man, who is of the earth, may terrify no more."[46] He knew that God defends the oppressed. He had plenty of examples from history to prove his point, but the exodus from Egypt was probably at the top of his mind. For 430 years the Israelites suffered under the oppression of Pharaohs in Egypt who subjected them to slavery. After the Egyptian people endured nine plagues, the tenth was truly devastating. In every Egyptian home, from the least to the greatest, the first born son died on the night the Spirit of God passed over the homes of the Israelites. God passed over the oppressed, but he afflicted the oppressors. This illustrates a timeless truth that God watches over the weak. If you want to be on God's side, do not ignore the plight of the oppressed, but rescue them.

No doubt we all believe that we are on God's side. Few of us would say that we actively support God's enemies: the rich, oppressors, threat-makers, schemers, proud, or abusers. This affirmation of the mind is not enough to ensure that we are on God's side. Our actions must prove that we actively oppose the oppressors. Further, to ensure we're on God' side we must make sacrifices to defend the oppressed. If you are not actively supporting those whom God defends, you are not on his side.

D. Sermon #4: Make Your Complaint Clear

To make the imprecatory psalms come alive for us we must identify our enemy, and specifically name our complaint to God about what our enemy is doing. In Psalm 35 The psalmist complains to God that his enemies fight against him, pursue him, seek his life, plot his ruin, hide a net for him, dig a pit without cause, and rob the poor. He charges that his enemies are ruthless

---

46. Ps 10:17–18

Preaching the Imprecatory Psalms

witnesses, they make false accusations, repay him evil for good, they gather in glee, they slander him, they ravage others, they mock, wink, and gloat. Obviously David had given a great deal of thought to what his enemy was doing. He knew that he would have God's ear, because he appealed to the things that God cared about. And he had a heart for the things God cared about because he was primarily concerned for God's reputation.

Unfortunately today God still has no shortage of enemies (after all, we were each one of them). And our enemies are not very different from King David's. David asks God to fight with those who fight with him.[47] Religious persecution comes to mind. Though thousands of Christians (and Jews) were put to death during the first century due to the Roman persecution, nowadays there are more martyrs for their Christian faith than then. Groups such as Voice of the Martyrs, Christian Solidarity International, and Open Doors speak out for contemporary victims of persecution. Some estimate that as many as half a million Christians are put to death each year for their faith, while 200 million Christians live with the threat of violence or imprisonment, and 400 million live with the deprivation of some liberty due to their faith. According to the Open Doors 2008 World Watch list, the ten countries most hostile to Christians are: Saudi Arabia, Iran, Somalia, Maldives, Yemen, North Korea, Vietnam, Laos, China and Bhutan.

One of the functions of making our complaint clear to God is that we remember the plight of the suffering. Memory is an act of love. Psalm 137:5 invokes a curse upon the worshiper if he *forgets* Jerusalem. Therefore, not to pray for justice to come to the oppressed is to "forget," and this would be a sin.

We also make our complaints known to God because we desire for Him to act. Adams writes, "We must be candid enough to acknowledge that to pray for the extension of God's kingdom is to solicit the destruction of all other kingdoms."[48] We echo the Lord's prayer by saying: "your kingdom come, your will be done."

When Peter was persecuted and imprisoned for his faith he may have prayed for the conversion of his captors. If he did, that prayer wasn't recorded. What is recorded is that he prayed God would consider the threats of his enemy.[49] Then he prayed for increased boldness to speak the name of Jesus, for deliverance from prison, and for miracles to aid the Christians and prove their message. Prayer for the conversion of enemies is a biblical theme. Wesley wrote that as we pray for our enemies, even for their plans to fail, we should take no pleasure in their destruction. He said,

---

47. Ps 35:1
48. Adams, *War Psalms of the Prince of Peace*, 52.
49. Acts 4:29

Part Three: Application

> Love does not rejoice in injustice. Unfortunately it is common among some Christians to rejoice over their enemy when he has fallen into affliction error or sin. . . . Who does not rejoice when his adversary makes a false step, which he thinks will be an advantage to his own cause? Only a man of love can avoid this. He alone weeps over the sin and folly of his enemy. He gets no pleasure in hearing or repeating those things. Rather, he desires this may be forgotten forever.[50]

Jesus instructed that we should pray for our enemies. This may include a prayer that their plans fail, but it should always mean that we pray for them to change, repent, and be saved.

> *Imprecatory prayer regarding the persecution of Christians:* Lord, we pray for the strength of persecuted Christians. May they maintain their strength, their confession of you as their one and only Lord, and may they be assured of your presence and blessing. God we ask that our country would be able and willing to prevent this persecution, if it is your will. Lord, we pray that you would remove the dictators from power who carry out persecution of your saints. May the tormentors fall in the pit that they have dug for others. We pray that the people of these hostile countries would be favorable to Christians, and no longer turn a blind eye or tolerate the persecution. Amen.

David said that his enemy "seeks my life."[51] It has become clear to many Westerners that we have had an enemy seeking our lives while we were unaware. The terrorist attacks of Sept 11, 2001, revealed that we too have an enemy seeking our life, pursuing us, and plotting our ruin. Sometimes the enemy is hiding in secrecy, like Al Qaeda. Other times the enemy is state sponsored (like Hezbollah in Lebanon) or even the very government itself (like Hamas in Palestine). These groups plot the ruin of innocent people. They do it to gain power, or to attract worldwide attention, or to further Islamic Jihad with the ultimate goal of eliminating all non-believers in Islam.

> *Imprecatory prayer regarding terrorists*: God, we pray that you foil the plans of terrorists. Close the camps that train people in terrorism. Remove the government leaders who sponsor or support terrorism from leadership. Protect us from their attacks, and may you confuse these groups in their plans. May they be like chaff and remembered no more. Give our government wisdom and strength

---

50. Wesley, *The Nature of the Kingdom*, 77.
51. Ps 35:4

Preaching the Imprecatory Psalms

to take a strong and wise stand against them. May their plans come to nothing. Amen.

David complained that his enemy robs the poor.[52] Today we have the same complaint about guerrillas, dictators, and leaders who rob the poor. The communist regimes in China, North Korea, Vietnam, and Cuba have fallen short of their promise to help the poor, and instead have proved detrimental.

> **Prayer:** *God, we pray for the victims of oppressive regimes in China, North Korea, Vietnam, and Cuba. We pray that the leaders of these countries would be removed from power, and that you would replace them with righteous leaders. If the dictators in these countries are planning violence, spoil their plans. Bring the one-child policy in China that has led to the death of millions of babies to an end. Allow your name to be proclaimed freely in these countries. Open the borders of these countries up to the rest of the world so that relief for the poor may be brought in. Amen.*

The psalmist complained that his enemy continued to repay him evil for the good that he had done.[53] In the book of Nehemiah we read of two such enemies, named Tobiah and Sanballat. Cyrus gave Nehemiah permission to rebuild the city walls of Jerusalem. But Tobiah and Sanballat wrote letters to the king saying that this work was illegal and never authorized. Then when construction began Tobiah and Sanballat threatened violence, Nehemiah had to command the people to build with one hand, while holding a sword in the other. When the wall was nearing completion, Tobiah and Sanballat ridiculed the workers, saying that if a fox walked on the wall, it would fall. Having endured this opposition, Nehemiah prayed, "Remember Tobiah and Sanballat, O my God, because of what they have done; remember also the prophetess Noadiah and the rest of the prophets who have been trying to intimidate me."[54] Clearly, Nehemiah was prepared to pray against his enemies by making his complaint clear and asking God to repay his enemy.

When Jesus was on his way to Jerusalem, he was going to stop through Samaria, but the people would not welcome him there. Angry at their rudeness, James and John asked Jesus if he wanted them to command fire from heaven to come and consume the city.[55] Jesus rebuked them, but it's interesting that James and John saw such an act of immanent vengeance from God's hands as a real possibility. Most of us today would never ask God if he

---

52. Ps 35:10
53. Ps 35:12
54. Neh 6:14
55. Luke 9:54

Part Three: Application

wants us to command fire from heaven to consume a city. Why is it that we tend to be reluctant to pray such a prayer? Or more importantly, why would such a prayer never occur to us? Some may claim that we have evolved in our understanding of God, and James and John had a primitive view. Some may say that we've gotten nicer over the years. Another possibility is that we have become more apathetic. In any case, recapturing the passion from the imprecatory psalms requires that we recapture the assurance of God's promise: "Vengeance is mine. I will repay." While initially this may sound like terrible news, and a barbaric view of God, consider the alternative. It goes without saying that man will take vengeance, if given the opportunity. Since vengeance will be had, wouldn't you rather God be the one to exact it? King David faced this very dilemma. Because of his sin of intending to go to war (signified by counting his troops) when God had not asked him to do so, God gave David a choice of what type of punishment he would rather incur: death at the hands of his enemies, famine, or plague. David said he would rather fall into the hands of God than man, for perhaps God would be merciful. He evidently chose the plague, and 70,000 men died.[56]

David complained that his enemies ravaged him and others like lions, and he prayed for rescue.[57] During the resistance to Apartheid in South Africa, many Christian leaders offered up imprecatory prayers. Desmond Tutu admits, "We prayed earnestly that God would bless our land and would confound the machinations of the children of darkness."[58] Similarly, Margaret Nash, an Anglican layperson in Cape Town, joined black workers in resisting the bulldozing of their shack. A young man named Nkwenke Nkomo was one of thousands of young people who were jailed without trial. She wrote,

> O God whose Son in anger drove the money changers from the temple let the anger of Nkwenkwe Nkomo and his fellow detainees be to the cleansing of this land. O God I hold before you the anger the rage the frustration the sorrow of Mrs. Nkomo and all black mothers who demand for their children the same change to grow up strong and tall, loving and unafraid, as any white mother wants for her children; In penitence I offer you my own mixed-up anger that it, with theirs, may be taken up into your redemptive will in which the clash between anger and fear, oppressed and oppressor, can give way to the incomprehensible action of agape-love, bringing about the reconciliation, the embrace of the other, the alien, the enemy, creating the festival of shalom in which the

---

56. 1 Chr 21:14
57. Ps 35:17
58. Tutu, *No Future Without Forgiveness*, 4.

wolf shall lie down with the lamb and the whole of life on earth shall rejoice in the spender of your glory.[59]

David said that his enemies mocked, winked, and gloated.[60] I think of false teachers today who mock the beliefs of the faithful. Jude warned that false teachers would secretly slip in among us.[61] This has no doubt been the case since the beginning. Jesus said "If anyone causes one of these little ones who believe in me to sin, it would be better for him to have a large millstone hung around his neck and to be drowned in the depths of the sea."[62] Obviously there is a judgment in store for false teachers. It is fitting for us to pray against false teaching.

> **Prayer:** *God, we pray against false teaching in our churches. We pray for discernment, so that your faithful will recognize the wolves in sheep's clothing. Help us to stop supporting their message and reveal the false motives of these teachers. If they are motivated by pride or profit, let that be an obvious warning. And take away our own pride that attracts us to legalistic preaching.*

Pray That the Plans of the Enemy Would Be Foiled.

When we make our complaint clear to God, we remember that our complaint is against the injustice, not against the person. There are some important guidelines to keep in mind when we bring our complaint to God. McKenzie gives us four of them:

> 1. Hatred must not be directed at the person of one's neighbor; he is hated for his evil quality. 2. One may desire that the divine justice be accomplished in the sinner; but it must be a desire for divine justice, not a desire for the personal evil of another out of personal revenge. 3. The infliction of evil may not be desired absolutely, but only under the condition that the sinner remains obdurate and unrepentant. 4. It must be accompanied by that true supernatural charity which efficaciously desires the supreme good—the eternal happiness—of all men in general, not excluding any individual who is capable of attaining it.[63]

---

59. Tutu, *The African Prayer Book*, 45–46.
60. Ps 35:16, 19
61. Jude 4
62. Matt 18:6
63. McKenzie, "The Imprecations of the Psalter," 92–93.

Part Three: Application

David prayed that his enemies would be disgraced, put to shame, and turned back in dismay. He asked that they be like chaff; remembered no more.[64] Jesus indicated that some of his enemies would be like chaff. When he was rejected by the people of Korazin, Bethsaida, and Capernaum, he said that it would be more tolerable for Tyre, Sidon, and Sodom on the Day of Judgment, because the people in those cities would have repented if they saw the things that Jesus did.[65] Instead, Jesus says that these cities will go down to the depths.

David prayed that the path of his enemy would be dark.[66] Similarly, Jude warned false teachers of impending darkness. He said that these false teachers are clouds without water, trees without fruit, waves of the sea casting up foam of shame, and wandering stars for whom blackest darkness is reserved forever. David also prayed that his enemy would be overtaken by ruin, entangled, fall in a pit.[67] He asked God that his enemy would be filled with shame, confusion, and disgrace.[68]

When we make our complaint clear to God, we remember that the imprecatory psalms have more than therapeutic and preaching value: they are prayers. And as such, they have the value that other prayers have. Jesus told us to keep asking, keep seeking, and keep knocking.[69] He said this because prayer makes a difference. James tells of the example of Elijah, who prayed that it would not rain, and it did not for three and a half years. Then he prayed that it would rain, and it did.[70] James' point is that Elijah was a man just like us. We can pray with confidence that God hears us. Jesus never said "prayer is a good way to adjust your attitude." He said, "Truly I tell you, if you have faith and do not doubt, not only can you do what was done to the fig tree, but also you can say to this mountain, 'Go, throw yourself into the sea,' and it will be done."[71] As we pray, we expect that things will happen that would not have happened if we did not pray. So we have a great opportunity and responsibility to make our complaint clear to God.

64. Ps 35:4–5
65. Matt 11:20
66. Ps 35:6
67. Ps 35:8
68. Ps 35:26
69. Matt 6:33
70. Jas 5:17–18
71. Matt 21:21

E. Sermon #5: Take Responsibility for Your Part

Jesus told us that before we attempt to take the speck out of a neighbor's eye, we should take the log out of our own.[72] This is a command that keeps us humble and potentially builds great friendships. Instead of following this command, some take the path of pride and never remove the log out of their own eye. Others follow the path of avoidance, and never take the speck out of their neighbor's eye (though this is clearly a loving and compassionate thing to do). Some people think the log is so big in their own eye that they can never remove it, so they hide behind it as an excuse never to confront others ("who am I to judge?"). But the imprecatory psalms imply that it is possible to remove the log. There is a time for self-examination, and there is a time for confrontation. A time to work on the log, and a time to work on the speck.

In these cursing psalms the author seems keenly aware of the difference. Often the psalmist is confident that his enemy charges against him without cause, and he appeals to God on the basis of his innocence. He says his enemy "hid a net without cause,"[73] and his enemies gloat and oppose him "without reason."[74] He says this opposition is "no offense of mine,"[75] and complains that they question him about things "I do not know."[76] He says, "I have done no wrong"[77] and "I have kept myself from sin."[78] He claims, "you won't find sin in my heart"[79] and offers as proof, "If I had sinned, God would not listen."[80] There are times when an enemy opposes us, or others, or God, with no fault of our own. The fetal victims of abortion are opposed without cause. Girls enslaved into sexual trade are mistreated without reason. Perhaps some of your enemies oppose you, and in this particular situation you are without sin.

On the other hand, perhaps some of the enemies in your life are the result of your sin. The psalmist was keenly aware of this reality, too. When the Jews were exiled and enslaved in Babylon, there were two responses. There was an outward, earthly, prideful response of hatred for a human enemy: Look what these barbarians have done to us! But there was also an introspective, mature,

---

72. Matt 7:4
73. Ps 35:7
74. Ps 35:19
75. Ps 59:3
76. Ps 35:11
77. Ps 55:4
78. Ps 18:23
79. Ps 17:3
80. Ps 66:18

and spiritual response. Look how God is using our enemies to discipline his children, because of our sin! Perhaps your enemy who opposes you is an instrument of God to purify you of sin. If this is the case, as you pray for your enemy, reflect upon your own contribution to the problem.

Deserve Wrath

Desmond Tutu is mindful that we are all guilty. He wrote, "There is no room for gloating or arrogant finger-pointing. We have supplied God with enough evidence, if God had needed it, to want to dispatch us all, to wipe the slate clean as when he tried to make a fresh start with the Flood."[81]

In Psalm 38:1 David begins with "Lord, do not rebuke me in your anger or discipline me in your wrath." David knew that he was deserving of God's wrath. Coming to grips with this reality is a sign of maturity. When the prodigal son contemplated returning to his father after he had shamed and rejected the family, he knew he was deserving of his father's wrath. He did not intend to justify himself, or even beg to be restored to his former position. Instead, he rehearsed, "Father, I have sinned against heaven and against you. I am no longer worthy to be called your son; make me like one of your hired men."[82] As the story goes, his father was ready to forgive and restore his son, but evidently his son learned a great deal about maturity since he was willing to receive the wrath he was due. King David knew that as he prayed for his enemies he must also be willing to receive the punishment that he deserved. He prayed, "if I have done this and there is guilt on my hands—if I have done evil to him who is at peace with me or without cause have robbed my foe—then let my enemy pursue and overtake me; let him trample my life to the ground and make me sleep in the dust."[83]

Be Accountable to God Alone

Later in Psalm 38 David recognized that the arrows that pierced him were God's, and it was the Lord's hand that came down upon him. This spiritual insight is an impressive sign of maturity. What did it look like when God's arrows pierced King David? Most likely, it was the attack of an enemy. God often uses natural means as his instrument of correction. This means that anyone else in David's situation, when attacked by an enemy, could easily

---

81. Tutu, *No Future without Forgiveness*, 144.
82. Luke 15:19
83. Ps 7:3–5

have missed the work of God. They could have concentrated solely on the irritation and grief caused by another human being. But David looked deeper at his enemies, and saw the work of God. The reverse is also true. When he was the enemy, he saw God as the one offended. When David prayed for repentance after he committed adultery with Bathsheba and had her husband Uriah killed, he said, "Against you, you only, have I sinned."[84] David knew that he was accountable to God alone.

Be Troubled by Sin

I have a friend who is meticulously careful with everything he eats and drinks. He almost never drinks a soda. When he does, he feels it profoundly throughout his body. I, on the other hand, feel in my body the lack of caffeine by 10 am. Likewise, Christians who have been careful with their conduct can feel profoundly, even in their body, the effects of succumbing to temptation. David was deeply troubled about his sin. He wrote, "Because of your wrath there is no health in my body; my bones have no soundness because of my sin. My guilt has overwhelmed me like a burden too heavy to bear. My wounds fester and are loathsome because of my sinful folly. I am bowed down and brought very low; all day long I go about mourning. My back is filled with searing pain; there is no health in my body."[85]

It can be painfully obvious when someone is troubled by sin and experiences the effects in their countenance. I received in the mail from an organization called the Initiative Against Sexual Trafficking a picture worth a thousand words. It was eight photos of the same woman: her mug shots from when she was booked for prostitution on eight separate occasions. The deterioration in her countenance told a painful story, and was clear enough that it needed no explanation. In each subsequent photo was she not only more disheveled, but also more aloof, and evidently more under the influence of drugs. Jesus warned that the thief comes to steal, kill, and destroy,[86] and this is exactly what the thief had done to this woman. That sin will have harmful effects is certain, so the mature Christian must learn to be troubled by these effects, rather than ignore them or become used to them.

84. Ps 51:4
85. Ps 38:3–7
86. John 10:9

Part Three: Application

Stop Defending Yourself

David said, "I am feeble and utterly crushed; I groan in anguish of heart."[87] Many people spend their entire lives avoiding the feeling of being crushed by their sin. Instead at all costs they defend themselves and attempt to stand justified. In the comedy *Monty Python's Holy Grail,* the Black Knight is a prime example of one who can never admit defeat. Each time his adversary cut off a limb during a sword duel, he had the audacity to claim "It's just a flesh wound." Finally he is reduced to a man with no arms and no legs bobbing on the ground, still yelling threats. What the knight needed instead, was to admit defeat.

Ironically, though many of us avoid the feeling of defeat at all costs, with the admission comes relief. Jesus told the story of two men who came to the temple to pray. The Pharisee prayed, "God, I thank you that I am not like other men—robbers, evildoers, adulterers—or even like this tax collector. I fast twice a week and give a tenth of all I get." But the tax collector prayed in desperation, "God have mercy on me, a sinner."[88] Jesus said that the tax collector went home justified. But he also went home relieved. It is a relief to no longer try to pretend that you are perfect, or worry that someone will figure out that you have sinned. The Apostle John said that if we say we have no sin we deceive ourselves, but if we confess our sin God is faithful and just to forgive us and cleanse us from all unrighteousness.[89] Rather than avoid the feeling of being crushed, as mature Christians we should welcome the feeling with relief and resignation.

Be Transparent

Not only does relief come with admission of defeat, but it also comes when something formerly hidden is brought into the open. During youth group the high schoolers were reading a passage, and one of the youth mispronounced a word. What came out instead was an accidental profanity. He was embarrassed, and the slip was not missed by anyone in the group. Yet in a surprising show of maturity, no one laughed, even though I could tell it was with great difficulty that the laughter was restrained at the tight gate of the lips. It was obvious to me that teaching could not continue under these circumstances, so I said "could we all just laugh for a minute, and then

---

87. Ps 38:8
88. Luke 18:11–13
89. 1 John 1:8–9

continue." The group laughed in great relief, now that the obvious embarrassment was out in the open.

Each year on Ash Wednesday Christians throughout the world write our sins on white cards, and then nail them to the cross. Afterwards, we collect them and burn them in a fire. Then we draw some ash out of the fire and receive a cross on our heads. This is a moving experience of confession and repentance. Have you ever cheated when writing down your sins on a piece of paper? I've asked around at our church, and some admitted to me that they have. It's fruitless, of course, to cheat, because nothing is hidden from the eyes of God. King David prayed, "All my longings lie open before you, O Lord, my sighing is not hidden from you."[90] David knew well that he could neither hide his anguish nor his sin from God. So the advantage of transparency with God is honesty with ourselves, and permission for God to work repentance within us. It was with the same transparency that we should mimic David, "My guilt is not hidden from you."[91]

Confess

Continuing in Psalm 38 David said, "I confess my iniquity, I am troubled by my sin."[92] The King knew that this was a necessary step in taking responsibility for his own sin, and his role in the adversarial relationship with his enemy. The resignation of defeat and transparency bring relief, and so does confession.

In Dostoyevsky's *Crime and Punishment* the main character Raskolnikov committed two murders. He became troubled by his sin, to the point where his body greatly suffered. He was delirious, famished, parched, angry, aloof, and clearly in the greatest anguish. He admitted his guilt to one person, a prostitute named Sonia. Though he seemed to have an idea what to do, of which the reader is not quite certain, he asks Sonia what to do. Her answer was emphatic, quick, and certain. "Go to the cross roads, bow down to the people, kiss the earth because you have sinned against it too, and say aloud to the whole world, 'I am a murderer.'"[93] Raskolnikov didn't seem to have any intention of following through with this prescription, but when he found himself at the crossroads later, this is exactly what he did. And it was this confession which led to his ultimate healing, repentance, and recovery of mental and physical health.

90. Ps 38:9
91. Ps 69:5
92. Ps 38:18
93. Dostoyevsky, *Crime and Punishment*, 498.

Part Three: Application

David prayed, "For the sake of your name, O LORD, forgive my iniquity, though it is great."[94] He knew that his sin was great, but he also knew that confession would yield a great reward both for God and for himself.

The psalmist was willing to give God permission to search him, know him completely, and see if there is any offensive way in him.[95] As mature Christians, we will give God the same free access to convict us of sin. When he does so, we will admit that we deserve his wrath, be accountable to him alone, allow ourselves to be troubled by our sin, stop defending ourselves, be transparent, and confess.

Furthermore, the psalmist also asks God to "lead me in the way everlasting."[96] This is not just a confessional prayer looking to the past sins committed, but a covenantal prayer looking toward the future. There is a strong connection in this psalm to Jesus' teaching in the Sermon on the Mount: "And forgive us our debts, as we also have forgiven our debtors. And lead us not into temptation, but deliver us from the evil one."[97]

Conclusion

The language of the imprecatory psalms is unquestionably passionate. It evokes a level of anger which most of us spend our whole life suppressing. All the psalms, including the imprecatory ones, increase our level of passion for the things that God cares about: They make us zealous for what is right, and for his holy name. They give us passion against God's enemies and develop hatred for sin and injustice. When our passions mirror God's passions our worship becomes even more powerful and authentic. Give these psalms another look, and let them foster a new passion.

---

94. Ps 25:11
95. Ps 139:23
96. Ps 139:24
97. Matt 6:12–13

10

Conclusion

The problem of the imprecatory psalms is that they present a way of dealing with enemies that seems inconsistent with Christ's teaching, especially in the Sermon on the Mount. At first glance, these psalms appear to advocate violence, hatred, revenge, and retaliation. Jesus, on the other hand, told us to love our enemies, pray for them, and not take revenge.

Scholars have attempted to resolve or at least explain this apparent inconsistency in a number of ways by creating a variety of interpretive models. The best interpretive model will uphold the following criteria: It will be faithful to the original context, realistic about human nature and experience, considerate of the integrity of the canon, mindful of God's inspiration, and have a legitimate contemporary application. Many of the historic models of interpretation fail in one or more of these criteria. Interpretations which are solely historical (but not theological) do not wrestle with the doctrine of inspiration, and do not offer the contemporary reader any application. The assertion that these psalms contain latent forms of magic or spells also poses problems for inspiration, and requires us to imagine that a behavior expressly prohibited by the Hebrew Bible was nevertheless maintained to some degree in Hebrew worship. The therapeutic limit of catharsis in general likewise limits the value of the cathartic interpretation of the psalms. The quotation hypothesis and prophetic hypothesis seem contrived, and require too much forcing of the texts. In addition, neither is realistic about human nature: Why should the psalmist not have had a justifiable reason to hate and curse real enemies? This is also a deficiency of allegorical models. The notion that these psalms belong to an earlier dispensation (or were the prior stage of progressive revelation) requires us to imagine too much discontinuity both in the mind of God and in the canon.

Part Three: Application

The dependence model, expressed by Erich Zenger's *A God of Vengeance?* sufficiently addresses the criteria I have proposed for any sound interpretive model of the imprecatory psalms. Simply put, the dependence model states that "the psalms of enmity are a way of robbing the aggressive images of the enemies of their destructiveness, and transforming them into constructive forces."[1] Brueggemann notes that the curses in these psalms are actually prayers directed to God, rather than at demons or at the enemy: "These elements [of lament] serve to characterize how desperate is the need. On the other hand, these elements serve to lodge that need at the throne of Yahweh, so that it is made unambiguously Yahweh's problem, about which Yahweh must do something."[2] Israel's understanding of warfare was unique in that it called for complete dependence upon God, to the point that the warrior is often an unnecessary observer. Lind writes of the Old Testament vision of utter dependence:

> The root of this vision of the way of Yahweh, a way that alienated Israel from her own environment and made her a suffering people, was not a late spiritualization but an event happening at the beginning of Israel's existence, an event that transformed warfare itself from a manipulation of power to a prophetic act and a patient waiting upon Yahweh's deliverance.[3]

The imprecatory psalms were written by victims of violence who were indeed angry, even to the point of feeling retributive and just hatred. But they did not direct their curses to their enemies, nor to demons, nor to soldiers. Instead, they directed their prayers containing these curses to God, depending upon God to supervene, avenge, and resolve the situation. They depended on God because they had no other resource, and because appealing to God fit their worldview. They were God's chosen people, the people of the covenant promise. They had reason to believe that God would uphold their case, preserve them, and avenge them. Furthermore, they had reason to believe they could depend upon God because they knew their pleas were consistent with God's character.

The authors of the imprecatory psalms were victims of violence, and for that reason the modern application of these psalms should arise from contemporary victims as well. Today's oppressed Christians are not loathe to pray imprecatory prayers. Zephania Kameeta's *Why O Lord? Psalms and Sermons from Namibia* is a prime example of the contemporary practice. Contemporary theologians who have experienced oppression have

1. Zenger, *A God of Vengeance?* vii.
2. Brueggemann, *Message of the Psalms*, 55–56.
3. Lind, *Yahweh Is a Warrior*, 174.

contributed many insights into understanding this part of the Psalter. Liberation theologians, for instance, capture the eschatological hope in these prayers that are often neglected by the traditional models of interpretation. The victims of oppression in this study have no need to allegorize or spiritualize the enemy. They wrestle honestly with their own hatred and anger. We should allow that the ancient psalmist did the same. The contemporary practice of imprecatory prayer has many similarities to the ancient psalter: They name their oppressors, and express their complaints to God in complete dependence. Out of their weakness they forsake revenge, and ask God to rectify the injustice. At the same time they are not blind to their own faults and ask God to examine and purify them. Often they pray for the conversion of their enemies, but always they pray with confidence that God will bring about the triumph of justice and righteousness.

To a large extent, the apparent contradiction between the imprecatory psalms and the Sermon on the Mount can be explained by the differences in genre. The Sermon on the Mount is prescriptive in nature, while the psalms are descriptive. The Sermon on the Mount is the voice of God, and in many cases the Psalter is the voice of God's people. But the difference in form does not dismiss the theological contribution of the psalter, nor does it render the practice of imprecatory prayer completely irrelevant. Instances of imprecation are found in the New Testament, even in the mouth of Jesus. The Sermon on the Mount, therefore, is not the only place that treatment of enemies is addressed, nor does it offer the one and only way to deal with them.

The reason that imprecation appears in the New Testament, and elsewhere in Scripture, is that it is consistent with the character and attributes of God. The love of God is wholly compatible with the justice of God. God is love, and yet God hates evil. Scripture presents a paradox: Since God judges, but is also completely loving, we must conclude that judgment is loving. Asking God to judge, therefore, is asking God to be consistent with his character. Incredibly, this paradox and consistency was acted out on the cross. Jesus bore the wrath of God and maintained the love and justice of God. To a large extent, therefore, the New Testament does represent a new dispensation. But this does not mean that God's character has in any way changed. The imprecatory psalms appeal to God's character—his justice, his covenant-love, and his solidarity with the oppressed. Contemporary imprecatory prayer can appeal to these same attributes of God. Additionally, despite the satisfaction of God's wrath in Christ, the Bible teaches that future judgment and reconciliation awaits at the *eschaton*. The new dispensation marked by Christ's death does not wholly negate God's future actions of judgment. Nor does it negate immediate forms of it. Instances of judgment occur after Christ's resurrection:

Part Three: Application

King Herod was struck dead by God and eaten by worms.[4] Similarly, Ananias and Sapphira died after they lied to the Holy Spirit.[5]

To rightly understand the imprecatory psalms, we must rightly interpret many of the theological categories and terms. I have set this discussion within a theological anthropology. From that examination, it is clear that the psalms do not express a personal desire for revenge. Additionally, the pleas of the innocent are not individualistic. Instead, the psalms are thoroughly corporate: they are the songs of a community, and part of their liturgy. One of the reasons that the imprecatory psalms have been problematic (and therefore neglected from liturgy) is that many of us have not personally experienced enemies on the scale of those addressed in the psalter, we are reluctant to declare ourselves innocent, and we are reticent to cultivate feelings of revenge toward personal enemies. This is all noble and advisable, and indeed consistent with the Psalter, although not representing the entirety of its teaching. Consequently, if we place ourselves in the middle of our community, certainly in the middle of a global community, we can see oppression on the scale of the Psalter. We can ask God to hear the call of his people.

A practical theology of the imprecatory psalms seeks to guide the Christian community in several activities and in a new understanding of the Psalter. First, it calls Western Christians to abandon the notion of personal enemies, personal revenge, and personal innocence. To rightly understand the contribution of this section of Scripture we must see and practice a more communal voice in the Psalter and in liturgy. Second, a practical theology of the Psalms invites Christians to identify enemies. This exercise demands confidence that we understand the heart of God, and how he defines an enemy. Inevitably we will begin by identifying ourselves. "For if, while we were God's *enemies*, we were reconciled to him through the death of his Son, how much more, having been reconciled, shall we be saved through his life!"[6] In addition, by understanding the heart of God, and by reading the imprecatory psalms closer, we will see that God has an abiding heart for the broken, needy, oppressed, fatherless, widows, etc. A call to identify God's enemies is a call to align ourselves correctly with God's passions. In this identification process, we will see that at times we have been the oppressor, either by what we have done or left undone. And as we identify enemies of God's program elsewhere, it is a call to solidarity with God's people and his agenda.

I conclude that it is at least permissible to pray imprecatory prayers. I agree that, "We can trust the psalmist not to mislead us into a prayer that

4. Acts 12:23
5. Acts 5:10
6. Rom 5:10

in the final analysis would be incorrect to pray."[7] Brueggemann says of this sort of prayer:

> It is bold because it insists that all such experiences of disorder are a proper subject for discourse with God. There is nothing out of bounds, nothing precluded or inappropriate. Everything properly belongs in this conversation of the heart. To withhold parts of life from that conversation is in fact to withhold part of life from the sovereignty of God.[8]

I offer several reasons that the imprecatory psalms have therapeutic value. First, these psalms admonish us to make God's fame and glory our primary concern (replacing personal desires for fame or vengeance). This exercise of humility is clearly also a recipe for health. Second, the psalms impart serenity by affirming the sovereignty of God: "God, grant me the serenity to accept the things I cannot change, courage to change the things I can, and wisdom to know the difference." The psalmist ought not change his situation of oppression; it is God's prerogative alone to avenge. The acceptance of what is beyond one's control also contributes to health. On the other hand, the psalmist can change his own heart. That leads us to the third therapeutic contribution: the Psalms teach us to appeal to the things God cares about. The psalms invoke a healthy reorientation of priorities. Similarly, the imprecatory psalms also give occasional reminders of self-examination: "Search me, God, and know my heart; test me and know my anxious thoughts. See if there is any offensive way in me, and lead me in the way everlasting."[9] Fourth, the imprecatory psalms make a case for the therapeutic value of anger and hatred. When denied, these emotions tacitly perpetuate injustice and they perpetuate feelings of impotence. When identified, feelings of anger and hatred can lead to redemptive action, efforts of reconciliation, self-examination, and repentance. Finally, the imprecatory psalms are *prayers*. Christians pray with expectation that God will answer. We pray with the belief that it makes a difference. So as we make our complaints known to God in prayer, we have the eager expectation that God will bring about justice.

The imprecatory psalms offer a wealth of value for contemporary preaching. Many of these themes are probably already addressed by preachers who are unaware of their presence in the Psalter. Concern for God's reputation is a pervasive biblical thought, and we can preach this theme since the imprecatory psalms are replete with it. The imprecatory psalms can be

---

7. Sire, *Learning to Pray through the Psalms*, 164.
8. Brueggemann, *Message of the Psalms*, 52.
9. Ps 139:23–24

Part Three: Application

preached with affirmation of the sovereignty of God and assurance that God is more willing and able to handle the instances of injustice than we could ourselves. Preachers have no trouble using the Psalter to remind their congregations that it is God's prerogative alone to avenge. We can preach about the heart of God, and how God keeps his covenant promises with His people. We can see in the imprecatory psalms that his people are not an ethnic group but a disadvantaged group. By examining the imprecatory psalms, preachers can call congregations from apathy about injustice or impotence in taking action. That may mean self-examination, or identification with the oppressed, or work toward reconciliation with enemies. In any case, that action will certainly involve prayer: prayer for God's intervention, prayer for a change in the situation, prayer for the conversion of the enemy, prayer for attenuation toward the enemy, prayer that God would bring an end to the enemies' activities. I have examined the therapeutic and preaching value of the imprecatory psalms, but we must not forget that these psalms are more than therapeutic, and more than fodder for preaching: They are prayers. Prayer has the effect of realigning one's own attitude, but when James said "The prayer of a righteous person is powerful and effective"[10] he meant that prayer changes more than the person praying. Prayer is a petition to God to change the course of history. Of all the redeeming value that can be gleaned from the imprecatory psalms, this would be the greatest.

---

10. Jas 5:16

Appendix

WHAT FOLLOWS IS JESUS' Sermon on the Mount from Matthew 5. I include the material here for several reasons. First, as a reference because I refer to the sermon several times in this study. Second, because the imprecatory psalms must be understood and lived with this sermon in mind. Without this sermon, this study of the imprecatory psalms would be incomplete and out of balance. Third, to reiterate the message in chapter 4, which is that Jesus speaks with more authority to people than people speak to God. Though all scripture is inspired, the genre of sermons is more prescriptive than the genre of psalms. It has been my argument that the psalms model an acceptable way to pray, but Jesus teaches us how to act.

Matthew 5

1 Now when Jesus saw the crowds, he went up on a mountainside and sat down. His disciples came to him, 2 and he began to teach them.

The Beatitudes

He said:
3 "Blessed are the poor in spirit,
for theirs is the kingdom of heaven.
4 Blessed are those who mourn,
for they will be comforted.
5 Blessed are the meek,
for they will inherit the earth.
6 Blessed are those who hunger and thirst for righteousness,
for they will be filled.
7 Blessed are the merciful,
for they will be shown mercy.

Appendix

8 Blessed are the pure in heart,
for they will see God.
9 Blessed are the peacemakers,
for they will be called children of God.
10 Blessed are those who are persecuted because of righteousness,
for theirs is the kingdom of heaven.

11 "Blessed are you when people insult you, persecute you and falsely say all kinds of evil against you because of me. 12 Rejoice and be glad, because great is your reward in heaven, for in the same way they persecuted the prophets who were before you.

13 "You are the salt of the earth. But if the salt loses its saltiness, how can it be made salty again? It is no longer good for anything, except to be thrown out and trampled underfoot.

14 "You are the light of the world. A town built on a hill cannot be hidden. 15 Neither do people light a lamp and put it under a bowl. Instead they put it on its stand, and it gives light to everyone in the house. 16 In the same way, let your light shine before others, that they may see your good deeds and glorify your Father in heaven.

17 "Do not think that I have come to abolish the Law or the Prophets; I have not come to abolish them but to fulfill them. 18 For truly I tell you, until heaven and earth disappear, not the smallest letter, not the least stroke of a pen, will by any means disappear from the Law until everything is accomplished. 19 Therefore anyone who sets aside one of the least of these commands and teaches others accordingly will be called least in the kingdom of heaven, but whoever practices and teaches these commands will be called great in the kingdom of heaven. 20 For I tell you that unless your righteousness surpasses that of the Pharisees and the teachers of the law, you will certainly not enter the kingdom of heaven.

21 "You have heard that it was said to the people long ago, 'You shall not murder, and anyone who murders will be subject to judgment.' 22 But I tell you that anyone who is angry with a brother or sister will be subject to judgment. Again, anyone who says to a brother or sister, 'Raca,' is answerable to the court. And anyone who says, 'You fool!' will be in danger of the fire of hell.

23 "Therefore, if you are offering your gift at the altar and there remember that your brother or sister has something against you, 24 leave your gift there in front of the altar. First go and be reconciled to them; then come and offer your gift.

25 "Settle matters quickly with your adversary who is taking you to court. Do it while you are still together on the way, or your adversary may hand you over to the judge, and the judge may hand you over to the officer,

and you may be thrown into prison. 26 Truly I tell you, you will not get out until you have paid the last penny.

27 "You have heard that it was said, 'You shall not commit adultery.' 28 But I tell you that anyone who looks at a woman lustfully has already committed adultery with her in his heart. 29 If your right eye causes you to stumble, gouge it out and throw it away. It is better for you to lose one part of your body than for your whole body to be thrown into hell. 30 And if your right hand causes you to stumble, cut it off and throw it away. It is better for you to lose one part of your body than for your whole body to go into hell.

31 "It has been said, 'Anyone who divorces his wife must give her a certificate of divorce.' 32 But I tell you that anyone who divorces his wife, except for sexual immorality, makes her the victim of adultery, and anyone who marries a divorced woman commits adultery.

33 "Again, you have heard that it was said to the people long ago, 'Do not break your oath, but fulfill to the Lord the vows you have made.' 34 But I tell you, do not swear an oath at all: either by heaven, for it is God's throne; 35 or by the earth, for it is his footstool; or by Jerusalem, for it is the city of the Great King. 36 And do not swear by your head, for you cannot make even one hair white or black. 37 All you need to say is simply 'Yes' or 'No'; anything beyond this comes from the evil one.

38 "You have heard that it was said, 'Eye for eye, and tooth for tooth.' 39 But I tell you, do not resist an evil person. If anyone slaps you on the right cheek, turn to them the other cheek also. 40 And if anyone wants to sue you and take your shirt, hand over your coat as well. 41 If anyone forces you to go one mile, go with them two miles. 42 Give to the one who asks you, and do not turn away from the one who wants to borrow from you.

43 "You have heard that it was said, 'Love your neighbor and hate your enemy.' 44 But I tell you, love your enemies and pray for those who persecute you, 45 that you may be children of your Father in heaven. He causes his sun to rise on the evil and the good, and sends rain on the righteous and the unrighteous. 46 If you love those who love you, what reward will you get? Are not even the tax collectors doing that? 47 And if you greet only your own people, what are you doing more than others? Do not even pagans do that? 48 Be perfect, therefore, as your heavenly Father is perfect.

Bibliography

Adams, James E. *War Psalms of the Prince of Peace: Lessons from the Imprecatory Psalms*. Phillipsburg, NJ: Presbyterian and Reformed, 1991.
Allen, Leslie. *A Liturgy of Grief: A Pastoral Commentary on Lamentations*. Grand Rapids: Baker, 2011.
———. *Psalms 101–150*. Word Biblical Commentary. Waco, TX: Word, 2002.
Anderson, Ray. *The Soul of Ministry*. Louisville: Westminster John Knox, 1997.
Anderson, Bernhard. *Out of the Depths*. Louisville: Westminster John Knox, 2000.
Asensio, Felix. "Encuentro de la Oracion del Salmista con la Cristiana en la Vision del Crisostomo." *Estudios Biblicos* 39.3–4 (1981) 201–21.
Augsburger, David W. *Conflict Mediation across Cultures*. Louisville: Westminster John Knox, 1992.
———. *Hate-Work*. Louisville: Westminster John Knox, 2004.
———. *Helping People Forgive*. Louisville: Westminster John Knox, 1996.
Ballard, Harold Wayne. *The Divine Warrior Motif in the Psalms*. North Richland Hills, TX: Bibal, 1999.
Basset, Lytta. *Holy Anger*. Grand Rapids: Eerdmans, 2007.
Birkeland, Harris. *The Evildoers in the Book of Psalms*. Oslo: I Kommisjon Hos Jacob Dybwad, 1955.
Bonhoeffer, Dietrich. *Letters and Papers from Prison*. New York: Touchstone, 1971.
———. *Life Together*. San Francisco: Harper San Francisco, 1954.
———. *Meditating on the Word*. Cambridge, MA: Cowley, 1986.
———. *Psalms: The Prayer Book of the Bible*. Minneapolis: Augsburg, 1970.
Brichto, H. C. *The Problem of Curse in the Hebrew Bible*. Philadelphia: Society of Biblical Literature and Exegesis, 1963.
Browning, Don S. *A Fundamental Practical Theology*. Minneapolis: Fortress, 1991.
Brueggemann, Walter. *Israel's Praise*. Philadelphia: Fortress, 1988.
———. *The Message of the Psalms*. Minneapolis: Augsburg, 1984.
———. *Praying the Psalms*. Eugene, OR: Cascade, 2007.
Calvin, John. *Commentary on the Book of Psalms*. Edinburgh: Calvin Translation Society, 1849.
Cheong, Eun Chae. *Biblical Basis of the Imprecatory Psalms: Special Attention to Psalms 109 and 35*. M.A. thesis for Columbia Biblical Seminary, South Carolina, 1987.
Chrysostom, John. *Commentary on the Psalms*. Translated by Robert Charles Hill. Brookline, MA: Holy Cross Orthodox Press, 1998.
Cooper, John. *Body, Soul and Life Everlasting*. Grand Rapids: Eerdmans, 1989.
Corcoran, Kevin J. *Rethinking Human Nature*. Grand Rapids: Baker Academic, 2006.

Bibliography

Cortese, Enzo. "Salmo 37: Una Interpretacion en Dialogo con el Tercer Mundo." *Estudios Biblicos* 51 (1993) 31–40.
Culbertson, Diana. "Preaching the Word in a Culture of Violence." *Word and World* 24.1 (2004) 58–65.
Day, John. "The Imprecatory Psalms and Christian Ethics." *Bibliotheca Sacra* 159 (2002) 166–86.
DePuy, Norman R. "Desert Storms and Suffering Servants." *Christian Century*, 108.26. September 18–25, 1991, 843.
Dostoyevsky, Fyodor. *Crime and Punishment*. New York: Barnes and Noble Classics, 2007.
Driver, Samuel Rolles. *Studies in the Psalms*. London: Hodder and Stoughton, 1915.
Edwards, Jonathan. *The Sermons of Jonathan Edwards*. New Haven: Yale University Press, 1999.
Erickson, Millard. *Christian Theology*. Grand Rapids: Baker, 1985.
Gerstenberger, E. "Enemies and Evildoers in the Psalms: A Challenge to Christian Preaching." *Horizons in Biblical Theology* 4 (1983) 61–77.
Gilkes, Cheryl Townsend. "'Mother to the Motherless, Father to the Fatherless': Power, Gender, and Community in an Afrocentric Biblical Tradition." *Semeia* 47 (1989) 57–85.
Greehy, John J. "The Cursing Psalms." *The Furrow* 29.3 (1978) 170–74.
Green, Joel B. *Body, Soul, and Human Life*. Milton Keynes, UK: Paternoster, 2008.
———. *What about the Soul?* Nashville: Abingdon, 2004.
Green, Joel B., and Stuart Palmer. *In Search of the Soul*. Downers Grove, IL: InterVarsity, 2005.
Griggs, Donald L. *Praying and Teaching the Psalms*. Nashville: Abingdon, 1984.
Groome, Thomas. *Sharing Faith*. San Francisco: Harper San Francisco, 1991.
Grudem, Wayne. *Systematic Theology*. Grand Rapids: Zondervan, 1994.
Gunkel, Hermann. *The Psalms, a Form-Critical Introduction*. Philadelphia: Fortress, 1967.
Gunn, George. *God in the Psalms*. Edinburgh: Saint Andrew, 1956.
Gutierrez, Gustavo. "A Spirituality of Liberation." *Other Side* 21.3 (1985) 40–43.
Hefner, Philip. *The Human Factor*. Minneapolis: Fortress, 1993.
Heitink, Gerben. *Practical Theology*. Grand Rapids: Eerdmans, 1993.
Henry, Matthew, and Thomas Scott. *Matthew Henry Commentary with Comments of Thomas Scott*. Bloomington, IN: Royal, 1970.
Hodge, A. A. *Outlines of Theology*. Grand Rapids: Eerdmans, 1949.
Inch, Morris. *Psychology in the Psalms*. Waco, TX: Word, 1969.
Kalluvettil, Paul. "The Warrior God and the Prince of Peace: Biblical Perspectives on War and Peace." *Journal of Dharma* 27.3 (2002) 291–308.
Kameeta, Zephania. *Why O Lord? Psalms and Sermons from Namibia*. Risk Book Series. Geneva: World Council of Churches, 1986.
Katz, Robert. *Empathy*. New York: Free Press of Glencoe, 1963.
Kelley, Page H. "Prayers of Troubled Saints." *Review and Expositor* 81.3 (1984) 377–83.
Kidner, Derek. *Psalms 73–150*. Tyndale Old Testament Commentaries. Downers Grove, IL: InterVarsity, 1975.
———. *The Wisdom of the Proverbs, Job, and Ecclesiastes*. Downers Grove, IL: InterVarsity, 1985.

Bibliography

Kim, Jungho. *A Literary and Theological Study of Imprecatory Psalms 35 and 137 as a Defense for Their Integrity*. D.Phil. dissertation for Bob Jones Seminary, 2004.

King, Jr., Martin Luther. *Strength to Love*. Philadelphia: Fortress, 1981.

Kraybill, Donald. *Amish Grace: How Forgiveness Transcended Tragedy*. San Francisco: Jossey Bass, 2007.

LaMothe, Ryan. "A Psychodynamic Perspective and Theological Implications of Hate and Hostility in Pastoral Counseling." *American Journal of Pastoral Counseling* 1.3 (1998) 27–46.

Laney, J Carl. "A Fresh Look at the Imprecatory Psalms." *Bibliotheca Sacra* 138.549 (1981) 35–45.

Lessing, Reed. "Broken Teeth, Bloody Baths, and Baby Bashing: Is There Any Place in the Church for Imprecatory Psalms?" *Concordia Journal* 32.4 (2006) 368–70.

Lester, Andrew D. *The Angry Christian*. Louisville: Westminster John Knox, 2003.

Lewis, C. S. *Reflections on the Psalms*. New York: Phoenix, 1985.

Lind, Millard. *Yahweh is a Warrior*. Scottdale, PN: Herald, 1980.

Luther, Martin. *Commentary on the Sermon on the Mount*. Translated by Charles A. Hay. Philadelphia: Lutheran Publication Society, 1892.

———. *Luther's Works*. Edited by Jaroslav Pelikan. Saint Louis: Concordia, 1956.

Martin, Chalmers. "Imprecations in the Psalms." *Princeton Theological Review* 1 (1903) 537–53.

Mays, James L. *The Lord Reigns: A Theological Handbook of the Psalms*. Louisville: Westminster John Knox, 1994.

McKenzie, J. L. "The Imprecations of the Psalter." *American Ecclesiastical Review* 111 (1944) 81–96.

Milne, Bruce. *Know the Truth*. Downers Grove, IL: InterVarsity, 1998.

Moreland, J. P., and Scott Rae. *Body and Soul*. Downers Grove, IL: InterVarsity, 2000.

Mowinckel, Sigmund. *The Psalms in Israel's Worship*. Nashville: Abingdon, 1962.

Murphy, Jeffrie G., and Jean Hampton. *Forgiveness and Mercy*. Cambridge: Cambridge University Press, 1988.

Murphy, Nancey. *Bodies and Souls or Spirited Bodies?* Cambridge: Cambridge University Press, 2006.

Nichols, Michael P., and Melvin Zax. *Catharsis in Psychotherapy*. New York: Gardner, 1977.

Niebhur, Reinhold, *The Nature and Destiny of Man*. Louisville: Westminster John Knox, 1996.

Niemoller, Martin. *First Commandment*. London: Hodge, 1937.

———. *God is My Fuehrer*. New York: Philosophical Library and Alliance Book Corporation, 1941.

———. *Here Stand I*. Translated by Jane Lymburn. New York: Willett, Clark and Co., 1937.

Osgood, Howard. "Dashing the Little Ones against the Rock." *Princeton Theological Review* 1 (1903) 23–37.

Raj, J. R. John Samuel. "Cosmic Judge or Overseer of the World-Order? The Role of Yahweh as Portrayed in Psalm 7." *Bangalore Theological Forum* 34.2 (2002) 1–15.

Ringgren, Helmer. *Faith of the Psalmists*. Philadelphia: Fortress, 1963.

Rubenstein, Richard. *After Auschwitz*. Baltimore: Johns Hopkins University Press, 1992.

Salomon, Alvaro. "Reflexiones Pastorales Sobre algunos Salmos." *Cuadernos de Teologia* 20 (2001) 259–74.

Bibliography

Shepherd, John. "The Place of the Imprecatory Psalms in the Canon of Scripture." *The Churchman* 111 (1997) 27–47, 110–126.

Schökel, Luis and Cecilia Camiti. *Salmos I-II-Traducción, Introducción y Comentario*. Estella, Verbo Divino, 1992.

Shriver, Donald W. *An Ethic for Enemies*. New York: Oxford University Press, 1995.

Shults, LeRon. *Reforming Theological Anthropology*. Grand Rapids: Eerdmans Publishing Company, 1993.

Sire, James. *Learning to Pray through the Psalms*. Downers Grove, IL: InterVarsity, 2005.

Sittser, Gerald. *A Grace Disguised*. Grand Rapids: Zondervan, 1996.

Solberg, Richard W. *God and Caesar in East Germany*. New York: Macmillan, 1961.

Spurgeon, Charles, John Calvin, and Matthew Henry. *Parallel Classic Commentary on the Psalms*. Chattanooga, TN: AMG, 2005.

Spurgeon, C. H. *The Treasury of David*. Grand Rapids: Baker, 1977.

Tutu, Desmond. *The African Prayer Book*. New York: Doubleday, 1995.

———. *Crying in the Wilderness: Struggle for Justice in South Africa*. Grand Rapids: Eerdmans, 1982.

———. *No Future without Forgiveness*. New York: Doubleday, 1999.

———. *Hope and Suffering: Sermons and Speeches*. Grand Rapids: Eerdmans, 1983.

Vos, Johannes G. "Ethical Problems of the Imprecatory Psalms." *Westminster Theological Journal* 4 (1942) 123–38.

Waltke, Bruce. "Theology of the Psalms." In *New International Dictionary of Old Testament Theology*, vol. 4, edited by Bruce Waltke, 1100–1114. Grand Rapids: Zondervan, 1997.

Ward, Keith. *Religion and Human Nature*. Oxford: Oxford University Press, 1998.

Wesley, John. *The Nature of the Kingdom: Wesley's Messages on the Sermon on the Mount*. Minneapolis: Bethany House, 1986.

Wiesel, Elie. *Night/Dawn/Day*. New York: Aronson B'nai B'rith, 1985.

Wiesenthal, Simon. *The Sunflower*. New York: Schocken, 1976.

Wikarsa, Dedy. *An Exegetical Study of Psalm 137: Praying the Imprecatory Psalms as Christians Today*. Th.M. thesis for Reformed Theological Seminary, 1998.

Williams, Donald M. *Psalms 1–72. The Preacher's Commentary*. Nashville: Thomas Nelson, 1986.

Zenger, Erich. *A God of Vengeance? Understanding the Psalms of Divine Wrath*. Translated by Linda M. Maloney. Louisville: Westminster John Knox, 1996.

www.ingramcontent.com/pod-product-compliance
Lightning Source LLC
Chambersburg PA
CBHW070252230426
43664CB00014B/2510